THE REGISTER
OF
OVERWHARTON PARISH
STAFFORD COUNTY
VIRGINIA
1723-1758

AQUIA CHURCH
Built 1757

THE REGISTER
OF
OVERWHARTON PARISH
STAFFORD COUNTY
VIRGINIA
1723-1758
AND
SUNDRY HISTORICAL
AND
GENEALOGICAL NOTES

* * *
* *
*

Compiled and Published
By
George Harrison Sanford King
Fellow, American Society of Genealogists
Fredericksbury, Virginia
1961

SOUTHERN HISTORICAL PRESS, INC.
P.O. Box 738
Easley, South Carolina 29641-0738

ISBN 0-89308-576-6

TO MY FRIEND

CATHERINE LINDSAY (SMITH) KNORR

(Mrs. Hermann August Knorr)

President General

The Order of the Crown in America

and

Honorary Governor General

Hereditary Order of Descendants of Colonial Governors

CONTENTS

ILLUSTRATIONS

PREFACE

OVERWHARTON PARISH REGISTER 1720 to 1760 was published in 1899 by William F. Boogher, Esq. from a copy of the original made by Powhatan Moncure, Esq., of Stafford County, then custodian of the old records of Overwharton Parish. This volume, long out of print, contains innumerable errors and omissions. I hope that the present volume will correct those faults.

Mr. Boogher indicates that his version of the Register covers the years 1720 - 1760, though neither date appears in the manuscript volume. The Register actually begins in 1723 and terminates in 1758; there are, however, a few entries after 1758 regarding the Reverend Mr. Moncure's immediate family.

The Register begins in 1723 during the rectorship of the Reverend Mr. Alexander Scott (1686-1738), but it is unlikely that the manuscript is contemporary with his term [1711-1738] as curate of Overwharton Parish. For the years 1723-1735 there are no entries of marriages or deaths, and relatively few births or baptisms were recorded in the existing volume. I believe there was an earlier Register from which someone transcribed a few recordings for the period 1723-1738. It was not until after the death of the Reverend Mr. Alexander Scott that his successor, the Reverend Mr. John Moncure (circa 1714-1764), began a systematic record of births, baptisms, marriages and deaths. The presence of many blank spaces and pages for the period 1723-1738 strengthens this assumption.

As in other colonial registers, there is evidence of errors and inconsistencies in both names and dates but these, for the most part, are negligible. We must be grateful to the Reverend Mr. John Moncure for keeping the Register and to his descendants who preserved it.

Many families mentioned in The Register of Overwharton Parish 1723-1758 are also mentioned in The Register of Saint Paul's Parish 1715-1798, published in 1960 by the present compiler. Therefore persons interested in families in colonial Stafford County should consult both Registers. These Registers not only contain records concerning inhabitants of these parishes, but also of some persons in adjoining counties, as well as a few across the Potomac River in Maryland.

These two colonial parish registers of Stafford County go far toward bridging the many gaps caused by the mutilation and theft of the county court records during the Civil War. The court house was not burned, however, and we are now left with a few books covering the period 1664-1860. The record books prior to 1860 once at Stafford County Clerk's Office and those now there are detailed in The Virginia Magazine of History and Biography, Volume 53, pages 215-218.

The Register usually records both births and baptisms but does not mention the sponsors except in the case of the children of the Reverend Mr. John Moncure. When the birth and baptismal dates are both entered, I have recorded only the birth date,

ix

but when the birth date is absent, I have recorded the baptismal date. To differ-
entiate between these recordings, the birth date is designated by the letter B and
the baptismal or christening date by the letter C. The other abbreviations are
the usual: M. (married) and D. (died). The Gregorian Calendar was in use until
1752, however, in this version of the Register all double dates have been altered
to the style of the Julian Calendar. For example: The Reverend Mr. Moncure recorded the birth of William Withers, son of John and Hannah Withers, as March 21,
1746/7, while William Withers recorded his own birth in his family Bible as March
21, 1747. In the presently presented volume I have followed this practice by ex-
pressing the year as it is now reckoned by the Julian Calendar.

The Register abounds with recordings of the births and baptisms of Negro slaves.
This seems to have been required in order that their owners could be taxed when they
came to proper age to be tithables. A study of these recordings indicate that many
gentlemen, who resided elsewhere, had plantations [often referred to as a "quarter"]
in Overwharton Parish. Among these may be mentioned Colonel Charles Carter of
Stanstead in Brunswick Parish, later of Cleve in Hanover Parish, King George County;
Landon Carter, Esq., of Sabine Hall, Richmond County; Colonel Henry Fitzhugh of Bedford and Major John Fitzhugh of Marmion, both in Saint Paul's Parish, Stafford County; Colonel Thomas Lee and his son Colonel Philip Lee, both of Stratford, Westmoreland County; Worden Pope, Gentleman, of Washington Parish, Westmoreland County; and
the Reverend Mr. David Stuart and his son the Reverend Mr. William Stuart, rectors
of Saint Paul's Parish, Stafford County, Virginia.

Since it would be impracticable to detail all of the Negro recordings, I have
in Section II alphabetically listed the names of the slave owners. The date following a name indicates the first year that person had a slave baptized in Overwharton
Parish.

It will be observed that the Reverend Mr. John Moncure's first slave entry is
in 1730 [see page 140], at which time he was not a resident of Overwharton Parish.
This is another evidence that the recordings for 1723-1738 were made after the death
of the Reverend Mr. Alexander Scott (1686-1738). The Parson probably purchased the
slave and entered the birth after he became curate of the parish.

The Register records the birth of Helen Scott, daughter of the Reverend Mr.
James Scott on June 7, 1739, and on January 22, 1741 there is an entry of the birth
of "Moll, a Negro female slave by Jean belonging to Helen Scott, a daughter of the
Rev? Mr. James Scott." Thus at the age of eighteen months the little girl became a
mistress. This was not an uncommon practice among the wealthy families of colonial
Virginia and thus we see that infants could hold property in their own names.

To make up for the sparseness of the early period of the Register, I have presented in Section III a transcription from a Stafford County Quit Rent Roll for
1723. The names of the Tenders of Tobacco in Overwharton Parish in 1724, presented
in Section IV, also assist in filling the gap in the sparse recordings for the early
years of the Register.

In Section V the reader will find a historical sketch of Overwharton Parish
and a little of the history of Stafford County. My purpose there has been to vest
some of those mentioned in The Register of Overwharton Parish with more than their

PREFACE

mere names and to supplement the information usually found in the now lost colonial vestry books. Much of this material has been found in primary sources, although I have drawn heavily upon some secondary sources which I consider reliable. Among the latter are: Doctor George MacLaren Brydon, Virginia's Mother Church [1947]; Edward Lewis Goodwin, The Colonial Church in Virginia [1927]; Ralph Happel, Stafford and King George Courthouses and the Fate of Marlborough, Port of Entry, in The Virginia Magazine of History and Biography, Volume 66, pages 183-194; Fairfax Harrison, Landmarks of Old Prince William [1924]; the Reverend Mr. Horace Edwin Hayden, Virginia Genealogies [1891]; George Carrington Mason, The Colonial Churches of Westmoreland and King George Counties, Virginia, in The Virginia Magazine of History and Biography, Volume 56, pages 280-293 and Bishop William Meade, Old Churches and Families of Virginia [1857].

Section VI records the verbatim inscriptions on the several handsome marble memorial tablets which appropriately adorn the walls of Aquia Church.

The church wardens and vestrymen of Overwharton Parish in 1757, when Aquia Church was completed, represented the most influential families in the parish at that time and in Section VII will be found some account of them, their families and their connections. I have appended an account of the family of the Reverend Mr. John Waugh (1630-1706).

The register of Overwharton Parish is now on deposit in the Archives Division of the Virginia State Library. I am indebted to Mr. John W. Dudley, Assistant Archivist, for making the manuscript available to me, as well as for other courtesies extended. Many pages of the manuscript volume are tattered, worn, faded and torn, and this condition has presented preplexing problems at times. It is one of the many colonial manuscript volumes in dire need of restoration.

I am indebted to Ralph Happel, Esq., Park Historian, Fredericksburg and Spotsylvania National Military Park, for advice in preparing this volume and to my friend Mrs. Hermann August Knorr of Pine Bluff, Arkansas, for her unceasing encouragement in my several undertakings. It is to her, my dear Kitty, that I affectionately dedicate this volume.

George H.S. King

November 11, 1961
1301 Prince Edward Street
Fredericksburg
Virginia

A

B. ABBOT, John son of John Abbot, January 6, 1755.

M. ABBOT, Rachel and Peter Knight, December 19, 1756.

B. ABBOT, George son of John Abbot, May 11, 1757.

M. ABBOT, John and Margaret Lyon, January 15, 1758.

M. ABBOT, Anne and Ephraim Knight, February 12, 1758.

M. ABRAM, Mary and Walter Morgan Lewis, August 27, 1738.

D. ADAMS, George March 1, 1745.

M. ADAMS, John and Honora Carty, September 23, 1750.

B. ADAMS, William son of John and Honorah Adams, April 17, 1751.

D. ADIE, Martha wife of Hugh Adie, October 19, 1749.

M. ADIE, William and Elizabeth Parender, July 25, 1754.

B. ADIE, Ann Fisher daughter of William and Elizabeth Adie, November 29, 1756.

ALLAN : ALLEN

D. ALLEN, William January 13, 1741.

M. ALLEN, William and Bridget Withers, February 15, 1743.

B. ALLAN, John son of Archibald and Abigail Allan, August 12, 1743.

D. ALLAN, Margaret September 8, 1743.

B. ALLEN, James son of William and Bridget Allen, January 2, 1744.

B. ALLAN, Elizabeth daughter of William and Bridget Allan, April 26, 1746.

D. ALLAN, George December 3, 1754.

ALLENTHORP : ALLENTHROP : ALLENTROP

C. ALLENTROP, Jacob son of John and Anne Allentrop, December 24, 1742.

M. ALLENTHORP, Benjamin and Elizabeth Fletcher, August 19, 1746.

M. ALLENTHORP, Sarah and William Price, August 5, 1748.

1

M. ALLENTHORP, Margaret and John Read, March 5, 1754.

M. ALRIDGE, John and Anne Hamilton, June 11, 1738.

M. AMELY, Bridget and Thomas Biddle, February 5, 1758.

M. ANDERSON, John and Sarah Carney, November 28, 1752.

B. ANDERSON, Bailey son of John and Sarah Anderson, November 13, 1753.

B. ANDERSON, Scarlet son of John and Sarah Anderson, June 20, 1756.

B. ANDERSON, Sela daughter of John and Sarah Anderson, March 1, 1758.

   ANGEL : ANGELL

M. ANGELL, Samuel and Anne Hornbuckle, August 14, 1745.

B. ANGEL, Jannet December 29, 1746 at William Black's.

B. ANGEL, Margaret daughter of Samuel and Anne Angel, May 29, 1750.

M. ANGELL, John and Milly Harvey, October 5, 1750.

B. ANGEL, Ann daughter of Samuel and Ann Angel, April 2, 1752.

B. ANGEL, George son of John and Mildred Angel, October 20, 1752.

B. ANGELL, Franky daughter of Samuel and Anne Angell, February 7, 1754.

B. ANGEL, Frances daughter of John and Milley Angel, August 18, 1754.

B. ANGLIS, William son of Christian Anglis, May 9, 1749.

M. ANKERUM, Jean and William Asbury, January 13, 1749.

D. ANONYMUS, Thomas November 1, 1754, a servant of John Peyton.

   ASBEE : ASHBEE : ASHBIE : ASHBY   SEE: ASHBY &c. PAGE 3

   ASBERRY : ASBURY : ASBURRY : ASHBURY

M. ASBERRY, John and Jean Boalin, February 25, 1745.

D. ASBURY, Anne daughter of George and Hannah Asbury, February 5, 1747.

B. ASBURY, Ann daughter of George and Hannah Asbury, October 6, 1747.

M. ASBERRY, Ann and John Wilson, August 16, 1748.

M. ASBURY, William and Jean Ankerum, January 13, 1749.

B. ASHBURY, Henry son of George and Hannah Ashbury, February 10, 1750.

B. ASBURY, Mary daughter of John and Jean Asbury, September 20, 1750.

M. ASBURY, Thomas and Martha Jennings, December 1, 1751.

B. ASBURY, William son of George and Hannah Asbury, March 24, 1752.

B. ASBERRY, Ann Harris daughter of Benjamin and Sarah Asberry, April 21, 1753.

B. ASBURRY, Benjamin son of John and Jean Asburry, July 26, 1753.

B. ASBURY, Nelly daughter of George and Hannah Asbury, June 13, 1754.

B. ASBURY, William Boling son of John and Jane Asbury, January 20, 1755.

D. ASBURY, Frances wife of Benjamin Asbury, May 8, 1755.

D. ASBURY, Mary daughter of George Asbury, July 5, 1755.

B. ASBURY, Eliza daughter of Benjamin Asbury, December 23, 1756.

B. ASBURY, Jeremiah son of George and Hannah Asbury, June 21, 1757.

B. ASBURY, [mutilated] son of John and Jean Asbury, May 10, 1758.

B. ASBROOK, Nancy daughter of Jane Asbrook, June 11, 1754.

ASHBY : ASHBIE : ASHBEE : ASBEE &c.[1]

M. ASHBY, John and Jean Combs, May 11, 1741.

B. ASBEE, Elizabeth daughter of John and Jean Asbee, July 9, 1742.

B. ASBEE, Stephen son of Robert and Mary Asbee, October 19, 1742.

D. ASBEE, Stephen son of Robert and Mary Asbee, September 5, 1744.

B. ASHBIE, Anne daughter of Robert and Mary Ashbie, January 10, 1745.

M. ASHBY, Elias and Winifred Million, September 4, 1745.

B. ASBEE, William son of Elias and Winifred Asbee, April 23, 1746.

B. ASHBEE, Sarah daughter of Robert and Mary Ashbee, January 17, 1747.

B. ASHBY, Thomas son of Robert and Mary Ashby, March 5, 1749.

---

1 - The will of Robert Asbee, Senior, was proved at Stafford County Court in
    1764; it is indexed Ashby.

B. ASHBY, Fransisina daughter of Elias and Winifred Ashby, March 15, 1749.

B. ASHBY, Jesse son of Margery Ashby, May 20, 1750.[1]

B. ASHBY, Milly daughter of Robert and Mary Ashby, September 11, 1751.

M. ASHBY, Thomas and Mary MacCullough, November 14, 1751.

B. ASBEE, Mary Ann daughter of Thomas Asbee, July 30, 1752.

B. ASHBY, Elisha son of Elias Ashby, December 26, 1752.

B. ASHBY, Wilmoth daughter of Robert Ashby, Jun[r], October 28, 1753.

D. ASBEE, Elizabeth wife of Robert Asbee, October 15, 1754.

B. ASBEE, Elizabeth daughter of Thomas and Mary Asbee, November 3, 1754.

M. ASHBY, Catherine and Isaac Murphy, January 1, 1756.

M. ASHBY, John and Sarah MacCullough, February 26, 1756.

B. ASHBY, John son of John Ashby, June 6, 1756.

C. ASHBY, [mutilated] son of Robert Ashby, July 25, 1756.

B. ASHBY, Hankuson son of Thomas and Mary Ashby, February 6, 1757.

B. ASHBY, Balley son of John and Sarah Ashby, November 22, 1758.

ASHBURY   SEE: ASBERRY : ASBURY : ASBURRY : ASHBURY   PAGE 2

M. ATCHISON, Adam and Elizabeth Byram, October 20, 1742.

B. ATCHISON, Mary daughter of Adam and Betty Atchison, April 11, 1744.

B. ATCHISON, John son of Adam Atchison, January 9, 1746.

B. ATCHISON, Lucy daughter of Adam and Elizabeth Atchison, December 26, 1747.

B. ATCHISON, Rosenah daughter of Adam and Elizabeth Atchison, May 6, 1750.

B. ATCHISON, Jean daughter of Adam and Elizabeth Atchison, April 18, 1752.

B. ATCHISON, Nathan son of Adam and Elizabeth Atchison, February 1, 1756.

---

1 - The last will and Testament of Robert Asbee, Senior, of Stafford County was
    dated April 17, 1762; therein he says he is aged and infirm. The will was
    admitted to probate November 12, 1764, and is indexed Ashby. He mentions
    his son John Asbee and his grandson Jess, son of Margery Asbee. The infer-
    ence is these spellings were used interchangeably.

B

M. BAILEN, Peter and Martha Parker, August 6, 1738.

 BAILES   SEE: BAYLES : BAYLIS : BAILES : BAILIS   PAGE 6

B. BAKER, Anne daughter of Edward Baker, April 1, 1737.

B. BAKER, Eleanor daughter of Edward Baker, March 6, 1739.

B. BAKER, Jean daughter of Edward Baker, December 29, 1740.

D. BAKER, Jean daughter of Edward Baker, January 21, 1741.

B. BAKER, Edward son of Edward and Ann Baker, January [blank], 1742.

M. BAKER, John and Rebecca Lunsford, June 8, 1747.

B. BAKER, John son of John Baker, January 4, 1750.

D. BALIEWEL, Martha April 13, 1740.

B. BALL, William son of Edward and Sarah Ball, January 14, 1740.

D. BANNISTER, John son of William Bannister, March 20, 1742.

B. BANNISTER, Henry son of Susannah Bannister, April 29, 1746.[1]

M. BANNISTER, Nathan and Anne Eaves, May 24, 1752.

 BARBEE : BARBY

B. BARBY, Joseph son of Thomas Barby, February 11, 1744.

M. BARBEE, Mary and William Cotney, February 24, 1745.

M. BARBEE, Thomas and Margaret Fant, September 29, 1748.

B. BARBEE, Catherine November 1, 1749.

B. BARBEE, Judy daughter of Thomas and Margaret Barbee, December 16, 1749.

M. BARBEE, Betty and William Smith, January 1, 1750.

M. BARBY, Anne and Garner Burges, February 19, 1751.

B. BARBEE, William son of Thomas Barbee, April 3, 1751.

B. BARBEE, Thomas son of Thomas Barbee, October 18, 1752.

---

1 - See page 111

B. BARBEE, John son of Thomas Barbee, November 12, 1754.

B. BARBY, Sarah daughter of Thomas and Margaret Barby, January 28, 1756.

B. BARBEE, Betty daughter of Thomas Barbee, March 25, 1757.

B. BARBEE, Joseph son of Thomas and Margaret Barbee, May 17, 1758.

B. BARBER, James son of John and Elizabeth Barber, August 16, 1742.

    BARBY   SEE: BARBEE : BARBY   PAGES 5-6

M. BARRET, Ellen and Reverend Daniel McDonald, July 26, 1740.

M. BARRY, Thomas and Catherine Jones, August 5, 1749.

    BASNET : BASNETT : BASNIT

M. BASNIT, Isaac and Mary Rhodes, May 18, 1745.

D. BASNET, Abraham February 8, 1749.

B. BASNETT, Ann daughter of Isaac and Mary Basnett, September 3, 1749.

M. BATEY, Simson and Elizabeth Maccarty, December 24, 1747. [SEE: BETTY, PAGE 9]

M. BATTOO, James and Winny Holliday, February 12, 1747.

B. BATTOO, Mary daughter of James and Winifred Battoo, April 29, 1747.

B. BATTOO, Sithy daughter of James and Winifred Battoo, February 17, 1752.

C. BATTOO, John Holliday son of James Battoo, May 19, 1754.

M. BAXTER, Alexander and Mary Byram, November 28, 1751.

    BAYLES : BAYLIS : BAILES : BAILIS

B. BAYLES, John son of Mulrain and Winifred Bayles, February 19, 1743.

D. BAYLIS, John son of Mulrain Baylis, July 16, 1743.

B. BAYLES, Peggie daughter of Mulrain Bayles, February 2, 1745.

D. BAILIS, John December 8, 1746.

M. BAYLIS, John and Mary Baylis, October 8, 1747.

M. BAYLIS, Mary and John Baylis, October 8, 1747.

B. BAYLIS, Winy daughter of John and Mary Baylis, November 1, 1747.

M. BAILIS, Winifred and Henry Robinson, August 1, 1750.

B. BAYLIS, Betty daughter of John and Mary Baylis, October 20, 1751. [The name
is spelled Bailis in the baptismal recording.]

B. BAILIS, Jesse son of John and Mary Bailis, February 4, 1754.

B. BAYLIS, Christopher son of John and Mary Baylis, September 9, 1756.

M. BAYLIS, William and Anne Gough, January 19, 1757.

B. BAZELL, William son of Hannah Bazell, January 13, 1743.

D. BEACH, James December 17, 1752 at William Wright's.

M. BEACH, George and Susanna Duke, December 23, 1753.

C. BEACH, [blank] daughter of George and Susanna Beach, August 18, 1754.

B. BEEGLES, [blank] a child of Mary Beegles, August 3, 1745.

B. BEGELL, [blank] a child of Anthony and Mary Begell, September 16, 1742.

M. BEGOLEY, Jacob and Elizabeth Boan, August 4, 1746.

C. BEGOLEY, William Lariue son of Jacob and Elizabeth Begoley, November 30,1746.

M. BELL, Thomas and Mary Latham, June 25, 1741.

B. BELL, John son of Thomas and Mary Bell, July 2, 1743.

D. BELL, John son of Thomas and Mary Bell, October 27, 1744.

M. BELL, George and Anne Hanson, April 15, 1745.

B. BELL, Charity daughter of Thomas Bell, October 27, 1745.

B. BELL, Mary daughter of George and Anne Bell, January 7, 1746.

B. BELL, Elizabeth daughter of Andrew and Mary Bell, October 25, 1746.

B. BELL, Elizabeth daughter of George and Anne Bell, January 31, 1748.

B. BELL, William son of Andrew and Mary Bell, October 25, 1748.

B. BELL, Johnathan son of George and Anne Bell, January 7, 1751.

B. BELL, George son of George and Ann Bell, August 12, 1753.

B. BELL, John son of Thomas and Mary Bell, July 26, 1754.

B. BELL, Elijah son of George and Anne Bell, September 3, 1755.

B. BELL, Thomas son of Thomas Bell, December 24, 1756.

B. BELL, William son of James Bell, January 11, 1757.

M. BELSHER, Miriam and Alexander Maccatiar, December 24, 1751.

M. BENNET, Nicholas and Elizabeth Knight, June 12, 1749.

B. BENSON, Catherine daughter of Charles and Judith Benson, August 29, 1753.

M. BENSON, Enoch and Mary Doial, February 15, 1756.

B. BERRY, Lawrence Suddeth son of Sarah Berry, December 23, 1742.

M. BERRY, Sarah and John Ellis, September 30, 1744.

B. BERRY, Benjamin son of Richard and Sarah Berry, June 10, 1748.

M. BERRY, Bridget and Samuel Mitchell, January 30, 1749.

B. BERRY, Mary daughter of Richard and Sarah Berry, January 19, 1750.

B. BERRY, Sarah daughter of Richard and Sarah Berry, January 13, 1752.

B. BERRY, William son of Richard and Sarah Berry, January 12, 1754.

M. BERRY, William and Anne Porch, February 26, 1754.

M. BETHANY, Thomas and Mary Ann Croswell, December 21, 1755.

M. BETHEL, William and Jean Hurst, December 26, 1739.

B. BETHEL, James son of Edward and Mary Bethel, January 7, 1740.

D. BETHEL, James son of Edward Bethel, January 17, 1741.

B. BETHEL, John son of Elizabeth Bethel, January 24, 1741.

B. BETHEL, Peggy daughter of William and Jean Bethel, November 30, 1741.

B. BETHEL, Henry son of Edward and Mary Bethel, February 6, 1742.

B. BETHEL, John son of Edward and Mary Bethel, June 23, 1744.

M. BETHEL, Mary and Joseph Lee, November 14, 1745.

B. BETHEL, Sary daughter of Edward and Mary Bethel, July 23, 1747.

D. BETHEL, Joseph September 15, 1748.

M.   BETHEL, Sythe and Robert Hammit, February 7, 1749.

B.   BETHEL, Samuel son of William Bethel, February 9, 1749.

B.   BETHEL, Elizabeth daughter of Edward and Mary Bethel, March 26, 1749.

D.   BETHEL, William February 19, 1750.

B.   BETHEL, Seth daughter of Edward and Mary Bethel, March 10, 1751.

B.   BETHEL, Edward son of Edward Bethel, April 30, 1754.

B.   BETHEL, Mary daughter of Edward Bethel, August 10, 1756.

M.   BETTSON, Thomas and Jane Merringham, April 14, 1748.

B.   BETTSON, Thomas son of Thomas and Jane Bettson, July 23, 1748.

     BETTY : BATTY : BATEY

M.   BATEY, Simson and Elizabety Mccarty, December 24, 1747.

B.   BETTY, William son of Simpson Betty, February 3, 1750.

B.   BETTY, Ann daughter of Simpson and Elizabeth Betty, February 9, 1753.

B.   BETTY, Lettice daughter of Simpson and Elizabeth Betty, April 11, 1756.

M.   BIDDLE, Thomas and Bridget Amely, February 5, 1758.

B.   BISCOE, Mary "daughter of Mary Biscoe, Marquis Calmee's serv^t:", January 1, 1741.

M.   BLACK, William and Anne Dent, October 17, 1745.

M.   BLACKBURN, Edward and Margaret Harrison, May 26, 1757.

M.   BLACKMAN, Hannah and Joshua Noble, September 7, 1746.

M.   BLAND, Moses and Jane Wiggonton, January 14, 1750.

M.   BLUEFORD, Jemima and Robert English, November 22, 1756.

D.   BLUFARD, Elizabeth the mother of Thomas Weathers, August 13, 1750.

M.   BOAN, Elizabeth and Jacob Begoley, August 4, 1745.

     BOLING : BOLLING : BOALIN

M.   BOLING, Edmund and Mary Sudduth, May 4, 1744.

M. BOALIN, Jean and John Asberry, February 25, 1745.

B. BOLLING, John son of Edmund Bolling, October 12, 1746.

B. BOLING, Nancy daughter of Edmund and Ann Boling, April 25, 1749.

M. BOLING, Johannah and William Fuell, February 17, 1750.

B. BOLING, William son of Edmund and Mary Boling, March 8, 1752.

M. BOLLING, Elizabeth and Robert Mays, December 27, 1756.

B. BOLING, Elizabeth daughter of Edmund and Mary Boling, October 30, 1757.

B. BOTTS, Elizabeth daughter of Seth and Sib Botts, October 3, 1741.[1]

D. BOTTS, Thomas March 9, 1742 at Robert Ashby's.

B. BOTTS, William son of Seth and Sibb Botts, April 16, 1744.

B. BOTTS, Aaron son of Seth Botts, July 30, 1746.

B. BOTTS, Joseph son of Seth Botts, June 23, 1748.

D. BOTTS, Elizabeth April 17, 1751.

B. BOTTS, Joshua son of Seth Botts, July 24, 1751.

B. BOTTS, John son of Seth and Seb Botts, October 25, 1754.

M. BOTTS, Sarah and James Wiggonton, February 9, 1756.

B. BOTTS, Jenny daughter of Seth and Sib Botts, January 8, 1757.

M. BOUCHARD, William and Mary Stringfellow, November 12, 1751.

M. BOURN, William and Sarah Ellen Gregg, December 11, 1756.

M. BOWMAN, John and Elizabeth Elliot, December 23, 1750.

B. BOX, Jeoffery August 17, 1738, "belonging to James Dillon."

M. BOX, Mary and Matthew Brooks, August 23, 1741.

B. BRADLEY, Nancy daughter of David and Margaret Bradley, April 26, 1749.

D. BRADLEY, Margaret wife of David Bradley, January 3, 1753.

---

1 - For information relative to the Botts family of Stafford County see Tyler's
    Quarterly Historical and Genealogical Magazine, Volume 31, pages 44-53 and
    Volume 33, pages 249-255.

M. BRADLEY, David and Elizabeth Simson, April 17, 1755.

M. BRADLEY, William and Margaret Fortick, March 26, 1758.

B. BRAGG, Peggy daughter of Joseph Bragg, April 9, 1750.

B. BRAGG, Phoebe daughter of Joseph Bragg, March 25, 1752.

B. BRENT, Innis son of Charles and Hannah Brent, July 24, 1727. [1]

B. BRENT, Catherine daughter of Charles and Hannah Brent, January 12, 1729.

B. BRENT, Mary daughter of Charles and Hannah Brent, May 25, 1732.

B. BRENT, Charles son of Charles and Hannah Brent, June 11, 1735.

B. BRENT, Anne daughter of Charles and Hannah Brent, December 5, 1737. [2]

B. BRENT, Jean daughter of George and Catherine Brent, April 10, 1738.

B. BRENT, Hugh son of Charles and Hannah Brent, November 3, 1739.

B. BRENT, Susannah daughter of Benjamin and Mary Brent, November 29, 1739.

B. BRENT, George son of George and Catherine Brent, October 23, 1740.

B. BRENT, William son of Charles and Hannah Brent, May 19, 1742.

D. BRENT, Captain William August 17, 1742 at Acquia.

B. BRENT, Mary daughter of Benjamin and Mary Brent, March 13, 1744.

B. BRENT, George son of Charles and Hannah Brent, June 7, 1744.

D. BRENT, Catherine wife of George Brent, January 12, 1751.

---

1 - There were two Brent families in Stafford County which have been the subject
of genealogies by Mr. Chester Horton Brent: The Descendants of Coll? Giles
Brent, Cap. George Brent and Robert Brent, Gent. [1946], and The Descendants
of Hugh Brent [1936]. The former is supplemented by Dr. George Mason Graham
Stafford in his work, General George Mason Graham [1947].

2 - It is an error in The Descendants of Hugh Brent, page 59, where it is stated
that Anne Brent (1737-1802) married Hugh Atwell. She married on November 14,
1762 Thomas Atwell, Gentleman, (1737-1788) of Prince William County, Virginia and both of their last wills and Testaments remain of record in Prince
William County. Their children were: (1) Mary, born August 31, 1763; (2)
Charles Brent, born September 5, 1765 [Revolutionary pensioner #S.10064];
(3) Ann (November 2, 1766 - October 10, 1831) married Col. Johnston Smith and
David Gibson; (4) Margaret, born April 16, 1768; (5) William, born January 16,
1770, d.s.p., 1797; (6) Thomas born 19 November 1771; and (7) Hugh Atwell born
June 2. 1774.

M. BRENT, Catherine and James Wren, March 27, 1753.

M. BRENT, Mary and William Wright, October 18, 1753.

D. BRENT, Innes [Innis] son of Charles Brent, September 6, 1754.

M. BRENT, Catherine and James Douglass, October 1, 1754.

D. BRENT, Charles January 13, 1756.

M. BRENT, Mary and Zacharias Lewis, August 24, 1756.

M. BRENT, Susanna and Dr. John Sutherland, September 15, 1756.

M. BRENT, Jane and Richard Graham, February 10, 1757.

M. BRIAND, Mary and John Fling, December 31, 1744.

M. BRIDWELL, Isaac and Abigail Green, January 20, 1740.

M. BRIDWELL, Elizabeth and Aaron Garrison, May 18, 1740.

B. BRIDWELL, William son of John and Lucy Bridwell, October 19, 1740.

B. BRIDWELL, Sarah daughter of John Bridwell, January 13, 1743.

D. BRIDWELL, William son of Abraham Bridwell, April 5, 1743.

B. BRIDWELL, Sarah daughter of Isaac and Abigail Bridwell, May 23, 1743.

B. BRIDWELL, Isaac son of Abraham and Mary Bridwell, June 17, 1743.

M. BRIDWELL, Ann and John Davis, September 11, 1744.

B. BRIDWELL, Millie daughter of Samuel and Mary Bridwell, December 2, 1744.

B. BRIDWELL, John son of Isaac and Abigail Bridwell, December 7, 1744.

M. BRIDWELL, Robert and Elizabeth Jones, January 13, 1745.

B. BRIDWELL, Mary daughter of John and Lucy Bridwell, June 19, 1745.

B. BRIDWELL, Thomas son of Jacob and Elizabeth Bridwell, January 21, 1746.

D. BRIDWELL, Mary daughter of John and Lucy Bridwell, February 22, 1746.

D. BRIDWELL, Mildred daughter of Samuel and Mary Bridwell, March 23, 1746.

B. BRIDWELL, William son of Isaac and Abigail Bridwell, February 10, 1747.

B. BRIDWELL, Sarah daughter of Abraham Bridwell, July 25, 1747.

B. BRIDWELL, Margaret daughter of Jacob Bridwell, January 12, 1748.

B. BRIDWELL, Mealy son of Samuel Bridwell, August [blank], 1749.

B. BRIDWELL, John son of John and Lucy Bridwell, August 10, 1749.

D. BRIDWELL, Mealy son of Samuel Bridwell, November 8, 1749.

B. BRIDWELL, George son of Isaac and Abigail Bridwell, January 26, 1750.

D. BRIDWELL, Isaac son of Abraham Bridwell, May 2, 1750.

M. BRIDWELL, Betty and Richard Simms, October 15, 1750.

M. BRIDWELL, Margaret and Henry Wigginton, November 12, 1750.

B. BRIDWELL, Benjamin son of John Bridwell, April 15, 1752.

D. BRIDWELL, Samuel November 27, 1753. He was drowned in Quantico Run.

B. BRIDWELL, Isaac son of Isaac and Abigail Bridwell, December 9, 1753.

B. BRIDWELL, Elizabeth daughter of Jacob and Elizabeth Bridwell, December 25, 1753.

B. BRIDWELL, George son of John and Lucy Bridwell, December 15, 1754.

B. BRIDWELL, Samuel son of Jacob and Elizabeth Bridwell, March 6, 1756.

B. BRIDWELL, Simon son of John and Lucy Bridwell, August 11, 1757.

M. BRIDWELL, [mutilated] and Lucy Lea, April 9, 1758.

M. BRODERICK, Christopher and Sarah Hammet, December 19, 1744.

M. BRODERICK, Sarah and John Cannon, July 8, 1745.

B. BRODERICK, Mary daughter of Christopher and Sarah Broderick, October 20, 1745.

B. BROMLEY, Betty daughter of William and Judith Bromley, January 3, 1750.

M. BROOKE, Hannah and Alexander Taylor, February 24, 1757.

M. BROOKES, Sarah and John Wilson, February 7, 1752.

M. BROOKS, Matthew and Mary Box, August 23, 1741.

M. BROOKS, Matthew and Jean Jack, February [blank], 1743.

M. BROWN, Frances eldest daughter of Dr. Gustavus Brown of Charles County, Maryland, and the Rev. John Moncure, Rector of this Parish, June 18, 1741.

M. BROWN, John and Hannah Cooke, November 28, 1751.

B. BROWN, Rawleigh Travers son of John and Hannah Brown, July 13, 1753.

M. BROWN, Joshua and Alice Lunsford, July 21, 1754.

M. BROWN, John and Jean Nowland, August 24, 1755.

C. BROWN, Cicy January 18, 1756.

C. BROWN, Pearson March 6, 1757.

M. BRUING, William and Keziah Simmons, February 4, 1753.

M. BRUING, Ann and [?]isfield Noxal, August 1, 1757.

B. BURCHEL, Nanney daughter of Charles and Margaret Burchel, October 12, 1741.

B. BURCHELL, Charles son of Charles Burchell, July 10, 1744.

D. BURCHELL, Charles March 25, 1745.

M. BURCHELL, Margaret and George Hinson, December 29, 1746.

D. BURCHEL, William April 14, 1753 at George Hinson's.

M. BURGES, Garner and Anne Barby, February 19, 1751.

B. BURGES, Peggy daughter of Garner and Ann Burges, July 27, 1751.

C. BURGES, Molly daughter of Garner Burges, December 9, 1753.

M. BURGES, William and Bathsheba Courtney, January 19, 1755.

M. BURK, John and Elizabeth Farlow, August 31, 1755.

M. BURN, James and Catherine Champ, October 14, 1748.

B. BURN, Elizabeth daughter of James and Catherine Burn, March 4, 1749.

B. BURN, Judith daughter of James Burn, May 24, 1751.

B. BURN, Catherine daughter of James and Catherine Burn, August 3, 1753.

B. BURRIS, William, son of Thomas and Mary Burris, December 19, 1744.

B. BURRIS, [blank] a child of Thomas Burris, July 26, 1747.

M. BURTON, Lettice and Alexander Jefferies, September 30, 1741.

B. BURTON, Priscilla daughter of William Burton, January 17, 1746.

M. BURTON, William and Rachel Porch, October 7, 1753.

B. BURTON, Samuel son of William and Rachel Burton, April 20, 1756.

B. BUSH, Elizabeth daughter of George and Mary Bush, February 20, 1746.

B. BUSH, George son of George Bush, August 10, 1748.

B. BUSH, John son of George and Mary Bush, December 20, 1752.

    BUSSEL : BUSSELL

B. BUSSEL, Betty daughter of Hannah Bussel, February 7, 1746.

B. BUSSEL, James son of Winifred Bussel, May 20, 1747.

M. BUSSEL, Hannah and John Honey, February 2, 1748.

M. BUSSELL, Winifred and Philip Peyton, September 15, 1748.

M. BUSSEL, George and Catherine Randal, January 8, 1754.

C. BUSSEL, Agathy daughter of William Bussel, October 26, 1755.

M. BUSSELL, [mutilated] and Sarah Day, February 5, 1758.

D. BUTCHER, Ann November 24, 1747 "a servant of Rawleigh Travers."

B. BUTCHER, James son of William and Mary Butcher, September 10, 1757.

M. BUTLER, Thomas and Mary Mason, April 7, 1741.

D. BUTLER, Thomas December 3, 1743.

M. BUTLER, Mary and John Carter, February 4, 1745.

M. BUTLER, Margaret and Alexander Nelson, February 21, 1745.

M. BUTLER, Joseph and Anne Carter, November 28, 1745.

    BYRAM : BYROM

B. BYROM, Sarah daughter of Cuthbert and Sarah Byrom, November 14, 1740.

M. BYRAM, Elizabeth and Adam Atchison, October 20, 1742.

B. BYRAM, John son of Cuthbert and Sarah Byram, January 19, 1743.

D. BYROM, John son of Cuthbert and Sarah Byrom, March 20, 1743.

M. BYRAM, Lucy and William Gough, October 19, 1743.

B.   BYRAM, Winifred daughter of Cuthbert and Sarah Byram, September 26, 1744.

B.   BYRAM, Milly daughter of Elizabeth Byram, December 10, 1746.

B.   BYRAM, Lucy daughter of Cuthbert Byram, January 29, 1747.

M.   BYRAM, William and Sarah Gough, May 14, 1747.

B.   BYRAM, Mille daughter of William and Sarah Byram, March 28, 1748.

B.   BYRAM, Cuthbert son of Cuthbert Byram, January 6, 1750.

B.   BYRAM, Lizy daughter of William and Sarah Byram, March 12, 1750.

M.   BYRAM, Mary and Alexander Baxter, November 28, 1751.

B.   BYROM, Sarah daughter of William and Sarah Byrom, May 28, 1753.

M.   BYRAM, Winifred and William Routt, November 27, 1753.

B.   BYROM, Nancy daughter of William and Sarah Byrom, October 5, 1755.

M.   BYRAM, Peter and Martha Horton, March 26, 1758.

C

M.   CAMMEL, William and Mary Smith, July 25, 1742.

B.   CAMP, Hannah daughter of Mary Camp, March 26, 1746.

M.   CAMPBELL, James and Elizabeth Millener, September 27, 1741.

M.   CANNADAY, William and Margaret Lince, January 16, 1747.

B.   CANNADAY, Frankey daughter of John and Rose Cannaday, May 29, 1751.

M.   CANNADAY, Lettice and Edward Gill, February 4, 1753.

B.   CANNADAY, Ann daughter of John and Rosanna Cannaday, March 2, 1753.

M.   CANNON, John and Sarah Broderick, July 8, 1745.

B.   CANNON, Ellis son of John and Sarah Cannon, January 3, 1748.

B.   CANNON, John son of John Cannon, February 1, 1750.

B.   CANNON, Henry son of John and Sarah Cannon, April 10, 1752.

B.   CANNON, William son of John and Sarah Cannon, July 4, 1754.

B. CANNON, Sarah, daughter of John Cannon, June 9, 1757.

D. CARBERRY, Edward February 24, 1741.

B. CARBERRY, James son of Edward and Mary Carberry, November 17, 1740.

B. CARNEY, Thomas son of John and Mary Carney, December 18, 1741.

B. CARNEY, Daniel son of John and Mary Carney, January 17, 1744.

D. CARNEY, Daniel son of John and Mary Carney, January 28, 1744

B. CARNEY, Absolom son of John and Mary Carney, January 27, 1745.

B. CARNEY, Mary daughter of John and Mary Carney, October 16, 1747.

B. CARNEY, Jane daughter of John and Mary Carney, December 21, 1749.

M. CARNEY, Sarah and John Anderson, November 28, 1752.

B. CARNEY, Onesby son of John and Mary Carney, January 2, 1755.

B. CARNEY, Anthony son of John and Mary Carney, October 13, 1756.

    CARON   SEE: CARROW   PAGE 17

D. CARON, Frances February 25, 1756 at Richard Fristoe's.

B. CARPENTER, Stephen son of John and Mary Carpenter, June 24, 1737.

B. CARPENTER, John son of John and Mary Carpenter, May 15, 1739.

B. CARPENTER, William son of John and Mary Carpenter, May 5, 1742.

B. CARPENTER, Thomas son of John and Mary Carpenter, August 7, 1744.

B. CARPENTER, Benjamin son of John and Mary Carpenter, October 5, 1746.

B. CARPENTER, Ann daughter of John and Mary Carpenter, October 16, 1748.

B. CARPENTER, George son of John and Mary Carpenter, March 24, 1753.

B. CARPENTER, Charles son of John and Mary Carpenter, September 6, 1756.

D. CARPENTER, Charles son of John and Mary Carpenter, October 10, 1756.

M. CARR, Esther and Peter Reynolds, June 2, 1745.

    CARROW   SEE: CARON   PAGE 17

B. CARROW, Frances daughter of Mary Carrow, June 29, 1754 at Richard Fristoe's.
    CARTEE   SEE: CARTEE : CARTY   PAGE 19

B. CARTER, John son of James and Mary Carter, May 7, 1727. [1]

B. CARTER, James son of James and Mary Carter, March 31, 1729.

B. CARTER, William son of James and Mary Carter, January 11, 1731.

B. CARTER, George son of James and Mary Carter, March 25, 1733.

B. CARTER, Catherine daughter of James and Mary Carter, April 1, 1735.

B. CARTER, Hugh son of James and Mary Carter, November 8, 1740.

B. CARTER, Charles son of James Carter, October 10, 1743.

D. CARTER, James October 24, 1743 "An honest, Good man."

B. CARTER, Dale son of Charles and Lucy Carter, August 9, 1744.

M. CARTER, John and Mary Butler, February 4, 1745.

M. CARTER, Anne and Joseph Butler, November 28, 1745.

M. CARTER, Joseph and Margaret Mason, November 27, 1746.

B. CARTER, Judith daughter of Charles and Lucy Carter, March 17, 1747.

B. CARTER, Mary Ann daughter of Joseph and Margaret Carter, December 7, 1747.

B. CARTER, Robert son of Robert and Winifred Carter, February 14, 1748.

B. CARTER, Lucy daughter of Charles and Lucy Carter, January 16, 1750.

B. CARTER, Mary daughter of Robert and Winifred Carter, May 21, 1750.

D. CARTER, Judith daughter of Charles and Lucy Carter, December 18, 1750.

B. CARTER, Margaret daughter of Joseph and Margaret Carter, March 11, 1751.

D. CARTER, Margaret wife of Joseph Carter, March 12, 1751.

M. CARTER, Solomon and Mary Marony, May 26, 1751.

D. CARTER, Lucy daughter of Charles and Lucy Carter, August 22, 1751.

B. CARTER, James son of John and Leanna Carter, July 17, 1752.

---

1 - The Carter family of Stafford County is discussed by Dr. Joseph L. Miller
    in The Descendants of Captain Thomas Carter [1912]. James Carter (1684-1743)
    married as his second wife, August 10, 1724, Mary Brent and their family is
    also discussed by Chester H. Brent in The Descendants of Hugh Brent [1936].

C. CARTER, James son of John Carter, Junior, August 30, 1752.

B. CARTER, Jedesiah son of Robert Carter, July 29, 1752.

B. CARTER, Catherine daughter of Jeremiah Carter, January 28, 1753.

C. CARTER, Elizabeth daughter of Solomon Carter, July 15, 1753.

B. CARTER, Catherine daughter of Charles Carter, October 15, 1753.

B. CARTER, Catherine daughter of James Carter, April 21, 1754.

B. CARTER, John son of John and Leana Carter, June 1, 1754.

D. CARTER, Margaret daughter of Joseph Carter, October 11, 1754.

M. CARTER, Joseph and Lettice Linton, February 5, 1755.

B. CARTER, Milly daughter of Robert Carter, March 22, 1755.

B. CARTER, Henry son of Jeremiah Carter, September 1, 1755.

B. CARTER, William son of John and Leana Carter, November 22, 1755. [In the
    baptismal record he is called the son of John Carter, Junior.]

M. CARTER, Catherine and William Davis, November 27, 1755.

B. CARTER, Anthony son of Joseph Carter, December 14, 1755.

B. CARTER, Tabitha daughter of Jeremiah Carter, December 11, 1757.

B. CARTER, Alexander son of Joseph Carter, June 16, 1758.

    CARTEE   :   CARTY

D. CARTY, Peter Murphy son of Honour Carty, December 1, 1748.[See Page 85]

B. CARTY, [blank]. "Honour Cartee delivered of a male child which died soon,
D. November 20, 1749."

M. CARTY, Honora and John Adams, September 23, 1750.

D. CARTEE, Thomas June 18, 1751 at Stephen Pilcher's.

B. CASH, Peter son of Peter and Charity Cash, July 17, 1746.

M. CASH, Elizabeth and Calvert Porter, September 21, 1749.

B. CASH, Elizabeth daughter of Peter and Charity Cash, May 26, 1750.

D. CASH, Elizabeth March 9, 1751.

M. CASH, Jean and William Waters, April 6, 1751.

B. CASH, James son of Peter and Charity Cash, October 26, 1753.

M. CASSITY, Catherine and Philip Matthews, January 4, 1742.

M. CASTELLO, Anne and Richard Sayas, September 30, 1746.

B. CAVE, James son of William and Anne Cave, April 24, 1741.

D. CAVE, William August 14, 1742.

D. CAVE, James son of William and Anne Cave, January 6, 1743.

M. CAVE, Anne and Thomas Dent, December 3, 1747.

M. CAVE, Elizabeth and Keene Withers,   December 21, 1747.

D. CAVENAUGH, Edward January [blank], 1742 at Rawleigh Chinn's.

M. CEARNES, Anne and Andrew Kenny, November 30, 1744.

M. CHAMBERS, Sarah and William McDuell, December 26, 1739.

    CHAMP : CHIMP : CHIMPE

M. CHIMP, William and Catherine Taylor, January 31, 1739.

B. CHIMP, John son of William and Catherine Chimp, March 10, 1743.

D. CHAMP, John son of William Champ, August 6, 1743.

B. CHAMP, Lansdell daughter of William and Catherine Champ, December 1, 1744.

B. CHIMPE, Rosamond daughter of William and Catherine Chimpe, November 18, 1746.

D. CHAMP, William November 13, 1747.

M. CHAMP, Catherine and James Burn, October 14, 1748.

M. CHAPMAN, Taylor and Margaret Markham, September 13, 1739.

B. CHAPMAN, Jane daughter of Taylor and Margaret Chapman, January 25, 1740.

D. CHAPMAN, Jane daughter of Taylor Chapman, November 12, 1740.

B. CHAPMAN, Jane daughter of Taylor and Margaret Chapman, January 25, 1741.

B. CHAPMAN, William son of Taylor and Margaret Chapman, September 12, 1741.

D. CHAPMAN, Taylor November 10, 1749.

CHIMP : CHIMPE : CHAMP   SEE: CHAMP : CHIMP : CHIMPE PAGE 20

B. CHINN, Lettice daughter of Rawleigh and Elizabeth Chinn, October 17, 1740.

B. CHINN, Lizzey daughter of Betty Chinn, October 18, 1745.

M. CHINN, Betty and Solomon Waugh, April 13, 1748.

M. CHINN, Rawleigh and Sarah Lacy, September 2, 1748.

B. CHINN, Margaret daughter of Rawleigh and Sarah Chinn, May 14, 1749.

M. CHINN, Hannah and John Risen, October 20, 1750.

M. CHINN, [blank] and Matthew Gregg, August 15, 1751.

B. CHINN, [blank] son of Rawleigh Chinn, Junior, November 18, 1751.

B. CHINN, Ann daughter of Rawleigh Chinn, Junior, December 15, 1754.

D. CHINN, Joseph January 28, 1754.

D. CLARK, Catherine May 7, 1741 at James Suddeth's.

M. CLARKE, Lucy and Stephen Pilcher, December 7, 1748.

B. CLUTTERBUCK, Mary daughter of William and Mary Clutterbuck, October 25, 1740.

M. COCKLEN, Margaret and William Todd, October 23, 1752.

M. COCKLEY, Robert and Sarah Sinclair, September 21, 1740.

COFFEE : COFFEY : COFFY : COFY

B. COFY, James son of Peter and Susannah Cofy, February 27, 1740.

D. COFFY, Frances daughter of Peter Coffy, January 5, 1741.

B. COFFEE, Lydia daughter of Peter and Susannah Coffee, January 25, 1742.

B. COFFEE, Benjamin son of Peter and Susannah Coffee, October 9, 1743.

M. COFFEY, Mary and James Kendal, February 25, 1745.

D. COLBURN, John son of John Colburn, February 3, 1754.

M. COLE, Catherine and Philip Pritchet, June 24, 1742.

B. COLEMAN, John son of John and Isabel Coleman, August 6, 1753.

B. COLEMAN, Lizy daughter of John and Isabel Coleman, February 13, 1755.

B.   COLEMAN, Jesse son of John and Isabel Coleman, September 3, 1757.

M.   COLLIE, James and Anne Cornwall, February 21, 1751.

B.   COLLIE, Charles son of James and Anne Collie, January 25, 1756.

M.   COLSON, Charles and Elizabeth Norton, February 1, 1739.

B.   COMBS, William son of Mason and Sarah Combs, November 28, 1740.

M.   COMBS, Jean and John Ashby, May 11, 1741.

B.   COMBS, Anne daughter of Mason and Sarah Combs, March 18, 1743.

B.   COMBS, Sarah daughter of Mason and Sarah Combs, February 25, 1745.

B.   COMBS, Mason son of Mason and Sarah Combs, February 21, 1747.

B.   COMBS, Winny daughter of Mason and Sarah Combs, May 14, 1749.

B.   COMBS, Wilmot daughter of Mason Combs, October 5, 1751.

D.   CONALLY, John January 18, 1750 at the house of Hannah Bailis.

B.   CONDRING, Jane daughter of Richard Condring, January 11, 1752.

M.   CONNALLY, Dorothy and Robert Read, November 10, 1747.

     CONWELL   SEE: CORNWEL

M.   CONYERS, Sarah Pattison alias and Thomas Hampton, June 1, 1749. [1]

M.   CONYERS, Anne Holland and Edward Payne, February 27, 1750.

M.   CONYERS, Theodosia and James Oduneal, October 19, 1755.

---

1 - Henry Conyers (16 -1733) appears in Stafford County circa 1700. By an unknown first wife he had (1) Hester Conyers who married John Mauzey and left
issue. Out of wedlock by Jannett Patterson [Pattison] he had (2) Sarah Patterson alias Conyers who married Thomas Hampton on June 1, 1749. Henry Conyers
married the said Jannett Patterson in 1727 and had (3) Ann Holland Conyers
(1728-1806) who married Edward Payne, Gentleman, (1726-1806); and (4) Theodosia Conyers (born circa 1730, per her deposition) who married James Oduneal [Duneale - Deneale]. Jannett Patterson Conyers, widow, married secondly in 1733 shortly after the death of Henry Conyers, Randall Holbrook. Dr.
A.J. Mauzey gives considerable genealogical information in regard to the Mauzey - Conyers family in his article on The Mauzey-Mauzy Family in The Virginia
Magazine of History and Biography, Volume 58, pages 112-119. Colonel Brooke
Payne in The Paynes of Virginia, pages 235-238 gives an excellent account of
the family of Edward Payne, Gentleman, with notes on the Conyers family.

M.   COOK, Jane and William Pritchet,   January 26, 1742.

D.   COOKE, Mildred   October 20, 1745.

M.   COOKE, Margaret and William Horton,   December 21, 1749.

M.   COOKE, Hannah and John Brown, November 28, 1751.

M.   COOKE, Travers and Mary Doniphan,   February 26, 1754.

D.   COOKE, John September 27, 1754 at Robert Fristoe's.

B.   COOKE, John son of Travers and Mary Cooke,   February 5, 1755.

M.   COOKE, Anne and Thomas Roach,   December 28, 1755.

B.   COOKE, Mott son of Travers and Mary Cooke,   March 17, 1757.

B.   COOPER, Joseph son of Joseph and Elizabeth Cooper,   July 22, 1740.

B.   COOPER, Juhonias son of Joseph and Betty Cooper,   February 20, 1742.

B.   COOPER, John son of Joseph and Elizabeth Cooper,   December 4, 1743.

B.   COOPER, Enos son of Joseph and Elizabeth Cooper,   April 26, 1745.

D.   COOPER, John   March 3, 1745.

B.   COOPER, [blank] son of Bridget Mary Cooper, March 6, 1747 at John Hayes'.

B.   COOPER, Thomas Timmons son of Joseph Cooper,   May 29, 1748.

D.   COOPER, Thomas Timmons son of Joseph Cooper,   February 2, 1749.

B.   COOPER, Spencer son of Joseph Cooper,   October 22, 1749.

M.   COOPER, Bridget and John Sylva,   July 1, 1750.

B.   COOPER, Vincent son of Joseph and Elizabeth Cooper,   October 10, 1751.

D.   COOPER, Vincent son of Joseph Cooper,   March 15, 1752.

B.   COOPER, Jesse son of Joseph and Elizabeth Cooper,   April 14, 1753.

B.   COOPER, Thomas son of Joseph and Elizabeth Cooper,   September 20, 1756.

M.   COOPER, William and Elizabeth Oliford,   January 5, 1758.

M.   CORBIN, William and Sarah Jenkins,   January [blank], 1743.

B.   CORBIN, Anne daughter of William and Sarah Corbin,   June 22, 1743.

M. CORBIN, William and Sarah Want, August 2, 1744.

B. CORBAN, Peter son of William and Sarah Corban, April 23, 1746.

B. CORBIN, John son of William and Sarah Corbin, November 22, 1747.

C. CORBIN, Mary daughter of William and Sarah Corbin, April 9, 1749.

B. CORBIN, [blank], a child of William Corbin, November 10, 1749.

M. CORBIN, John and Frances Fant, December 7, 1749.

B. CORBIN, William son of John and Frances Corbin, February 7, 1751.

B. CORBIN, Margaret daughter of William and Sarah Corbin, January 17, 1752.

B. CORBIN, James son of John and Frances Corbin, November 8, 1756.

M. CORNISH, Charles and Elizabeth Smith, December 17, 1738.

M. CORNWALL, Anne and James Collie, February 21, 1751.

    CORWEL   :   CONWELL

B. CORNWEL, John son of Margaret Cornwel, March 31, 1750.

B. CONWELL, Barnet son of Margaret Conwell, April 17, 1752.

M. COTNEY, William and Mary Barbee, February 24, 1745.

B. COTNEY, John son of William and Mary Cotney, November 10, 1745.

M. COTTON, John and Susannah Smith, February 17, 1743.

M. COURTNEY, Anne and Henry Foley, December 24, 1738.

B. COURTNEY, Elizabeth daughter of William Courtney, January 1, 1748.

M. COURTNEY, Bathsheba and William Burges, January 19, 1755.

M. CRAP, James and Joyce Hinson, June 3, 1750.

B. CRAP, John son of James Crap, Junior, October 7, 1753.

M. CRAVEN, Francisina and Samuel Mahanes, November 14, 1742.

B. CROSBY, Uriel son of George and Sarah Crosby, August 19, 1738.[1]

_____

1 - Uriel Crosby (August 19,1738 - February 8, 1799) married January 11, 1764 in
    Fauquier County, his cousin, Susannah Conway (March 17, 1745 - August 19,
    1805), daughter of Thomas Conway and Elizabeth Mauzey, his wife; they had
    fourteen children.

C.   CROSBY, Anna daughter of George and Sarah Crosby,   October 4, 1741.

M.   CROSBY, George and Mary Hughes,   January 6, 1744.

B.   CROSBY, Sally daughter of George and Sarah Crosby,   March 3, 1744.

B.   CROSBY, Anne daughter of George Crosby, Junior, and Mary, his wife, May 30, 1745.

D.   CROSBY, Sally daughter of George Crosby,   October 28, 1745.

D.   CROSBY, Ann daughter of George Crosby,   October 31, 1745.

D.   CROSBY, George   December 5, 1745.

B.   CROSBY, George son of George and Mary Crosby,   September 1, 1747.

M.   CROSBY, Sarah and Edward Ralls,   November 24, 1748.

B.   CROSBY, Mary daughter of George and Mary Crosby,   November 14, 1757.

M.   CROSEWEL, Ruth and Peter Stacey,   May 25, 1755.

M.   CROSWELL, Mary Ann and Thomas Bethany,   December 21, 1755.

M.   CRUMP, Benjamin and Hannah James,   February 2, 1749.

M.   CUBBAGE, John and Mary Jenkins,   July 10, 1750.

B.   CUBBIGE, Elizabeth daughter of John and Mary Cubbige,   April 7, 1751.

B.   CUBBIGE, Mary daughter of John Cubbige, April 15, 1753.

B.   CUBBIGE, William son of John and Mary Cubbige,   September 29, 1755.

M.   CUMMINGS, John and Lettice Phillips,   February 21, 1757.   "See Sept. 1741"[1]

M.   CUNIBERFORD, James and Elizabeth Holdbroke,   September 15, 1754.

B.   CUNNINGHAM, William son of Morris Cunningham,   March 21, 1744.

                                    D

M.   DABNEY, George and Mary Waller, September 11, 1754.

B.   DAFFIN, Keziah daughter of Henry and Judith Daffin,   March 3, 1751.

---

1 - The Rev. Mr. Moncure by this notation directs attention to the birth of Lettice, daughter of James and Elizabeth (Griffin) Phillips.   See Page 93.

B.   DALTON, Thomas son of James and Rachel Dalton,   July 10, 1741.

C.   DALTON, Anne daughter of John Dalton, September 29, 1745.

M.   DANIEL, Peter and Sarah Traverse,   July 15, 1736.

B.   DANIEL, Hannah daughter of Peter and Sarah Daniel,   September 9, 1737.

B.   DANIEL, Travers son of Peter and Sarah Daniel,   May 26, 1741.

B.   DANIEL, Elizabeth Travers daughter of Peter and Sarah Daniel,   May 16, 1745.

M.   DANIEL, Hannah and George Hedgman,   November 27, 1756.

M.   DANIEL, Travers and Frances Moncure, Junior, October 7, 1762 at Clermont, by the Rev. Mr. James Scott.

B.   DANIEL, Travers son of Travers and Frances Daniel, August 4, 1763.

M.   DARLOW, Thomas and Margaret Lynn,   April 9, 1758.

B.   DAVIDS, Elizabeth daughter of John and Anne Davids,   March 2, 1746.

M.   DAVIS, John and Ann Bridwell,   September 11, 1744.

B.   DAVIS, Thomas son of John Davis,   August 8, 1747.

B.   DAVIS, John son of John Davis,   November 11, 1748.

B.   DAVIS, Nanny daughter of John Davis,   March 28, 1750.

M.   DAVIS, Susannah and Richard Smith,   November 17, 1752.

B.   DAVIS, Isaac son of John Davis,   February 7, 1753.

M.   DAVIS, William and Catherine Carter,   November 27, 1755.

DAVIDSON   :   DAVISON

M.   DAVISON, Andrew and Sarah McInteer,   November 5, 1738.

B.   DAVIDSON, James son of Andrew and Sarah Davidson,   November 22, 1739.

B.   DAVIDSON, Andrew son of Andrew and Sarah Davidson,   January 9, 1742.

B.   DAVIDSON, William son of Andrew and Sarah Davidson,   October 25, 1745.

DAWSON   :   DOSON   :   DOYSON

M.   DAWSON, Jean and George Knight,   December 25, 1744.

M.   DAWSON, Christopher and Jane George,   February 16, 1750.

B. DOYSON, John son of Christopher and Jean Doyson, July 28, 1751.

B. DAWSON, Sarah daughter of Christopher and Jean Dawson, September 15, 1753.

M. DAWSON, Henry and Betty Turner, December 15, 1754.

B. DOSON, William and Henry sons of Christopher and Jane Doson, May 27, 1755.

D. DOSON, William and Henry sons of Christopher Doson, June 15, 1755.

D. DOSON, Sarah daughter of Christopher Doson, July 15, 1755.

B. DOSON, Henry son of Christopher Doson, June 27, 1756.

B. DAWSON, Jane daughter of Christopher and Jane Dawson, March 17, 1758.

B. DAY, Francis son of Francis and Mary Day, September 29, 1742.

B. DAY, John son of Francis and Mary Day, February 5, 1745.

B. DAY, Mary Ann daughter of Francis Day, September 28, 1747.

B. DAY, Constant daughter of Francis Day, January 2, 1751.

M. DAY, Robert and Mary Gum, January 16, 1757.

B. DAY, Winny daughter of Robinson and Mary Day, October 18, 1757.

M. DAY, Sarah and [mutilated] Bussell, February 5, 1758.

    DENEALE   SEE: DUNEAL PAGE 30 ALSO O'DUNEAL PAGE 89

M. DECKON, Margaret and James Reynolds, August 19, 1746.

    DENT : DINT

M. DINT, Arthur and Elizabeth Manuel, December 11, 1742.

B. DINT, Mary daughter of Arthur and Elizabeth Dint, November 8, 1743.

M. DENT, Anne and William Black, October 17, 1745.

B. DENT, James son of Arthur Dent, December 21, 1745.

M. DENT, Thomas and Anne Dave, December 3, 1747.

M. DEVANE, Mary and John Herrod, August 21, 1748.

D. DEVEENE, Margaret February 2, 1750 "the daughter of Mary Harod, surnamed
    Deveene."

M. DIAL, Mitchell and Mary Smith, November 19, 1752.

B.   DICK, Moses son of Jane Dick,   January 23, 1753.

B.   DICKINSON, Mary daughter of Edward and Anne Dickinson,   February 15, 1745.

M.   DILLON, Anne and William Hacker,   May 21, 1738.

M.   DILLON, James and Margaret Warner,   November 16, 1742.

M.   DILLON, James and Anne Suddeth,   July 24, 1746.

     DINT : DENT   SEE: DENT : DINT PAGE 27

M.   DINWIDDIE, Elizabeth and Gerrard Fowke,   November 26, 1745.

M.   DISKIN, John and Frances Mccarty,   June 19, 1755.

B.   DOBIE, Anne daughter of Anne Dobie,   October 25, 1744.

M.   DOIAL, Mary and Enoch Benson,   February 15, 1756.

M.   DONALDSON, John and Ann MacMurry,   December 31, 1747.

M.   DONIPHAN, Alexander and Mary Waugh,   June 17, 1740.[1]

B.   DONIPHAN, William son of Alexander and Mary Doniphan,   March 30, 1742.

M.   DONIPHAN, Anne and George White,   August 4, 1743.

B.   DONIPHAN, Elizabeth daughter of Alexander and Mary Doniphan,   April 18, 1744.

B.   DONIPHAN, Anne daughter of Alexander and Mary Doniphan,   February 28, 1747.

B.   DONIPHAN, Alexander son of Alexander and Mary Doniphan,   March 12, 1750.

B.   DONIPHAN, Mott son of Alexander and Mary Doniphan,   June 10, 1752.

M.   DONIPHAN, Mary and Travers Cooke,   February 26, 1754.

     DOOLING : DOELING : DOWLING

B.   DOOLING, Nancy daughter of Robert Dooling,   October 31, 1750.

B.   DOOLING, Margaret daughter of John Dooling,   December 25, 1751.

_____

1 - Some account of the ancestors and descendants of Captain Alexander Doniphan
     (171?-1768) will be found in Tyler's Quarterly Historical and Genealogical
     Magazine, Volume 26, pages 275-285. His wife, nee Mary Waugh, was the only
     child of Joseph Waugh, Gentleman, (circa 1660-1727) of Belle Plaine on Poto-
     mac Creek, and his second wife Mary (Crosby) Mountjoy Mauzey, and granddaugh-
     ter of the Rev. Mr. John Waugh (1630-1706). An account of her family connec-
     tions will be found in Tyler's Quarterly Historical and Genealogical Magazine,
     Volume 26, pages 99-104.

B.   DOELING, Mary Ann daughter of Robert Doeling, April 5, 1753.

B.   DOELING, James son of Robert Doeling, May 9, 1755.

M.   DOWLING, Nicholas and Elizabeth Dunnaway, June 30, 1754.

D.   DOOLING, Nancy daughter of Nicholas Dooling, October 24, 1756.

     DOSON   SEE: DAWSON : DOSON : DOYSON   PAGES 26-27

M.   DOUGLASS, James and Catherine Brent, October 1, 1754.

B.   DOUGLASS, George son of James and Catherine Brent, December 2, 1756.

D.   DOUGLASS, December 9, 1756.

     DOWLING   SEE: DOOLING : DOELING : DOWLING   PAGES 28-29

     DOYSON   SEE: DAWSON : DOSON : DOYSON   PAGES 26-27

M.   DRISCAL, Derby and Jean Noble, October 4, 1756.

M.   DRUO, Anne and William Miller, March 5, 1739.

D.   DUARS, Sarah March 5, 1749 at John Walters'.

B.   DUFFY, Stella, daughter of Margaret Duffy, November 28, 1740.

D.   DUFFY, Stella, daughter of Margaret Duffy, December 4, 1740.

M.   DUKE, Susanna and George Beach, December 23, 1753.

     DUNAWAY : DUNNAWAY

M.   DUNAWAY, Mary and James Stuart, February 12, 1740.

B.   DUNAWAY, Mary daughter of Samuel and Elizabeth Dunaway, January 6, 1740.

M.   DUNAWAY, Sarah and Thomas Martin, January 22, 1742.

D.   DUNAWAY, Laton son of Daniel Dunaway, January 31, 1744.

M.   DUNNAWAY, Daniel and Jean Judd, March 1, 1744.

B.   DUNAWAY, Charity daughter of Joseph Dunaway, March 7, 1745.

B.   DUNNAWAY, Hethe daughter of Joseph and Elizabeth Dunnaway, May 22, 1745.

B.   DUNNAWAY, Jean daughter of Joseph Dunnaway, January 2, 1748.

B.   DUNNAWAY, Eton son of Daniel Dunnaway, April 12, 1749.

C.　DUNNAWAY, Ezekial　July 23, 1749.

D.　DUNAWAY, Eton son of Daniel Dunaway, September 9, 1749.

B.　DUNNAWAY, Isaac son of Daniel Dunnaway,　September 20, 1750.

D.　DUNNAWAY,　Jane wife of Daniel Dunnaway,　October 28, 1750.

D.　DUNNAWAY, Daniel　December 12, 1751.

M.　DUNNAWAY, Elizabeth and Benjamin Tolson,　February 25, 1752.

M.　DUNNAWAY, Isaac and Mary Ann Tolson,　May 25, 1754.

M.　DUNAWAY, Elizabeth and Nicholas Dowling,　June 30, 1754.

B.　DUNAWAY, Benjamin son of Isaac and Mary Dunaway,　November 27, 1757.

D.　DUNCOMB, Samuel　November 30, 1740 "a servant belonging to John Jackson."

M.　DUNCOMB, Rosamond and Anthony Horton,　December 27, 1745.

　　DUNEAL　　SEE: O'DUNEAL　　PAGE 89

B.　DUNEAL, William Scott son of James and Theodosia Duneal,　August 10, 1756.

　　DUEST : DUWEST

M.　DUWEST, Elizabeth and Whorton Hooliday,　July 28, 1742.

B.　DUEST, Elizabeth daughter of Mary Duest, January 6, 1753.

M.　DUWEST, Elizabeth and George Mason,　October 21, 1755.

D.　DUWEST, Samuel son of Arthur Duwest,　September 1, 1740.

　　　　　　　　　　　　　　　E

M.　EARLE, Samuel and Elizabeth Holdbrooke, January 13, 1754. [1]

B.　EARLE, Theodosia Scott daughter of Samuel and Elizabeth Earle, November 14, 1754.

---

1 - She was the daughter of Randall Holdbrook(e) and Jannett Patterson Conyers, his wife, mentioned on page 22; see Stafford County Book "P", page 84, for a deed of gift dated 1755 from Randall Holdbrook to his son in law Samuel Earle and Elizabeth, his wife.　The Earle family, early domiciled in Westmoreland County, were property holders in Stafford County. Samuel Earle moved to Frederick County. See I.N. Earle, History and Genealogy of the Earles of Secaucus, with an account of other English and American branches [1925].

B. EARLE, Betty daughter of Samuel and Elizabeth Earle, September 6, 1756.

B. EATON, Mary daughter of William Eaton, May 22, 1744.

B. EATON, Sarah daughter of William Eaton, August 27, 1747.

B. EAVES, William son of Thomas Eaves, Junior, and Catherine, his wife, November 9, 1739.

B. EAVES, Thomas son of Thomas Eaves, Junior, and Catherine, his wife, August 15, 1742.

D. EAVES, Anne wife of Thomas Eaves, February 6, 1743.

M. EAVES, Winifred and Peter Wiggonton, October 13, 1746.

D. EAVES, Thomas March 10, 1752.

M. EAVES, Anne and Nathan Bannister, May 24, 1752.

M. EAVES, Hannah and John Stark, May 29, 1756.

B. EDGHILL, Jean daughter of Thomas Edghill, March 18, 1754.

B. EDRINGTON, Thomas son of William Edrington, August 17, 1743.

B. EDRINGTON, Christopher son of William Edrington, April 16, 1749.

B. EDRINGTON, Anne daughter of William Edrington, March 19, 1751.

B. EDRINGTON, John son of William Edrington, August 28, 1753.

B. EDRINGTON, James son of William and Betty Edrington, February 24, 1756.

M. EDWARDS, Elizabeth and William King, May 21, 1738.

B. EDWARDS, Jesse son of Ignatius and Mary Edwards, February 14, 1742.

B. EDWARDS, James son of Mearedy and Mary Edwards, February 22, 1744.

D. EDWARDS, John son of Ignatius Edwards, February 24, 1744.

B. EDWARDS, Anne daughter of Ignatius and Mary Edwards, July 17, 1745.

D. EDWARDS, James October 11, 1745.

B. EDWARDS, Elizabeth daughter of Meredith and Mary Edwards, December 22,1746.

B. EDWARDS, John son of Robert and Sarah Edwards, March 26, 1748.

B. EDWARDS, Sarah daughter of Ignatius and Mary Edwards, June 28, 1748.

B. EDWARDS, Meredith son of Meredith and Mary Edwards, September 12, 1749.

D. EDWARDS, Meredith October 16, 1749.

B. EDWARDS, Matthias son of Robert and Sarah Edwards, August 27, 1750.

D. EDWARDS, Ignatius October 15, 1750.

M. EDWARDS, Andrew and Betty Waugh May 7, 1751.[1]

B. EDWARDS, Betty daughter of Andrew and Betty Edwards, February 7, 1752.

D. EDWARDS, Betty daughter of Andrew and Betty Edwards, August 23, 1753.

B. EDWARDS, Billy son of Andrew and Betty Edwards, October 1, 1753.

D. EDWARDS, William Carter September 3, 1753 at Mary Edwards'.

B. EDWARDS, Jean daughter of Robert and Sarah Edwards, September 29, 1754.

M. EDWARDS, Bridget and Jeremiah Spilman, January 16, 1755.

B. EDWARDS, Robert son of Robert and Sarah Edwards, February 6, 1756.

M. EDWARDS, William and Eleanor Wheeler, February 12, 1756. [See page 128]

B. EDWARDS, Nancy daughter of Andrew and Betty Edwards, March 6, 1756.

M. EDWARDS, [mutilated]-her and Sarah Stacey, May 6, 1757.

M. EDWARDS, Andrew and Elizabeth Withers, January 19, 1758.[1]

M. EDZAR, James and Eleanor Grinnan, November 22, 1754.

B. EDZAR, Esdras son of James and Eleanor Edzar, August 25, 1755.

---

1 - Andrew Edwards (1725-1788) was probably thrice married: (1) unknown; (2) in
1751 to Betty (Brittingham) French Waugh, daughter of Nathaniel Brittingham
(16 -1741) of Pockomoke, Accomac County, and widow of Hugh French, Junior,
(17 -1740) and Captain James Waugh (17 -1750); and (3) in 1758 to Elizabeth
(Cave) Withers, daughter of William Cave who died testate in Stafford County
in 1742 and widow of Keene Withers (1728-1756) by whom she had five children.
The Withers issue are detailed by Gottschalk and Osler in Withers Family of
The County of Lancaster, England and of Stafford County, Virginia [1947] and
by Franz V. Recum in Withers -- America [1949]. Andrew and Elizabeth (Cave)
Edwards had an only child, Andrew Neale Monkister Edwards who married on October 13, 1803 in King George County, Sally Mason. Elizabeth (Cave) Withers
Edwards, widow, married thirdly Thomas Walker. The will of Andrew Edwards
was dated July 4, 1788 and proved July 14, 1788; he mentions his wife Elizabeth and her son Andrew N.M. Edwards, son Travers Edwards; and daughters Margaret wife of Robert Lowry, Mary wife of Alvin Mountjoy, Sarah and Anna Edward

B. ELKIN, David son of William and Martha Elkin, November 9, 1741.

B. ELKINS, Sally daughter of William Elkins, October 13, 1744.

B. ELKINS, Margaret daughter of William Elkins, August 7, 1747.

M. ELLIOT, Samuel and Esther Flood, August 8, 1742.

M. ELLIOTT, Samuel and Elizabeth Higgerson, May 20, 1747.

B. ELLIOTT, Anne daughter of Samuel and Elizabeth Elliott, July 10, 1748.

D. ELLIOTT, Samuel November 30, 1748.

M. ELLIOT, Elizabeth and John Bowman, December 23, 1750.

M. ELLIS, John and Sarah Berry, September 30, 1744.

B. ELLIS, Sith daughter of John and Sarah Ellis, July 22, 1745.

C. ELLIS, Milly September 30, 1750.

B. ELLIS, Jezreel son of Sarah Ellis, November 14, 1753.

B. ELLIS, [mutilated]-dey son of Sarah Ellis, March 15, 1756.

B. ENGLISH, [mutilated]-ze daughter of John and Mary English, May 30, 1756.

M. ENGLISH, Robert and Jemima Blueford, November 22, 1756.

B. ENGLISH, Sarah daughter of Robert and Jemima English, January 23, 1757.

M. EVANS, Elizabeth and Jeremiah Tongate, March 3, 1751.

F

B. FANT, Samuel son of William Fant, August 26, 1741.

M. FANT, Catherine and Alexander Simpson, July 17, 1743.

B. FANT, George son of William and Catherine Fant, June 5, 1745.

M. FANT, Margaret and Thomas Barbee, September 29, 1748.

B. FANT, Nathaniel son of William and Catherine Fant, January 10, 1749.

M. FANT, Frances and John Corbin, December 7, 1749.

M. FARLOW, Elizabeth and John Burk, August 31, 1755.

M. FARROW, Alexander and Ann O'Canion, October 5, 1753.

M. FERNSLEY, James and Sarah Robinson, November 3, 1748.

B. FERNSLEY, Sarah daughter of James and Sarah Fernsley, February 10, 1753.

D. FITZHUGH, Catherine wife of Thomas Fitzhugh, February 26, 1748.

C. FITZHUGH, Thomas son of John Fitzhugh, July 8, 1753.

C. FITZHUGH, Susanna daughter of John Fitzhugh, February 29, 1756.

B. FITZPATRICK, Lucy bastard daughter of Bridget Fitzpatrick, January 2, 1750
    at Charles Hinson's.

M. FITZPATRICK, John and Mary Waters, February 12, 1752.

B. FITZPATRICK, Thomas son of John and Mary Fitzpatrick, February 26, 1752.

B. FITZPATRICK, Ann bastard child of Bridget Fitzpatrick, June 4, 1753.

M. FLETCHER, George and Sarah Grigsby, January [blank], 1743.

B. FLETCHER, Sarah daughter of Charles Fletcher, May 31, 1743.

C. FLETCHER, Sarah daughter of Charles Fletcher, May 31, 1746.

M. FLETCHER, Elizabeth and Benjamin Allenthorp, August 19, 1746.

M. FLETCHER, Abraham and Priscilla Grigsby, November 28, 1746.

D. FLETCHER, George March 16, 1749.

M. FLETCHER, Moses and Sarah Martin, July 10, 1757.

M. FLING, John and Mary Briand, December 31, 1744.

    FLITTER   SEE: FRITTER : FLETTER : FLITTER   PAGE 38

M. FLOOD, Esther and Samuel Elliot, August 8, 1742.

C. FLOYD, Betty Ann daughter of James Floyd, June 7, 1752.

M. FOLEY, Henry and Anne Courtney, December 24, 1738.

B. FOLEY, Hannah daughter of John and Rosanna Foley, April 20, 1742.

M. FOLEY, Mary and Benjamin Stringfellow, June 15, 1743.

M. FOLEY, John and Sarah Poole, December 11, 1744.

B. FOLEY, Barnett son of John and Rosanna Foley, February 14, 1749.

B.   FORD, Mary daughter of David and Mary Ford, February 9, 1749.

B.   FORD, David son of David Ford, April 1, 1751.

D.   FOREGAST, James December 15, 1748 at William Wright's.

M.   FORTICK, Margaret and William Bradley, March 26, 1758.

     FORSTER : FOSTER

M.   FOSTER, George and Margaret Grigsby, December 22, 1746.

M.   FORSTER, William and Nanny Jordan, June 15, 1749.

B.   FORSTER, Isabell daughter of William and Anne Forster, February 16, 1753.

B.   FOSTER, Elizabeth daughter of William and Ann Foster, February 26, 1751.

B.   FOWKE, William Chandler son of Chandler and Mary Fowke, September 4, 1723.[1]

B.   FOWKE, John son of Chandler and Mary Fowke, January 17, 1725.

B.   FOWKE, Elizabeth daughter of Chandler and Mary Fowke, April 27, 1727.

B.   FOWKE, Anne daughter of Chandler and Mary Fowke, January 13, 1729.

B.   FOWKE, Chandler the younger son of Chandler and Mary Fowke, May 3, 1732.

D.   FOWKE, Ann daughter of Chandler and Mary Fowke, December 8, 1732.

B.   FOWKE, Sarah daughter of Chandler and Mary Fowke, August 10, 1734.

B.   FOWKE, Ann the younger daughter of Chandler and Mary Fowke, September 4, 1737.

D.   FOWKE, Sarah daughter of Chandler and Mary Fowke, October 14, 1739.

B.   FOWKE, Susannah daughter of Chandler and Mary Fowke, October 24, 1739.

D.   FOWKE, John son of Chandler and Mary Fowke, April 16, 1740.

---

1 - Captain Chandler Fowke (16 -1745) of Gunston Hall, Stafford County, was the
    son of Colonel Gerard Fowke (1662-1734) and Sarah Burdett, his wife, whose
    lineages are detailed by Jester and Hiden in Adventurers of Purse and Person,
    Virginia, 1607—1625, pages 192 and 331. He married Mary Fossaker, daughter
    of Colonel Richard Fossaker and his wife nee Mary Withers; she was the daught-
    er of Captain John Withers and married first Thomas Hathaway. The Reverend
    Horace Hayden in his Virginia Genealogies, pages 154—161) gives an account
    of the Fowke family and this account is supplemented in The Virginia Geneal-
    ogist, Volume 3, pages 60-64. The birth of William Chandler Fowke (1723-1742)
    is the first entry in The Register of Overwharton Parish; he married Jane
    [surname unknown] and had an only child, John Fowke.

B. FOWKE, Richard son of Chandler and Mary Fowke,   December 11, 1741.

D. FOWKE, William October 24, 1742.[1]

B. FOWKE, William son of Chandler and Mary Fowke,   May 31, 1743.

D. FOWKE, William son of Chandler and Mary Fowke,   December 2, 1743.

D. FOWKE, Captain Chandler of Gunston Hall,   February 10, 1745.

M. FOWKE, Gerard and Elizabeth Dinwiddie,   November 26, 1745.[2]

B. FOWKE, Robert Dinwiddie son of Garard and Elizabeth Fowke,   September 20, 1746.

M. FOXWORTHY, Sarah and Daniel Green,   October 16, 1750.

M. FOXWORTHY, John and Sarah Northcut,   September 29, 1751.

M. FOXWORTHY, Thomas and Sarah Nubal,   December 25, 1751.

M. FOXWORTHY, Nicholas and Mary Jordan,   January 26, 1752.

B. FOXWORTHY, John son of Thomas and Sarah Foxworthy,   February 2, 1753.

B. FOXWORTHY, Catherine daughter of Nicholas and Mary Foxworthy, March 28, 1753.

B. FOXWORTHY, William son of John and Sarah Foxworthy,   April 1, 1753.

B. FOXWORTHY, Suky daughter of John and Sarah Foxworthy,   February 1, 1756.

B. FOXWORTHY, [mutilated] son of Nicholas and Mary Foxworthy,   May 13, 1758.

B. FOXWORTHY, [mutilated] son of John Foxworthy,   May 13, 1758.

C. FOXWORTHY, Thomas June 4, 1758.

B. FRAZER, William son of Mary Frazer,   March 8, 1754.

B. FRAZER, Mary daughter of Isabel Frazer,   June 12, 1756.

---

1 - Captain Chandler and Mary (Fossaker) Fowke of Gunston Hall had several child-
    ren with identical names. This entry concerns his son William Chandler Fowke
    (September 4, 1723 - October 24, 1742) who died under age but left issue by
    his wife Jane a son John Fowke; they are named in the division of his estate
    at which time (June 15, 1743) Captain Chandler Fowke acted as guardian of his
    grandson. The will of Captain Chandler Fowke mentions his then living issue,
    viz: Gerard, Chandler, Richard, Elizabeth, Anne and Susannah Fowke.
2 - Elizabeth Dinwiddie was the daughter of Major John Dinwiddie (169?-1726) whose
    family is detailed in The Virginia Genealogist, Volume 3, pages 51-62.

M. FRENCH, Betty and James Waugh, August 22, 1740.

M. FRENCH, Margaret and Peter Hansbrough, February 26, 1745.

C. FRENCH, Mason mulatto son of Anne French, February 9, 1746.

D. FRENCH, Rachel daughter of Hugh French, January 16, 1755.

B. FRISTOE, Daniel son of Richard Fristoe, Junior, and Grace, his wife, December 7, 1739.[1]

B. FRISTOE, John son of Richard and Grace Fristoe, June 6, 1741.

D. FRISTOE, William son of Richard Fristoe, Senior, May 12, 1742.

B. FRISTOE, Richard son of Richard and Grace Fristoe, July 9, 1742.

B. FRISTOE, George son of Richard and Grace Fristoe, April 10, 1744.

B. FRISTOE, Jean daughter of Richard and Grace Fristoe, September 8, 1745.

B. FRISTOE, William son of Richard and Grace Fristoe, March 29, 1747.[2]

D. FRISTOE, George son of Richard Fristoe, May 12, 1748.

D. FRISTOE, Jean daughter of Richard and Grace Fristoe, July 5, 1748.

---

1 - The Reverend Daniel Fristoe (December 7, 1739 -November 3, 1774) was born on Chopawamsic Creek and professed the Baptist faith by baptism in 1755. He was ordained in 1771 and was minister at Chopawamsic Baptist Church. He married Mary Barker who was born September 11, 1735. He died testate in Stafford County and had seven children, viz: (1) Susannah (June 29, 1760 - July 18, 1821) who married first Edward Dulin and secondly Edmund Martin; (2) Lydia born November 17, 1761; (3) Mary born May 22, 1765, married Moses Daulton and moved to Mason County, Kentucky; (4) Thomas (November 27, 1767- April 23, 1815) died testate in Stafford County leaving issue by his wife nee Lydia Wells, daughter of Carty Wells, Junior, of Stafford and Prince William counties, Virginia, and Shelby County, Kentucky; (5) Tamar born January 17, 1770; (6) Ann (March 13, 1772 - October 30, 1817) married January 7, 1792 the Reverend William Grinstead (1772-1828) and moved to Mason County, Kentucky; (7) Catherine born June 19, 1774, married September 9, 1800 Rhodin Hord (1777-1822), son of Rhodin Hord (1740-1811) of Stafford and Spotsylvania counties, Virginia, and his wife nee Sarah Hord who was his first cousin. Rhodin Hord died testate in Mason County, Kentucky, leaving issue four children. Mary (Barker) Fristoe married secondly George Williams, Senior, who died testate in Stafford County, July 4, 1791 leaving issue (1) Henry Williams born March 10, 1779, moved to Mason County, Kentucky, where he died testate, 1826; and (2) George Williams, born April 1, 1781 who also moved to Mason County, Kentucky. For an extended account of Fristoe family see Mrs. Lula Reed Boss in D.A.R. Kentucky Genealogical Records Report, Volume 3 [1960].

2- The Reverend William Fristoe was ordained in 1771 and became a noted Baptist minister. He married Anne Barbee and left issue.

M. FRISTOE, Richard and Mary Hayes, November 24, 1748.

B. FRISTOE, George son of Richard and Grace Fristoe, January 8, 1749.

D. FRISTOE, George son of Richard and Grace Fristoe, December 7, 1750.

D. FRISTOE, Mary March 26, 1751.

B. FRISTOE, Robert son of Richard and Grace Fristoe, April 5, 1751.

M. FRISTOE, Martha and Josuah King, December 12, 1751.

M. FRISTOE, Robert and Anne Rhodes, February 23, 1752.

M. FRISTOE, Richard and Virgin Waters, February 28, 1757.

    FRITTER : FLETTER : FLITTER

M. FRITTER, Moses and Elizabeth Horton, December 1, 1751.

B. FLITTER, John son of Moses and Elizabeth Flitter, September 18, 1752.

B. FRITTER, Hugh Horton son of Moses and Elizabeth Fritter, January 8, 1754.

M. FLITTER, John and Bridget Riggins, March 16, 1755.

B. FLETTER, Moses son of Moses and Elizabeth Fletter, October 1, 1755.[1]

B. FLITTER, William son of John Flitter, October 22, 1755.

B. FLITTER, William son of Moses and Elizabeth Flitter, October 30, 1757.

M. FROGG, John and Elizabeth Strother, November 9, 1738.[2]

M. FUELL, William and Johannah Boling, February 17, 1750.

B. FUELL, Eleanor daughter of William and Hannah Fuell, October 9, 1750.

C. FURGUSON, Elizabeth daughter of John Furguson, May 19, 1754.

C. FERGUSON, Katy daughter of John Ferguson, October 17, 1756.

---

1 - Moses Fritter made Revolutionary War pension declaration #S-1201 in 1833.
    He was then a resident of Mason County, Kentucky.

2 - Captain John Frogg(e) (circa 1709-1795) of Prince William, Culpeper, Augus-
    ta and Bath counties, Virginia, married Elizabeth Strother, one of the six
    daughters and co-heiresses of William Strother, Gentleman, (circa 1696-1733)
    and Margaret Watts, his wife, of King George County, Virginia. Captain Frogg
    served in the colonial militia, was sheriff of Prince William County in 1757,
    and died testate in Bath County, 1795; his will names several children.

G

B. GAINES, Frances daughter of Humphrey and Sarah Gaines, November 14, 1753.

B. GAINES, Henry son of Humphrey and Sarah Gaines, April 11, 1755.

B. GAINES, Sarah daughter of Humphrey Gaines, February 25, 1757.

GALLAHAN : GALLAHON : GOLLOHON

B. GALLOHAN, Eleanor daughter of John and Penelope Gallohan, April 1, 1740.

B. GALLOHAN, Thomas son of John and Eleanor Gallohan, March 27, 1741.

B. GALLAHAN, Elizabeth daughter of Solomon and Mildred Gallahan, October 9,
    1741.

B. GALLOHAN, William son of Solomon Gallohan, April 26, 1743.

B. GALLOHAN, John son of John and Eleanor Gallohan, July 6, 1743.

B. GALLAHAN, Maleson daughter of Solomon Gallahan, May 2, 1745.

B. GALLOHAN, [blank] son of John Gallohan, June 18, 1746.

B. GOLLOHON, Solomon son of Solomon and Mary Gollohon, May 26, 1747.

B. GOLLOHAN, Alice daughter of John Gollohan, December 15, 1748.

B. GALLAHAN, Mary daughter of Solomon and Mary Gallahan, January 1, 1750.

B. GALLOHAN, Charles son of Solomon Gallohan, May 20, 1752.

B. GOLLAHAN, Margaret daughter of Solomon Gollahan, October 8, 1754.

B. GALLOHAN, Mary daughter of John Gallohan, February 4, 1755.

B. GALLOHON, Nelly daughter of John Gallohon, February 19, 1757.

M. GARNER, Parish and Margaret Sturdy, January 21, 1742.[1]

B. GARNER, James son of Parish and Margaret Garner, December 25, 1742.

B. GARNER, Thomas son of Parish Garner, August 25, 1744.

B. GARNER, John son of Samuel and Isabella Garner, November 13, 1756.

B. GARRET, Betty daughter of Robert and Mary Ann Garret, May 29, 1742.

---

1 - See The Garner and Keene Families of The Northern Neck of Virginia by
    Ruth Ritchie and Sudie Rucker Wood [1952].

B. GARRET, Constance daughter of Robert and Mary Garret, April 3, 1745.

M. GARRET, Daniel and Mary Holliday, September 4, 1745.

B. GARRET, Byram son of Robert and Mary Garret, November 28, 1747.

D. GARRET, Byram son of Robert Garret, December 18, 1748.

B. GARRET, Sarah daughter of Robert and Mary Ann Garret, March 4, 1751.

B. GARRET, Winifred daughter of Robert and Mary Garret, March 21, 1753.

B. GARRISON, John son of John and Nanny Garrison, May 17, 1740.

M. GARRISON, Aaron and Elizabeth Bridwell, May 18, 1740.

B. GARRISON, Mary Anne daughter of Aaron and Elizabeth Garrison, September 22, 1740.

B. GARRISON, Susannah daughter of John and Ann Garrison, May 21, 1742.

B. GARRISON, George son of Aaron Garrison, November 14, 1742.

B. GARRISON, William son of Mary Garrison, December 11, 1744.

B. GARRISON, John son of Aaron Garrison, January 1, 1745.

M. GARRISON, Mary and John Kelly, November 1, 1745.

B. GARRISON, William son of Aaron Garrison, October 23, 1746.

B. GARRISON, Sukey daughter of Aaron and Elizabeth Garrison, March 26, 1748.

B. GARRISON, Aaron son of Aaron Garrison, October 1, 1749.

B. GARRISON, Winny daughter of Aaron and Elizabeth Garrison, April 28, 1751.

B. GARRISON, Sarah daughter of Aaron and Elizabeth Garrison, April 24, 1753.

B. GARRISON, Moses son of Aaron and Elizabeth Garrison, March 5, 1755.

B. GARRISON, Milly daughter of Aaron and Elizabeth Garrison, June 27, 1758.

B. GASKINGS, Isaac son of Sarah Gaskings, July 29, 1754.

B. GEORGE, Elizabeth daughter of William and Eleanor George, May 13, 1740.

D. GEORGE, Elmore son of William George, November 25, 1740.

M. GEORGE, Nicholas and Margaret Whitson, December 25, 1740.

B. GEORGE, Nicholas son of Nicholas and Margaret George, November 2, 1741.

B. GEORGE, Elmore son of William and Eleanor George, May 14, 1742.

B. GEORGE, Sith daughter of Benjamin and Mary George, June 30, 1743.

B. GEORGE, Nanny daughter of Nicholas and Margaret George, December 3, 1744.

M. GEORGE, William and Mary Whitson, November 1, 1745.

B. GEORGE, John son of William and Mary George, March 1, 1747.

B. GEORGE, Elizabeth daughter of Nicholas and Margaret George, December 1, 1747.

B. GEORGE, Lydia daughter of William and Mary George, April 4, 1749.

M. GEORGE, Jane and Christopher Dawson, February 16, 1750.

B. GEORGE, Wilmoth daughter of Nicholas and Margaret George, March 4, 1751.

B. GEORGE, Franky daughter of William and Mary George, November 7, 1751.

B. GEORGE, Sarah Ann daughter of William George, April 1, 1754.

B. GEORGE, Sarah daughter of Nicholas and Margaret George, October 11, 1754.

B. GEORGE, William son of William George, December 1, 1756.

B. GEORGE, Lydia daughter of Nicholas and Margaret George, May 29, 1757.

D. GEORGE, William son of William George, June 3, 1758.

C. GERRARD, Mary Ann daughter of William Gerrard, February 17, 1754.

B. GERRARD, Anthony son of Jacob and Mildred Gerrard, September 6, 1756.

D. GILL, Spencer son of Elizabeth Gill, November 3, 1748.

M. GILL, Elizabeth and Joseph White, January 31, 1749.

M. GILL, Edward and Lettice Cannaday, February 4, 1753.

M. GILL, John and Elizabeth Williams, March 3, 1754.

B. GILL, Elsy daughter of John and Elizabeth Gill, January 28, 1755.

M. GLASS, Elizabeth and John Lindcey, January 15, 1750.

M. GLENDENING, John and Jane Grant, January 30, 1746.[1]

---

1 - This couple, first cousins, were residents of King George County. He was
    the son of John Glendening [died 1748] and Phoebe, his wife; she was the
    daughter of William Grant, Sr. [died 1733] and Margaret Glendening, his
    second wife.

M. GODFREY, William and Rebecca Robinson, October 26, 1746.

B. GODFREY, Jane daughter of William and Rebecca Godfrey, February 5, 1750.

B. GODFREY, James son of William Godfrey, July 26, 1752.

B. GODFREY, Elizabeth daughter of William and Rebecca Godfrey, October 28, 1754.

GOING   SEE :   GOWING : GOING PAGE 42

M. GOLDSMITH, John and Martha Powell, January 19, 1756.

B. GOLEMAN, Sarah daughter of Francis and Winifred Goleman, September 20, 1741.

GOLLAHON : GOLLOHON :   SEE : GALLAHAN : GALLAHON &c. PAGE 39

B. GOOLDING, Susanna "a bastard child", March 4, 1755.

M. GORMAN, Mary and James Steward, June 20, 1751.

B. GOUGH, Glady a child of Thomas and Sarah Gough, February 4, 1743.

M. GOUGH, William and Lucy Byram, October 19, 1743.

B. GOUGH, Joshua son of William and Lucy Gough, March 31, 1744.

M. GOUGH, Sarah and William Byram, May 14, 1747.

B. GOUGH, Sarah daughter of William Gough, August 15, 1749.

B. GOUGH, Nanny daughter of William Gouch, January 29, 1752.

B. GOUGH, William son of William Gough, February 17, 1755.

M. GOUGH, Anne and William Baylis, January 19, 1757.

B. GOUGH, Peggy daughter of William and Jemima Gough, September 25, 1757.

GOWING : GOING

D. GOWING, Isabel wife of Peter Gowing, March 11, 1745.

M. GOING, Peter and Mary Sullivant, May 28, 1745.

D. GOING, Peter May 22, 1753 at Priscilla Hayes [Hay's].

B. GRACE, Ellender daughter of Mary Grace, February 7, 1749.

B. GRACE, Sarah daughter of Mary Grace, January 8, 1751.

B. GRADY, William son of William and Anne Grady, November 11, 1744.

M. GRAHAM, Richard and Jane Brent, February 10, 1757.[1]

B. GRANT, Peter son of John and Margaret Grant, November 18, 1739.[2]

B. GRANT, William son of John and Lydia Grant, March 19, 1742.[3]

M. GRANT, Jane and John Glendening, January 30, 1746.

B. GRANT, Elizabeth daughter of John and Lydia Grant, July 25, 1747.

C. GRANT, Anne daughter of John and Lydia Grant, April 8, 1750.

D. GRANT, Mary wife of Jasper Grant, and also her child, February 27, 1752.

B. GRANT, Jane daughter of John and Lydia Grant, April 17, 1752.

B. GRANT, Mary daughter of John and Lydia Grant, September 15, 1754.

B. GRANT, John son of John and Lydia Grant, March 11, 1756.

B. GRASE, Ann a bastard child, December 12, 1746, at John Hughes'.

B. GRASE, John son of Mary Grase, November 14, 1753.

M. GRAVES, Sarah and George Jeffries, February 8, 1756.

M. GREEN, Abigail and Isaac Bridwell, January 20, 1740.

B. GREEN, Martha daughter of John and Abigail Green, April 15, 1741.

M. GREEN, William and Judith Harrel, January 21, 1742.

M. GREEN, William and Anne Robinson, December 18, 1743.

---

1 - For an account of the ancestors and descendants of Richard Graham (1736 -
1796) and Jane Brent (1738 - 1817) of Prince William County, Virginia, see
Doctor George Mason Graham Stafford, General George Mason Graham, page 46
et seq., [1947] and Chester Horton Brent, The Descendants of Coll. Giles
Brent, Capt George Brent and Robert Brent, Gent., page 120 [1946].

2 - There were several contemporary John Grants. This Captain John Grant (16 -
1747/8) of Stafford and Prince William counties married first August 17,
1727 Hester Foote and had issue (1) William Grant, Gent., of Prince William
and Fauquier counties, who married Judith Neale and (2) Ann Grant who married Felix Gilbert in Fauquier County per bond dated October 19, 1761. Capt.
John Grant married secondly Margaret (Watts) Strother, widow of William
Strother, Gent., and had issue (3) Peter Grant (1739-1815) who married in
Fauquier County on November 23, 1767 Susanna Winn and had no issue and (4)
Mary Grant who married John Hughes of Fauquier County, Virginia.

3 - John Grant married Lydia Barbee, daughter of Thomas Barbee (1690-1752).

B. GREEN, Sarah daughter of William and Anne Green, September 24, 1744.

M. GREEN, George and Elizabeth Whitson, December 23, 1744.

B. GREEN, Thomas son of George and Elizabeth Green, November 27, 1745.

M. GREEN, Patty and William Harding, January 28, 1746.

M. GREEN, Elizabeth and Richard Young, December 27, 1746.

B. GREEN, Dorcas daughter of William and Anne Green, December 30, 1746.

B. GREEN, James son of John Green, Junior, January 22, 1748.

B. GREEN, George son of George and Elizabeth Green, February 23, 1748.

M. GREEN, James and Lucy Martin, October 4, 1748.

B. GREEN, Annas daughter of William and Ann Green, March 15, 1749.

B. GREEN, George son of James and Lizzie Green, October 21, 1749.

D. GREEN, Lizzie wife of James Green, October 29, 1749.

B. GREEN, Sarah daughter of John Green, January 20, 1750.

D. GREEN, Sarah daughter of John Green, August 17, 1750.

M. GREEN, Daniel and Sarah Foxworthy, October 16, 1750.

B. GREEN, Mary daughter of William Green, July 21, 1751.

B. GREEN, Jesse son of John Green, Junior, and Jean, his wife, August 2, 1751.

M. GREEN, Mary and William More, November 28, 1751.

B. GREEN, Nancy daughter of John Green, July 19, 1753.

B. GREEN, Jael daughter of William Green, November 12, 1753.

B. GREEN, Lizy daughter of Daniel and Sarah Green, April 1, 1754.

B. GREEN, John son of John Green, Junior, April 4, 1755.

B. GREEN, William son of William and Ann Green, April 28, 1756.

B. GREEN, Mary daughter of Daniel and Sarah Green, August 25, 1756.

M. GREEN, Robert and Helen Lowry, November 23, 1756.

M. GREEN, Sarah and Snowdall Laytham, November 25, 1756.

M.   GREEN, John and Phillis Smith, December 19, 1756.

B.   GREEN, William son of John Green, January 18, 1757.

B.   GREEN, Elizabeth daughter of William and Anne Green, June 19, 1758.

M.   GREENLESS, Bathsheba and [mutilated], May 7, 1758.

D.   GREGG, Elizabeth daughter of William Gregg, May 12, 1740 at William Bethel's.

B.   GREGG, James son of Matthew and Catherine Gregg, May 15, 1740.

B.   GREGG, John son of Matthew and Catherine Gregg, January 10, 1745.

M.   GREGG, Matthew and [blank] Chinn, August 15, 1751.

C.   GREGG, Matthew son of Matthew Gregg, September 17, 1752.

M.   GREGG, Sarah Ellen and William Bourn, December 11, 1756.

B.   GREY, William son of Anne Grey, January 26, 1751.

B.   GREY, Richard son of John and Margaret Grey, May 15, 1751.

     GRIFFIN : GRIFFITH

M.   GRIFFIN, Elizabeth and James Phillips, September 27, 1741.

M.   GRIFFIN, Thomas and Sarah Suddeth, July 18, 1745.

B.   GRIFFITH, Daniel son of Thomas and Sarah Griffith, September 2, 1746.

D.   GRIFFIN, Phillis April 9, 1756 at James Hardwick's.

M.   GRIGSBY, Sarah and George Fletcher, January [blank], 1743.

M.   GRIGSBY, Alice and Benjamin Rush, April 1, 1744.

B.   GRIGSBY, William son of John and Anne Grigsby, October 30, 1744.

M.   GRIGSBY, Priscilla and Abraham Fletcher, November 28, 1746.

M.   GRIGSBY, Margaret and George Foster, December 22, 1746.

B.   GRIGSBY, Susannah daughter of John and Ann Grigsby, October 10, 1747.

M.   GRIGSBY, Lettice and Joshua Owens, November 19, 1747.

B.   GRIGSBY, Rachel daughter of John and Ann Grigsby, August 7, 1750.

M.   GRIGSBY, Sarah and William Rose, June 5, 1753.

M. GRIGSBY, Moses and Mary Matheny, August 26, 1753.

B. GRIGSBY, John son of Moses and Mary Grigsby, January 15, 1756.

M. GRIGSBY, Jane and William Rose, March 14, 1758.

B. GRIMES, Mary the daughter of Richard and Elizabeth Grimes, August 25, 1745.

M. GRINNAN, Eleanor and James Edzar, November 22, 1754.

B. GRINSTEAD, Lydia daughter of Peter Grinstead, January 26, 1751.

M. GROVES, Edward and Mary Hearne, September 15, 1748.

M. GROVES, William and Barbara Webster, February 2, 1749.

B. GUARD, [blank] the son of Mary Guard, March 14, 1755 at John Waters'.

B. GUARD, Sarah daughter of Mary Guard, January 15, 1757.

M. GUIN, Lizzy and James Matheny, December 12, 1751.

M. GUM, Mary and Robert Day, January 16, 1757.

M. GUNN, John and Martha Shamlin, September 30, 1753.

M. GWIN, James and Elizabeth Maccaboy, October 5, 1755.

M. GWODKIN, Jean and Henry Nelson, October 18, 1742.

H

D. HACKENEY, Dinah January 25, 1754.

M. HACKER, William and Anne Dillon, May 21, 1738.

B. HACKER, William son of William Hacker, December 9, 1739.

B. HACKER, John son of William and Anne Hacker, January 2, 1743.

   HAFFERNON   SEE :   HEFFERNON : HEFFERTON   PAGE 51

M. HALL, Mary and Charles Worral, November 16, 1751.

B. HALL, Lettice daughter of John Hall, March 2, 1757.

M. HALLEY, William and Catherine Jeffries, February 9, 1758.

M. HAMILTON, Anne and John Alridge, June 11, 1738.

C. HAMILTON, Henry February 24, 1754.

B. HAMILTON, Leanna daughter of Henry Hamilton, February 2, 1756.

HAMMET : HAMMIT : HAMMETH

B. HAMMETH, Margaret daughter of William and Mary Hammeth, February 10, 1739.

B. HAMMET, Charles son of William and Elizabeth Hammet, February 4, 1742.

B. HAMMET, Mary daughter of William and Elizabeth Hammet, February 4, 1744.

M. HAMMET, Sarah and Christopher Broderick, December 19, 1744.

M. HAMMIT, Robert and Sythe Bethel, February 7, 1749.

B. HAMMET, William son of Robert and Sith Hammet, November 14, 1749.

M. HAMMET, William and Rosamund Smith, May 6, 1755.

B. HAMOND, Charles son of John and Elizabeth Hamond, April 20, 1758.

M. HAMPTON, Thomas and Sarah Pattison alias Conyers, June 1, 1749.[1]

B. HANKINS, Diana daughter of Daniel and Hannah Hankins, December 6, 1740.

B. HANKINS, Margaret daughter of Daniel and Elizabeth Hankins, February 6, 1743.

B. HANKINS, Sarah daughter of Daniel Hankins, January 13, 1746.

B. HANSBROUGH, Peter son of James and Lettice Hansbrough, June 12, 1744.[2]

M. HANSBROUGH, Peter and Margaret French, February 26, 1745.[3]

B. HANSBROUGH, James son of James Hansbrough, November 11, 1746.

---

1 - See foot note page 22.

2 - James Hansbrough (died 1784) married on September 19, 1741 in Saint Paul's
    Parish, Lettice Sumner daughter of Joseph Sumner, Junior, (1   -1734) and
    their son Peter Hansbrough (June 12, 1744 - October 15, 1822) became a very
    wealthy land holder in Stafford, King George and Culpeper counties. He mar-
    ried on September 10, 1766 his first cousin Eleanor Minor (January 15, 1744-
    March 12, 1812), daughter of John and Margaret (Sumner) Minor. The will of
    James Hansbrough (circa 1719-1784) remains of record at Stafford County Court.

3 - Peter Hansbrough (17 -1781), believed to have been a brother of James Hans-
    brough, married first Margaret French and secondly Lydia Smith. He died
    intestate in Stafford County and in 1782 his estate was divided among his
    widow and his nine children.

D. HANSBROUGH, James son of James and Lettice Hansbrough, December 14, 1746.

B. HANSBROUGH, William son of Peter Hansbrough, August 4, 1747.

B. HANSBROUGH, Elizabeth Magdalen daughter of James and Lettice Hansbrough,
    February 22, 1748.

B. HANSBROUGH, Milly daughter of James Hansbrough, May 5, 1750.

M. HANSBROUGH, Peter and Lydia Smith, May 27, 1752.

B. HANSBROUGH, Gabriel son of James Hansbrough, November 27, 1752.

B. HANSBROUGH, Smith son of Peter and Lydia Hansbrough, May 25, 1753.

B. HANSBROUGH, James son of James Hansbrough, October 30, 1755.

B. HANSBROUGH, Sarah daughter of Peter and Lydia Hansbrough, March 13, 1756.

B. HANSBROUGH, Anna Violet daughter of James Hansbrough, April 24, 1758.

M. HANSFORD, Stephen and Margaret Maccarty, October 14, 1755.[1]

M. HANSON, Anne and George Bell, April 15, 1745.

B. HARDING, William son of Charles and Rachel Harding, March 12, 1738.

B. HARDING, Ann daughter of Charles and Rachel Harding, February 3, 1740.

B. HARDING, Wilmoth daughter of Henry and Wilmoth Harding, April 14, 1741.[2]

B. HARDING, Jane daughter of Charles and Rachel Harding, November 9, 1742.

B. HARDING, Franky daughter of George and Jenny Harding, March 7, 1743.

B. HARDING, Nicholas son of Henry and Wilmoth Harding, July 6, 1743.

B. HARDING, Charles son of Charles and Rachel Harding, April 6, 1745.

---

1 - On July 8, 1743 Stephen Hansford, late of the town of Abbotsbury in the
    County of Dorset, England, but now of King George County, Virginia, aged 44
    years, made a lengthy deposition in regard to the genealogy of the Chiches-
    ter family formerly of County Dorset who settled in Lancaster County, Vir-
    ginia. Stephen Hansford (1699-1772) purchased land in King George County in
    1730 and his last will remains of record there. He married Elizabeth Doni-
    phan, daughter of Captain Alexander Doniphan (circa 1653-1717). The above
    entry is presumed to be the second marriage of his father, Stephen Hansford
    (16 -1758), who died intestate in King George County, Virginia.

2 - Nicholas George by will 1738 mentioned his daughter Wilmoth Harding; this
    couple moved to Frederick County, Virginia, and in 1755 sold land in Stafford
    County formerly the property of Henry Harding, deceased, to George Harding.

M. HARDING, William and Patty Green, January 28, 1746.[1]

B. HARDING, Hall son of William and Patty Harding, October 25, 1746.

B. HARDING, Winny daughter of George and Jean Harding, December 1, 1746.

B. HARDING, John Scott son of Charles and Rachel Harding, August 3, 1747.

B. HARDING, Ann daughter of George and Jane Harding, May 29, 1749.

B. HARDING, Thomas son of Charles and Rachel Harding, August 11, 1749.

B. HARDING, Moses son of Charles and Rachel Harding, March 19, 1752.

B. HARDING, Henry son of George and Jane Harding, August 29, 1753.

B. HARDING, George son of Charles and Rachel Harding, July 3, 1754.

D. HARDING, Anne September 13, 1754.

M. HARDING, Ann and Mark Waters, July 20, 1756.

B. HARDING, Sarah daughter of George and Jean Harding, March 23, 1758.[2]

M. HARDWICK, Haswell and Mary Northcut, December 25, 1750.

B. HARDWICK, Ann daughter of Hasel and Mary Hardwick, February 22, 1752.

B. HARDWICK, William son of Hasel and Mary Hardwick, September 5, 1753.

B. HARDWICK, Elizabeth daughter of Hasel and Mary Hardwick, September 8, 1755.

    HAROD : HARROD   SEE: HEROD : HERROD   PAGE 52

B. HARPER, Sarah daughter of Michael and Mary Harper, April 24, 1741.

B. HARPER, Thomas son of Michael and Mary Harper, December 31, 1744.

B. HARPER, Mary daughter of Michael and Mary Harper, February 9, 1747.

B. HARPER, Margaret daughter of Michael and Mary Harper, November 9, 1749.

B. HARPER, Phoebe daughter of Michael and Mary Harper, April 13, 1752.

---

1 - William Harding died testate in Fairfax County, Virginia, in 1781.

2 - In 1755 Henry Harding and Wilmouth, his wife, of Frederick County deeded
    to George Harding of Stafford County, planter, 200 acres on Aquia Creek
    formerly the property of Henry Harding, deceased. The Virginia Gazette
    of February 6, 1768 states that Mr. George Harding of Halifax County died
    lately in Stafford County where he had gone on business. The inventory of
    the estate of George Harding, deceased, was filed in Halifax County, 1768.

M.   HARREL, Judith and William Green,   January 21, 1742.

D.   HARRISON, Captain William   December 1, 1745. [1]

M.   HARRISON, Thomas and Anne Peyton,   July 2, 1747. [2]

M.   HARRISON, Susannah and Robert Slaughter,   December 11, 1750.

M.   HARRISON, Sarah and John Monroe,   September 23, 1756.

M.   HARRISON, Margaret and Edward Blackburn,   May 26, 1757.

M.   HART, John and Rachel Oram,   March 23, 1746.

M.   HARVIE, Anne and Richard Wine,   July 23, 1738.

M.   HARVEY, Elizabeth and Thomas Johnson,   October 19, 1745.

M.   HARVEY, Milly and John Angell,   October 5, 1750.

M.   HAWES, Samuel and Mary Ann Ralls,   February 16, 1749.

M.   HAYES, Mary and Richard Fristoe,   December 24, 1748.

B.   HAY, Priscilla daughter of Thomas and Frances Hay,   November 8, 1755. [3]

B.   HAY, Catherine daughter of Thomas and Frances Hay,   October 12, 1757.

---

1 - Captain William Harrison (16 -1745), son of Captain William and Sarah
    (Hawley) Harrison, married in 1732 Isabella (Triplett) Hore, daughter of
    William and Isabella (Miller) Triplett and widow of Captain Elias Hore
    (16 -1730) of Westmoreland and Stafford counties, Va. by whom she had four
    children. Captain William and Isabella (Triplett) Harrison had four dau-
    ghters, viz: (1) Susannah who married Robert Slaughter in 1750; (2) Sarah
    who married John Monroe in 1756; (3) Margaret who married Edward Blackburn
    in 1757 and (4) Mary who married John Waller between 1760-1762. There is
    considerable record of these families in the Fairfax County records.

2 - Thomas Harrison (1724-1754) was the son of Burr Harrison (1699-1775) and
    Ann Barnes, his wife; grandson of Captain Thomas Harrison (1665-1746) and
    great-grandson of the immigrant Burr Harrison (1637-1697). He married Ann
    Peyton, daughter of John Peyton (1691-1760), on July 2, 1747 and their
    family is detailed by the Rev. Mr. Hayden in his Virginia Genealogies, page
    510 et seq. The tombstone of their son, the Rev.Thomas Harrison (1750-1811),
    is yet to be seen at the family seat, Fairview, on Chopawamsic Creek.

3 - Thomas Hay married Frances Thatcher, daughter of Thomas Thatcher who died
    testate in King George County in 1751 and Catherine Pannell, his wife.
    Frances Thatcher was the granddaughter of Sylvester Thatcher, Junior, (16 -
    1718) and Elizabeth Underwood, his wife, and of William Pannell (circa 1670-
    1716) and Frances Sterne, his wife, all of Richmond County, Virginia.

M.   HAYS, Catherine and Thomas Waters,   September 28, 1738.

B.   HAYNIE, Winifred, daughter of Charles and Elizabeth Haynie,   February 12,
     1754.

     HAYTER : HYTER

M.   HYTER, William and Anne Hewes,   April 3, 1743.

B.   HAYTER, James son of William and Anne Hayter,   January 22, 1744.

D.   HAYTER, Anne wife of William Hayter,   March 26, 1745.

B.   HAZEL, Fanny daughter of P. Hazel,   January 18, 1752.

B.   HEAD, Charles son of Mary Head,   May 13, 1745.

D.   HEAD, Mary May 21, 1745.

B.   HEAD, Joseph son of Robert and Dorothy Head,   October 27, 1746.

M.   HEARNE, Mary and Edward Groves,   September 15, 1748.

B.   HEASLON, Simon son of William Heaslon,   October 1, 1741.

B.   HEATH, Milian daughter of Thomas and Elizabeth Heath,   January 10, 1743.

M.   HEATH, Susanna Thomson and John Richards,   March 6, 1755.

B.   HEBRON, [mutilated] May 28, 1752 at Edward Ralls'.

B.   HEDGMAN, Nathaniel son of Peter and Margaret Hedgman,   February 6, 1729.

B.   HEDGMAN, William son of Peter and Margaret Hedgman,   July 21, 1732.

B.   HEDGMAN, George son of Peter and Margaret Hedgman,   December 11, 1734.

B.   HEDGMAN, John son of Peter and Margaret Hedgman,   October 13, 1741.

D.   HEDGMAN, Margaret wife of Major Peter Hedgman,   January 16, 1754.

M.   HEDGMAN, George and Hannah Daniel,   November 27, 1756.

B.   HEDGMAN, John son of George and Hannah Hedgman,   June 9, 1758.

     HEFFERNON : HAFFERNON : HEFFERTON

M.   HEFFERNON, James and Alander Payton,   May 20, 1740.

M.   HEFFERNON, William and Sarah Martin,   September 29, 1741.

B.   HAFFERNON, John son of James Haffernon,   November 20, 1741.

B. HEFFERTON, Mary Byford daughter of William Hefferton, April 23, 1743.

B. HAFFERNON, James son of James Haffernon, September 28, 1749.

M. HEFFERNUT, Sarah and William Wilkison, August 21, 1740.

M. HELMS, Mary and Gabriel Muffet, July 25, 1739.

B. HELMS, Sarah daughter of Samuel Helms, May 25, 1758.

M. HERNDON, Edward and Mary Waller, April 15, 1753. [1]

    HEROD : HERROD : HAROD

M. HERROD, John and Mary Devane, August 21, 1748.

B. HEROD, William son of John Herod, December 13, 1749.

D. HAROD, Margaret daughter of Mary Harod surnamed Deveene, February 2, 1750.

M. HEWES, Anne and William Hyter, April 3, 1743.

D. HEYDON, John December 22, 1751 "a servant of James Burns".

    HICKERSON : HIGERSON : HIGGERSON : HIGGISON

M. HIGGERSON, Hannah and James Whealy, July 8, 1739.

M. HIGGERSON, John and Jean Jackson, January 20, 1742.

D. HICKERSON, John February 2, 1743.

B. HIGERSON, Sarah Elwood daughter of Thomas and Sarah Higerson, March 27, 1743.

M. HIGGERSON, Elizabeth and John Waters, June 5, 1743.

M. HIGGERSON, Elizabeth and Samuel Elliot, May 20, 1747.

D. HIGGISON, Thomas February 21, 1755 at John Waters'.

    HIDEN   SEE : HYDEN PAGE 58

---

1 - Doctor John Goodwin Herndon in his genealogy, The Herndon Family of Virginia, Volume One, pages 23 and 44 errs in identifying the husband of Mary
Waller, daughter of George Waller (1703- circa 1768) of Spring Hill and
Elizabeth Allen, his wife. She married a man many years her senior, Edward
Herndon (circa 1702 - 1759) of Spotsylvania County as his second wife and
had no issue by him. She married secondly David Hening (17 -1798) of Culpeper County and had several children among whom was William Waller Hening
(1767-1828) compiler of The Statutes at Large...of Virginia [1809-1823].

B. HIGGINS, John Bayham son of Jane Higgins, May 28, 1742.

D. HILL, John March 19, 1743.

M. HILL, William and Catherine Stacy, September 17, 1745.

B. HILL, John son of William and Catherine Hill, October 11, 1751.

B. HILL, Martha daughter of James and Lydia Hill, May 5, 1753.

B. HILL, William son of William Hill, August 14, 1753.

M. HILL, Martha and James Russell, February 24, 1754.

B. HILL, George son of William and Catherine Hill, February 19, 1755.

D. HINSON, Edmund November 13, 1742.

M. HINSON, Isabell and James Yelton, November 13, 1743.

M. HINSON, George and Margaret Burchell, December 29, 1746.

D. HINSON, Mary March 16, 1747 at John Honey's.

B. HINSON, [blank] daughter of George and Margaret Hinson, October 4, 1747.

M. HINSON, Mary and Henry Threlkeld November 3, 1748.

D. HINSON, Charles February 22, 1750.

B. HINSON, Lettice daughter of George Hinson, May 21, 1750.

M. HINSON, Joyce and James Crap, June 3, 1750.

B. HINSON, Mary daughter of George and Margaret Hinson, October 28, 1752.

D. HINSON, Margaret wife of George Hinson, November 22, 1752.

M. HINSON, George and Sarah Sullivan, February 4, 1753.

B. HINSON, Elizabeth daughter of Lazarus and Sarah Hinson, March 31, 1753.

B. HINSON, Elijah son of George and Sarah Hinson, May 27, 1754.

B. HINSON, Sarah daughter of Lazarus and Sarah Hinson, November 21, 1755.

M. HOGG, John and Eleanor Savage, December 19, 1744.

M. HOLDBROOK, William and Elizabeth King, December 8, 1744.

M. HOLDBROOKE, Elizabeth and Samuel Earle, January 13, 1754.

M. HOLDBROOKE, Elizabeth and James Cuniberford, September 15, 1754.

HOLLIDAY : HOOLIDAY

M. HOOLIDAY, Whorton and Elizabeth Duwest, July 28, 1742.

M. HOLLIDAY, Mary and Daniel Garret, September 4, 1745.

B. HOLLIDAY, Mary daughter of Wharton Holliday, April 29, 1746.

M. HOLLIDAY, Winny and James Battoo, February 12, 1747.

B. HOLLIDAY, John son of Wharton and Elizabeth Holliday, December 11, 1747.

M. HOLLIDAY, Keziah and Robert Million, December 14, 1749.

B. HOLLIDAY, Mary daughter of Wharton Holliday, June 9, 1752.

B. HOLLIDAY, Janie daughter of Wharton Holliday, September 22, 1754.

B. HOLLIDAY, Betty daughter of Wharton Holliday, June 27, 1757.

D. HOMES, Henry November 16, 1743 at Anthony Murray's.

M. HONEY, John and Hannah Bussel, February 2, 1748.

B. HONEY, [blank] the daughter of John and Hannah Honey, December 5, 1750.

D. HONEY, [blank] the daughter of John and Hannah Honey, December 13, 1750.

C. HONEY, William son of John Honey, July 19, 1752.

B. HONEY, John son of John and Hannah Honey, July 31, 1755.

D. HOPS, Anthony April 24, 1751 at Alexander Nelson's.

M. HORD, Mary and [mutilated], May 13, 1758.

M. HORE, Catherine and Thomas Monroe, April 16, 1745.[1]

---

1 - Captain Elias Hore (16 - 1730) of Westmoreland and Stafford counties married in April 1711 IsabellaTriplett; she married secondly Captain William
Harrison (see page 50). Captain Hore died testate leaving issue four children, viz: Elias (171?-1782) of Stafford County; William (17 - 1753) who
died testate in Westmoreland County; Catherine who married Thomas Monroe;
and Sarah Hore who was unmarried in 1761 when she received a deed of gift
from her mother, Isabell Harrison. Captain Elias Hore was the son of
John Hore, merchant at Maddox, Westmoreland County, who by his will of
1712 bequeathed his son Elias all his lands in Stafford County. There is
considerable record of the Hore family in the records of Westmoreland,
Stafford and Prince William counties.

B. HORE, Elias son of Elias and Mary Hore, December 31, 1749.[1]

B. HORE, Betty daughter of Elias and Mary Hore, October 6, 1751.

B. HORE, Nathaniel Brown son of Elias Hore, December 18, 1755.

B. HORNBUCKLE, Franklin son of Richard Hornbuckle, April 11, 1741.

M. HORNBUCKLE, Anne and Samuel Angell, August 14, 1745.

D. HORNBUCKLE, Richard July 29, 1747.

M. HORNBUCKLE, Elizabeth and John Smith, December 31, 1747.

D. HORNBUCKLE, George September 10, 1749 at John Smith's.

B. HORTON, Townshend son of Snowdal and Sarah Horton, April 21, 1740.

B. HORTON, Housin daughter of Snowden and Sarah Horton, May 16, 1743.

B. HORTON, Venus daughter of Snowdel and Sarah Horton, July 14, 1745.

M. HORTON, Anthony and Rosamond Duncomb, December 27, 1745.

B. HORTON, Reuben son of Anthony and Rosamond Horton, April 27, 1747.

B. HORTON, Frances daughter of Elizabeth Horton, June 21, 1747.

B. HORTON, George a bastard son of Mary Horton, January 26, 1748.

B. HORTON, Aden son of Anthony and Rosamond Horton, June 4, 1749.

M. HORTON, William and Margaret Cooke, December 21, 1749.

B. HORTON, John son of John and Sarah Horton, December 23, 1749.

B. HORTON, Benjamin son of Martha Horton, August 26, 1750.

---

1 - Elias Hore (171? - 1782) married Mary, traditionally nee Brown, and had
issue: (1) Captain John Hore d.s.p. 1809 leaving will mentioning many relatives; (2) Elias Hore (1749-1832) married Theodosia Waller (1753-1829),
daughter of George Waller of Spring Hill, and left issue; (3) Elizabeth
("Betty") (1751-1792) married Henry Clifton of Stafford County; (4) Captain
James Hore d.s.p. in Stafford County leaving a large estate; his widow
Frances married secondly John Stewart; (5) Nathaniel Brown Hore d.s.p.
probably in infancy; (6) William Hore is mentioned in his brother's will
of 1809 above mentioned; (7) Mary Hore (1760-1820) married Cooper Chancel-
lor (1756-1845) of Prince William County [for an account of their family
see William and Mary College Quarterly, Second Series, Volume 15, pages
179-180]; and (8) Catherine Hore married Captain George Williams of Dumfries, Prince William County, Virginia.

B. HORTON, Thomas son of Mary Horton, January 4, 1751.

B. HORTON, Mary daughter of William Horton, March 22, 1751.

D. HORTON, Anthony September 21, 1751 at Hugh Horton's.

M. HORTON, Elizabeth and Moses Fritter, December 1, 1751.

B. HORTON, Phebe daughter of John and Sarah Horton, March 14, 1752.

B. HORTON, Turrel son of William and Margaret Horton, January 4, 1753.

B. HORTON, Orpah daughter of John and Sarah Horton, February 14, 1754.

B. HORTON, Winifred daughter of Martha Horton, July 28, 1754.

D. HORTON, Snowdall January 19, 1755.

D. HORTON, Phoebe daughter of John Horton, July 17, 1755.

D. HORTON, Orpah daughter of John and Sarah Horton, August 8, 1755.

B. HORTON, James son of John and Sarah Horton, August 10, 1755.

B. HORTON, Beverly son of William and Margaret Horton, April 8, 1757.

B. HORTON, Clara daughter of John and Sarah Horton, December 5, 1757.

M. HORTON, Martha and Peter Byram, March 26, 1758.

B. HOWARD, John son of James and Margaret Howard, September 2, 1739.

D. HOWARD, Grace February 7, 1751.

M. HOWARD, William and Elizabeth Stacey, May 29, 1751.

B. HOWARD, Elizabeth daughter of William and Elizabeth Howard, August 14, 1752.

D. HOWARD, Elizabeth wife of William Howard, July 12, 1755.

M. HOWARD, William and Martha Wheeler, April 25, 1756.

B. HUCKSEP, Samuel son of Samuel and Eliz.[a] Hucksep, June 11, 1742.

   HUGHES   SEE : HEWES PAGE 52

M. HUGHES, Mary and George Crosby, January 6, 1744.

M. HUGHES, James and Agnes MacCartee, May 6, 1744.

B. HUGHES, William son of James and Agnes Hughes, February 14, 1745.

D. HUGHES, Agnes March 4, 1747.

B. HUGHES, Elizabeth daughter of Ralph Hughes, June 30, 1753.

D. HUGHS, Loftus September 14, 1753 at Mary Suddeth's.

B. HUGHS, John son of Ralph Hughs, December 24, 1756.

M. HUMPHREYS, John Junior and Margaret Young, September 23, 1738.

B. HUMPHREYS, Jemima June 20, 1744.

B. HUMPHRYS, Franky daughter of William and Sarah Humphrys, March 8, 1755.

M. HUNTER, Elizabeth and John Renny, October 12, 1746.

D. HUNTER, John September 29, 1749 at Captain William Mountjoy's.

M. HURST, Jean and William Bethel, December 26, 1739.

B. HURST, James son of Thomas and Mary Hurst, November 13, 1740.

B. HURST, Landen son of Mary Hurst, July 25, 1741.

B. HURST, Nathaniel son of Mary Hurst, June 6, 1744.

B. HURST, Priscilla daughter of Thomas and Mary Hurst, June 21, 1745.

D. HURST, John December 6, 1747.

M. HURST, Mary and Owen Wingfield, November 9, 1748.

M. HURST, Henry and Anne Pyke, March 20, 1750.

B. HURST, Absalom son of Thomas Hurst, May 15, 1750.

B. HURST, Nancy daughter of Henry Hurst, April 20, 1751.

M. HURST, James and Rosannah Jones, April 21, 1751.

B. HURST, Elizabeth daughter of James and Rosanna Hurst, January 10, 1752.

B. HURST, Henry son of James and Rosanna Hurst, December 3, 1753.

B. HURST, Milly daughter of James and Rosanna Hurst, August 28, 1756.

B. HURST, Elijah son of John Hurst, February 16, 1758.

B. HURST, James son of Thomas and Mary Hurst, March 4, 1758.

B. HUSK, Nanny daughter of Thomas and Mary Husk, January 24, 1748.

M. HUTT, Aggy and William Ticer, December 15, 1754.

HYDEN : HIDEN [1]

B. HYDEN, Lucy daughter of William and Mary Hyden, December 28, 1731.

B. HYDEN, Samuel son of William and Mary Hyden, June 19, 1733.

B. HYDEN, Henry son of William and Mary Hyden, December 2, 1735.

B. HYDEN, Charity daughter of William and Mary Hyden, June 19, 1737.

B. HYDEN, Richard son of William and Mary Hyden, March 8, 1739.

B. HYDEN, William son of William and Mary Hyden, September 29, 1740.

B. HYDEN, Daniel son of William and Mary Hyden, April 6, 1743.

D. HYDEN, Daniel son of William Hyden, June 5, 1744.

B. HYDEN, Jacob son of William and Mary Hyden, August 18, 1745.

D. HYDEN, William son of William Hyden, October 21, 1745.

B. HYDEN, Nathaniel December 1, 1749.

M. HYDEN, Mary and John Nicolson, April 23, 1752.

B. HYDEN, Daniel March 17, 1753 "at his home".

B. HIDEN, William January 28, 1756.

HYTER   SEE :   HAYTER : HYTER   PAGE 51

I

B. INNIS, George son of John and Mary Innis, March 1, 1741.

B. INNIS, John son of John and Mary Innis, October 10, 1742.

B. INNIS, Patty daughter of John Innis, August 16, 1750.

D. INNIS, Patty daughter of John Innis, August 22, 1750.

B. INNIS, James son of John and Mary Innis, March 11, 1752.

---

1 - See "The Hiden Family" by Mrs. Martha (Woodroof) Hiden, F.A.S.G., in
    Tyler's Quarterly Historical and Genealogical Magazine, Volume 24, pages
    125-147.

B. INNIS, William son of John and Mary Innis, July 9, 1757.

M. ISAAC, Margaret and Alexander Suitor, July 21, 1745.

J

M. JACK, Jean and Matthew Brooks, February [blank], 1743.

M. JACK, Mary and Simon Robinson, August 3, 1755.

B. JACKSON, Sarah daughter of John and Sarah Jackson, November 2, 1740.

B. JACKSON, Henry son of William and Grace Jackson, October 8, 1741.

M. JACKSON, Jean and John Higgerson, January 20, 1742.

B. JACKSON, George son of John and Sarah Jackson, July 28, 1743.

B. JACKSON, Sith March 23, 1744.

D. JACKSON, William March 16, 1749. [See footnote page 74]

B. JACKSON, Diana daughter of William and Jane Jackson, May 9, 1749.

B. JACKSON, John son of Grace Jackson, April [blank], 1750.

D. JACKSON, John son of Grace Jackson, March 15, 1753.

D. JACKSON, Grace September 17, 1754 at John Peyton's.

C. JAMES, Margaret daughter of George James, November 21, 1742.[1]

---

1 - John James came to Virginia in 1650 and in 1670 patented land in Stafford
County where he died ante 1690; his widow, Elizabeth, married secondly
Thomas Norman. Thomas James, son and heir of John James, lived on Potomac
Creek. He patented land there in 1699 about which time he married Sarah,
widow of Andrew Barbee. Thomas James died testate circa 1727 leaving George
James (circa 1702-1753) his eldest son and heir-at-law. By inheritance,
purchase and marriage George James became a wealthy land holder in Stafford,
Prince William and Spotsylvania counties; he died intestate in Fredericksburg
in 1753. He married Mary Wheeler, only child of John Wheeler, Gentleman,
(1684-1746) a vestryman in Overwharton Parish and had ten children, viz: (1)
Thomas (circa 1729-1776) of Fauquier County, married Mary Bruce; (2) George
(circa 1730-1755); (3) John (circa 1732-circa 1794) married in 1763 Anne
Strother; (4) Esther, born circa 1734, married Henry Field of Culpeper County; (5) Mary (1736-1822) married first in 1754 Anthony Strother, Gentleman,
(1710-1765) and secondly in 1771 Colonel Henry Smith; (6) Diana born circa
1740; (7) Margaret (1742-1748); (8) Joseph born 1746; (9) Daniel born 1748,
married on April 5, 1773 in Orange County, Lucy Davis; and (10) Henry James,
born circa 1750, and his brother Joseph were living in Fauquier County, 1774.

B.   JAMES, Joseph son of George and Mary James, December 8, 1746.

D.   JAMES, Margaret daughter of George James, October 30, 1748.

D.   JAMES, William November 2, 1748.

B.   JAMES, Daniel son of George James, December 6, 1748.

M.   JAMES, Hannah and Benjamin Crump, February 2, 1749.

JEFFRIES : JEFFERIES : JEFFERYS

M.   JEFFRIES, Alexander and Lettice Burton, September 30, 1741.

B.   JEFFRIES, [blank] a child of Alexander Jeffries, September 6, 1742.

M.   JEFFERYS, Silent and Benjamin Suthard, January 19, 1744.

B.   JEFFRIES, James son of Alexander Jeffries, November 25, 1744.

M.   JEFFRIES, James and Sarah Matthews, December 23, 1746.

B.   JEFFRIES, Susannah daughter of James and Elizabeth Jeffries, April 8, 1747.

B.   JEFFRIES, Betty daughter of James and Sarah Jeffries, August 11, 1747.

D.   JEFFRIES, Betty August 17, 1747.

B.   JEFFRIES, Catherine daughter of James Jeffries, October 28, 1748.

B.   JEFFERIES, Mary daughter of James Jefferies, June 21, 1750.

M.   JEFFRIES, Elizabeth and Nelson Kelly, November 4, 1751.

B.   JEFFERIES, William son of James and Sarah Jefferies, September 20, 1752.

B.   JEFFRIES, Lydia daughter of James and Sarah Jeffries, September 17, 1754.

M.   JEFFRIES, Joseph and Margaret Smith, October 24, 1754.

B.   JEFFRIES, Sarah daughter of Joseph and Margaret Jeffries, August 22, 1755.

M.   JEFFRIES, George and Sarah Graves, February 8, 1756.

C.   JEFFRIES, Sarah daughter of James Jeffries, April 25, 1756.

M.   JEFFRIES, Catherine and William Halley, February 9, 1758.

M.   JENKINS, Sarah and William Corbin, January [blank], 1743.

M.   JENKINS, Mary and John Cubbage, July 10, 1750.

M.   JENKINS, Margaret and John Jones, November 20, 1752.

M.   JENNINGS, Martha and Thomas Asbury, December 1, 1751.

B.   JOHNS, Jane daughter of Elizabeth Johns, March 16, 1755.

    JOHNSON : JOHNSTON

B.   JOHNSON, Benoni son of William and Frances Johnson, February 4, 1740.

M.   JOHNSTON, Silent and John Simpson, August 17, 1740.

B.   JOHNSTON, Wilmoth daughter of William and Frances Johnston, May 17, 1742.

M.   JOHNSON, Thomas and Elizabeth Harvey, October 19, 1745.

B.   JOHNSTON, Archibald son of Charles Johnston, September 2, 1750.

D.   JOHNSON, William December 25, 1751 at John Prim's.

B.   JOHNSON, Rachel October 23, 1752.

D.   JOHNSON, Elizabeth November 13, 1752.

B.   JOHNSON, Eleanor daughter of William and Tabitha Johnson, December 8, 1755.

B.   JONES, Elizabeth Warner daughter of Brereton and Lettice Jones, October 7, 1741. [1]

M.   JONES, Sarah and William Matheney, March 22, 1744.

B.   JONES, Robert son of Brereton and Lettice Jones, June 29, 1744.

M.   JONES, Elizabeth and Robert Bridwell, January 13, 1745.

M.   JONES, Thomas and Frances Leftridge, December 16, 1746.

M.   JONES, James and Frances Mason, January 8, 1747.

---

1 -   Brereton Jones (January 4, 1716 - August   , 1795) was born in Saint
      Stephen's Parish, Northumberland County, the son of Colonel Robert Jones
      (16 -1749) who died testate in Lunenburg County, and Elizabeth Brereton,
      his wife. He married on November 15, 1740 Elizabeth Warner who was born
      in January 1727 and survived him. She was the only child to survive in-
      fancy of John Warner, prominent surveyor in the upper Northern Neck of
      Virginia, who died testate in Stafford County in 1742. Brereton Jones
      died testate in Fauquier County and from his Bible we have the births of
      his ten children, viz: (1) Elizabeth Warner, October 7, 1741; (2) Robert,
      June 29, 1744; (3) Lettice, March 26, 1747; (4) Henry Brereton, August 31,
      1753; (5) Charles, June 11, 1755; (6) William, February 15, 1758; (7) Robert,
      November 15, 1760; (8) John Warner, March 27, 1764; (9) Daniel, March 27,
      1767, and (10) Mary, June 5, 1769.

B.   JONES, Elijah son of Thomas and Frances Jones, September 22, 1747.

M.   JONES, Rose and John Robertson, October 15, 1747.

M.   JONES, Catherine and Thomas Barry, August 5, 1749.

M.   JONES, Charles and Elizabeth Sinclair, April 21, 1751.

M.   JONES, Rosannah and James Hurst, April 21, 1751.

M.   JONES, John and Margaret Jenkins, November 20, 1752.

M.   JONES, Phillis and William Sturdy, December 17, 1752.

B.   JONES, Mary daughter of John Jones, October 4, 1755.

B.   JONES, James the son of John Jones, March 17, 1758.

B.   JORDAN, Willoughby son of William and Sarah Jordan, May 8, 1748.

M.   JORDAN, Nanny and William Forster, June 15, 1749.

M.   JORDAN, Mary and Nicholas Foxworthy, January 26, 1752.

D.   JUDD, Mary May 23, 1740.

M.   JUDD, Jean and Daniel Dunnaway, March 1, 1744.

B.   JUTTLE, William son of Catherine Juttle, January 26, 1742.

K

KANNEY   SEE :   KENNY :   KANNEY   PAGE

M.   KEES, Catherine and John Kendall, January 9, 1752.

M.   KELLY, John and Mary Garrison, November 1, 1745.

D.   KELLY, Honour August 13, 1747 at William Wright's.

M.   KELLY, Margaret and George Kendal, June 5, 1748.

M.   KELLY, Sarah and William Sebastian, June 11, 1751.

M.   KELLY, Nelson and Elizabeth Jeffries, November 4, 1751.

B.   KEMP, John son of James and Elizabeth Kemp, August 28, 1742.

B.   KENDALL, Jesse son of William Kendall, Junior, November 4, 1740.

D. KENDALL, Jesse November 18, 1740.

B. KENDALL, Thomas son of William and Jemima Kendall, March 27, 1742.

B. KENDALL, George son of William and Jemima Kendall, January 13, 1744.

M. KENDALL, James and Mary Coffey, February 25, 1745.

B. KENDALL, Ann daughter of William and Jemima Kendall, December 6, 1745.

B. KENDALL, Jesse son of James and Mary Kendall, June 19, 1747.

B. KENDALL, John son of William and Jemima Kendall, March 2, 1748.

M. KENDALL, William and Jemima Kirk, May 10, 1748.

M. KENDAL, George and Margaret Kelly, June 5, 1748.

B. KENDALL, John son of James and Mary Kendall, February 26, 1749.

M. KENDALL, Joshua and Catherine Smith, April 4, 1749.

B. KENDALL, William and Samuel sons of William and Jemima Kendall, August
    30, 1749.

B. KENDALL, Henry December 25, 1749, and baptized February 4, 1750.[1]

D. KENDALL, Jesse son of James Kendall, April 17, 1750.

B. KENDALL, Jesse son of Joshua Kendall, August 21, 1751.

M. KENDALL, John and Catherine Kees, January 9, 1752.[2]

---

1 - In the Mountain View section of Stafford County is a Kendall family ceme-
    tery with the following tombstones: (1) In Memory of Henry Kendall, born
    December 25, 1749; died June 20, 1810; (2) In Memory of Lucy Kendall, born
    December 13, 1763; died September 22, 1841; (3) In Memory of Joshua Kendall,
    born March 30, 1796; died June 23, 1852; (4) In Memory of William Kendall,
    born January 27, 1792; died January 2, 1854; (5) an unmarked grave; (6) In
    Memory of Eleanor Kendall, born August 29, 1788; died January 12, 1859; and
    (7) In Memory of Lucy T. Kendall born February 3, 1795; died March 9, 1859.

2 - Catherine's maiden name was probably Key which spelling has been interchang-
    ed with Kay; she had a grandson James Key Kendall. John Kendall died test-
    ate in Stafford County, December 9, 1808; his wife survived him. Their child-
    ren were: (1) Moses; (2) Daniel; (3) Aaron of Fayette County, Ohio; (4) Char-
    les; (5) Elizabeth married Peter Knight and moved to Harrison County, Virgin-
    ia; (6) Mary (1759-1858) married Captain William Starke (1754-1838) of Staf-
    ford County; (7) Ann married Henry Starke [died intestate in Stafford County,
    1803] and predeceased her father leaving five infant children; (8) Sarah mar-
    ried Enoch Harding of Stafford County, Virginia.

B.   KENDALL, Mary Ann daughter of William and Jemima Kendall, April 9, 1752.

B.   KENDALL, Jess son of James and Mary Kendall, September 20, 1752.

B.   KENDALL, Daniel son of John and Catherine Kendall, January 1, 1753.

B.   KENDALL, Joshua son of Joshua and Catherine Kendall, May 27, 1753.

B.   KENDALL, Lizy daughter of William and Jemima Kendall, April 1, 1754.

B.   KENDALL, Charles son of John and Catherine Kendall, September 7, 1754.

B.   KENDALL, Bailey son of James and Mary Kendall, October 8, 1755.

B.   KENDALL, Nancy daughter of Joshua and Catherine Kendall, December 19, 1755.

B.   KENDALL, Jeremiah son of William and Jemima Kendall, February 6, 1758.

B.   KENDALL, Nelly daughter of Joshua and Catherine Kendall, February 11, 1758.

B.   KENDALL, Elizabeth daughter of John and Catherine Kendall, February 27, 1758.

B.   KENDRICK, James son of Patrick and Jane Kendrick, January 10, 1752.

B.   KENDRICK, Isabel daughter of Patrick and Jane Kendrick, October 13, 1754.

B.   KENNEDY, Jane daughter of Milly Kennedy, March 29, 1756.

M.   KENNEDY, Isabella and William Patten, December 19, 1756.

KENNY : KANNEY   SEE :   RENNY PAGE 101

B.   KENNY, John son of James and Anne Kenny, February 14, 1740.

B.   KENNY, Richard son of James Kenny, April 9, 1742.

B.   KANNEY, William son of James and Ann Kanney, December 22, 1743.

M.   KENNY, Andrew and Anne Cearnes, November 30, 1744.

B.   KENNY, Nancy daughter of Andrew and Anne Kenny, August 2, 1745.

B.   KENNY, Thomas son of James and Anne Kenny, October 15, 1745.

B.   KENNY, John son of Andrew Kenny, May 6, 1747.

B.   KENNY, Sarah daughter of James and Anne Kenny, April 15, 1749.

B.   KENNY, Elizabeth daughter of Andrew and Ann Kenny, August 31, 1749.
     "Elizabeth Kenny baptized at St.Andrew's Church, September 24, 1749."

B. KENNY, Reuben son of James and Ann Kenny, October 12, 1751.

B. KENNY, Mary Ann January 9, 1755.

B. KENTON, Mary daughter of Mark and Mary Kenton, August 9, 1740.

M. KING, William and Elizabeth Edwards May 21, 1738.[1]

B. KING, John son of William and Elizabeth King, December [blank], 1740.

M. KING, Elizabeth and William Holdbrook, December 8, 1744.

B. KING, William son of William and Elizabeth King, February 22, 1745.

D. KING, Weathers son of William King, August 20, 1747.

B. KING, Nimrod son of William King, November 29, 1750.

M. KING, Josuah and Martha Fristoe, December 12, 1751.

M. KING, Martha and Joseph Maccollough, February 9, 1752.

C. KING, Elizabeth daughter of William King, September 7, 1755.

B. KING, John Edwards son of William King, December 21, 1757.

KIRK : KIRKE

M. KIRKE, John and Sarah Robinson, June 23, 1741.

B. KIRKE, Winifred daughter of John and Sarah Kirke, April 21, 1742.

B. KIRKE, Randall son of John and Sarah Kirke, April 21, 1742.

B. KIRK, William son of William and Sarah Kirk, June 6, 1742.

B. KIRKE, John Hardy son of Sarah Kirke, March 30, 1743.

D. KIRK, Sarah wife of William Kirk, December 28, 1743.

B. KIRK, John son of John and Sarah Kirk, January 20, 1745.

---

1 - William King (17 - 1765) descended from a family seated in Stafford County since the formation of the county. He married Elizabeth Edwards who
long survived him and on October 15, 1784 relinquished her right of dower
in lands sold by her son William King and Lettice, his wife, which had
been purchased by her husband William King, Senior, deceased, in 1747 and
1759. The deed recites the right to these lands fell to William King [Jr.]
"by the death of my father William King who died intestate." William and
Elizabeth (Edwards) King were the parents of General John Edwards King
(1757-1828) of Kentucky.

B. KIRKE, Elisha son of John and Sarah Kirke, July 2, 1747.

D. KIRKE, Elijah son of John and Sarah Kirke, November 25, 1747.

M. KIRK, Jemima and William Kendall, May 10, 1748.

B. KIRKE, Lucretia daughter of John and Sarah Kirke, May 8, 1751.

D. KIRKE, William March 21, 1753.

B. KIRKE, Sarah daughter of John and Sarah Kirke, September 5, 1753.

B. KIRKE, Elizabeth Wornom daughter of John Kirke, November 23, 1755.

M. KIRK, Henry and Sarah Lunsford, May 23, 1756.

B. KIRK, Suky daughter of Henry and Sarah Kirk, April 25, 1757.

B. KITCHEN, Elizabeth daughter of James and Mary Kitchen, January 15, 1748.

B. KITCHEN, Richard son of James and Mary Kitchen, January 15, 1748.

B. KITCHEN, Merryman son of James Kitchen, March 26, 1750.

B. KITCHEN, Charles son of James and Mary Kitchen, March 7, 1752.

C. KITE, John son of John Kite, July 14, 1754.

B. KNIGHT, John son of Leonard and Eleanor Knight, February 15, 1740.

B. KNIGHT, Nelly daughter of Leonard and Nelly Knight, August 7, 1743.

B. KNIGHT, Mary Ann daughter of Christopher Knight, June 14, 1744.

M. KNIGHT, George and Jean Dawson, December 25, 1744.

B. KNIGHT, William son of Elizabeth Knight, February 28, 1746.

B. KNIGHT, Elizabeth daughter of George and Jean Knight, March 4, 1746.

B. KNIGHT, John son of George Knight, October 22, 1747.

D. KNIGHT, William November 27, 1747.

M. KNIGHT, Elizabeth and Nicholas Bennet, June 12, 1749.

M. KNIGHT, John and Charity Latimore, October 23, 1750.

B. KNIGHT, Samuel son of John and Charity Knight, August 15, 1751.

B. KNIGHT, Sarah Ann daughter of George and Jean Knight, October 2, 1753.

B. KNIGHT, Ephraim son of Isaac Knight, February 3, 1754.

M. KNIGHT, Peter and Rachel Abbot, December 19, 1756.

B. KNIGHT, Christopher son of Peter and Rachel Knight, November 2, 1757.

M. KNIGHT, Ephraim and Anne Abbot, February 12, 1758.[1]

M. KNIGHT, [mutilated] and Elizabeth Yates, February 4, 1758.

B. KNIGHT, [mutilated] son of Peter and Rachel Knight, November 2, 1758.[2]

                                    L

M. LACY, Sarah and Rawleigh Chinn, September 2, 1748.

D. LAING, Andrew at James Waugh's February 8, 1742.

M. LAMB, Mary and Edward Malphus, December 25, 1740.

D. LAMBETH, Elizabeth July [blank], 1755, a servant of John Ralls.

M. LANE, James Hardage and Mary Smith, January 15, 1758.[3]

    LATHAM : LAYTHAM : LAYTHEM

M. LATHAM, Mary and John Richards June 24, 1740.

M. LATHAM, Mary and Thomas Bell, June 25, 1741.

M. LATHAM, Mary and Henry Suddeth, June 25, 1745.

D. LATHAM, Jane January 7, 1746 at Mary Richards'.

---

1 - The Spotsylvania County records show the presence there in 1750 and after-
     wards of a Ephraim Knight. He purchased land in 1760 which was sold in
     1795 by his son John Knight then of Stafford County, Virginia.

2-   This is most likely the birth of Peter Knight who married Elizabeth Kend-
     all, born February 27, 1758. See pages 63 and 64.

3-   James Hardage Lane died testate in Loudoun County in 1787. His wife, nee
     Mary Smith (173? - December 26, 1796),was the daughter of Henry and Sarah
     (Crosby) Smith of Stafford County. They had eleven children, viz: (1)
     John; (2) William; (3) George; (4) James Hardage; (5) Daniel Crosby; (6)
     Enoch Smith; (7) Mary married Enoch Hansbrough; (8) Rebeckah married Asa
     Blanchard; (9) Deliah married Richard Newman; (10) Elizabeth married Joel
     Beach and (11) Sarah married Mr. Darrell.

D.   LATHAM, Frances October 1, 1746.

D.   LATHAM, John October 2, 1746.

M.   LAYTHAM, Sarah and William Mays, February 9, 1752.

M.   LATHAM, Snowdall and Sarah Green, November 25, 1756.

B.   LAYTHEM, Jemima daughter of Snowdall and Sarah Laythem, November 1, 1757.

M.   LATIMORE, Mary and Lewis Pritchet, March 31, 1744.

M.   LATIMORE, Charity and John Knight, October 23, 1750.

B.   LAWLESS, Thomas son of Mary Lawless, January 28, 1744.

D.   LAWLESS, Thomas son of Mary Lawless, September 10, 1744.

D.   LAWLESS, Mary September 14, 1744.

M.   LEA, Lucy and [mutilated] Bridwell, April 9, 1758.

M.   LEE, Joseph and Mary Bethel, November 14, 1745.

M.   LEFTRIDGE, Frances and Thomas Jones, December 16, 1746.

B.   LEMASTER, Elizabeth daughter of Thomas and Lettice Lemaster, January 14, 1753.

M.   LEMMON, John and Eleanor McCarty, April 10, 1748.

M.   LEWIS, Walter Morgan and Mary Abram, August 27, 1738.

M.   LEWIS, Zacharias and Mary Brent, August 24, 1756. [1]

B.   LIMBRICK, Susannah daughter of William Limbrick, October 12, 1739.

B.   LIMBRICK, Thomas son of William and Catherine Limbrick, May 10, 1744.

M.   LIMBRICK, Rachel and Thomas Porch, July 22, 1748.

D.   LIMBRICK, Vinson son of William Limbrick, April 28, 1749.

B.   LIMON, James son of John Limon, August 15, 1748.

M.   LINCE, Margaret and William Cannaday, January 16, 1747.

---

1 - Zacharias Lewis (17 -1798) died testate in Prince William County. His wife, Mary Brent, was born May 25, 1732 [see page 11]; her ancestry is detailed by Mr. Chester Horton Brent in The Descendants of Hugh Brent [1936], page 59.

M. LINDCEY, John and Elizabeth Glass, January 15, 1750.

M. LINTON, Mary and John Remy, April 6, 1740. [1]

M. LINTON, Lettice and Joseph Carter, February 5, 1755.

D. LOMACKS, Richard August 28, 1749 at John Peyton's, Aquia.

B. LOWRY, Judith daughter of William and Tabitha Lowry, February 13, 1742. [2]

B. LOWRY, George son of William and Tabitha Lowry, November 24, 1744.

M. LOWRY, Tabitha and Jeremiah Starke, January 29, 1747.

M. LOWRY, Helen and Robert Green, November 23, 1756.

B. LUNS, Letty daughter of Rebecca Luns, June 21, 1744.

B. LUNSFORD, Sarah daughter of William and Mary Lunsford, March 7, 1744.

B. LUNSFORD, Hannah daughter of William and Dinah Lunsford, June 5, 1744.

B. LUNSFORD, Mary daughter of William Lunsford, September 7, 1746.

B. LUNSFORD, Charlotte daughter of William and Dinah Lunsford, December 22, 1746.

M. LUNSFORD, Rebecca and John Baker, June 8, 1747.

B. LUNSFORD, Benjamin son of William Lunsford, February 10, 1749.

C. LUNSFORD, Jemima July 23, 1749.

M. LUNSFORD, Judith and John Pelter, February 27, 1750.

B. LUNSFORD, William had a bastard child named James born at his house on October 7, 1750.

B. LUNSFORD, Hannah daughter of William Lunsford, October 16, 1751.

---

1 - Anthony Linton [Lynton], son of William Linton and Johanna Lewis, his wife, inherited property in Richmond County from his maternal grandfather Edward Lewis; he sold this in 1735. Anthony Linton married Mary Page, daughter of William Page who died testate in Stafford County in 1716. He died testate in Stafford County in 1738 leaving two infant children, John Linton and Lettice Linton who married Joseph Carter. Mary (Page) Linton married secondly John Remy.

2 - William Lowry died intestate in Stafford County in 1745; Jeremiah Stark(e) married his widow Tabitha Lowry and was guardian to his two orphan children, Judith Lowry and George Lowry, in 1757.

M. LUNSFORD, Rowley and Joanna Sturdy, June 16, 1754.

M. LUNSFORD, Alice and Joshua Brown, July 21, 1754.

M. LUNSFORD, John and Margaret Martyn, January 6, 1756.

M. LUNSFORD, Lettice and William Simpson, January 18, 1756.

B. LUNSFORD, Jane daughter of Moses and Rachel, April 24, 1756.

M. LUNSFORD, Sarah and Henry Kirk, May 23, 1756.

B. LUNSFORD, Enoch son of John Lunsford, February 28, 1758.

M. LUNSFORD, Susanna and John Peyton, March 28, 1758.

LYNAUGH : LYNAH : LYNUM : LINAUGH : LINOUGH

B. LYNUM, Joseph son of Rose Lynum, March 24, 1748.

B. LYNUM, Frank son of Rose Lynum, April 21, 1751.

B. LYNAH, Margaret daughter of Rose Lynah, July 23, 1754 at Peter Rout's.

B. LINOUGH, [mutilated] , a mulatto son of Rose Linough, September 15, 1757.

M. LYNN, Margaret and Thomas Darlow, April 9, 1758.

M. LYON, Margaret and John Abbot, January 15, 1758.

Mc - Mac

MACABOY : MACCABOY

M. MACABOY, Morthough and Elizabeth Pumphrey, December 27, 1747.

D. MACABOY, Murthough January 17, 1750.

B. MACCABOY, Murthough son of Murthough and Elizabeth Maccaboy, January 19, 1750.

M. MACCABOY, Elizabeth and James Gwin, October 5, 1755.

MC CARTY : MAC CARTY : MACCARTY : MAC CARTEE : MACCARTEE

B. MC CARTY, John son of William and Agnes McCarty, March 29, 1741.

B. MC CARTY, James son of John McCarty, April 23, 1741.

D. MC CARTY, William September 15, 1743.

M.   MAC CARTEE, Agnes and James Hughes, May 6, 1744.

M.   MAC CARTY, Elizabeth and Simson Batey, December 24, 1747.

M.   MC CARTY, Eleanor and John Lemmon, April 10, 1748.

D.   MAC CARTY, Cornelius February 18, 1755 "at his own house." [1]

M.   MAC CARTY, Frances and John Diskin, June 19, 1755.

M.   MAC CARTY, Margaret and Stephen Hansford, October 14, 1755.

B.   MC COLIN, Mary daughter of John McColin, September 30, 1742.

M.   MC CONCHIE, William and Bridget Whitecotton, November 10, 1747.

B.   MC CONCHIE, Richard son of William and Bridget Mc Conchie, July 10, 1748.

M.   MC CONCHIE, Bridget and Stephen Pilcher, December [blank], 1750.

     MC COY : MACCOY : MACOY

B.   MC COY, Elizabeth daughter of Murdy and Ann McCoy, September 29, 1744.

B.   MACOY, Alexander son of Murdy and Ann Macoy, October 20, 1749.

B.   MACOY, William son of Murdy and Ann Mccoy, October 15, 1752.

D.   MACCOY, Elizabeth daughter of Murdy Maccoy, June 5, 1755.

M.   MACOY, Feanly and Jane Thomson, July 18, 1757.

B.   MACCOY, [mutilated] daughter of Murdy Maccoy, July 22, 1757.

B.   MC COY, Daniel son of Finlay Mc Coy, October 10, 1757.

     MC CULLOUGH : MC COLLOUGH : MACCOLLOUGH

M.   MC CULLOUGH, Mary and Thomas Ashby, November 14, 1751.

M.   MACCOLLOUGH, Benjamin and Elizabeth Whitson, December 19, 1751.

M.   MC COLLOUGH, Hannah and Benjamin Tolson, Junior, December 31, 1751.

---

1 - The last will and Testament of Cornelius McCarty of Dettingen Parish,
    Prince William County, was dated May 21, 1754; it was admitted to probate
    before the Stafford County court, April 8, 1755. By this instrument he
    made his wife Frances McCarty his sole heir and executrix. In May 1755,
    shortly before her marriage to John Diskin of Prince William County, she
    made a deed of gift to her niece Elizabeth Porter for a Negro slave call-
    ed Moll.

M.   MACCOLLOUGH, Joseph and Martha King, February 9, 1752.

B.   MACULOUGH, William son of Benjamin and Elizabeth Maculough, May 19, 1754.

M.   MACCULLOUGH, Sarah and John Ashby, February 26, 1756.

B.   MACCULLOUGH, James son of Benjamin and Elizabeth Maccullough, November 29, 1756.

MC DANIEL : MACDANIEL   SEE : MC DONALD

B.   MC DANIEL, Mary daughter of James and Martha McDaniel, January 6, 1740.

B.   MC DANIEL, Margaret daughter of James and Jane McDaniel, January 8, 1752.

M.   MACDANIEL, Margaret and John Powel, February 10, 1752.

B.   MACDANIEL, Reuben son of James and Jean Macdaniel, November 22, 1755.

B.   MC DONALD, William son of James and Martha Mc Donald, January 25, 1743.

M.   MC DONALD, Reverend Daniel and Ellen Barret, July 26, 1740.[1]

M.   MC DUELL,William and Sarah Chambers, December 26, 1739.

B.   MC DUELL, John son of William and Sarah McDuell, July 22, 1740.

B.   MC DUELL, Mary daughter of William and Sarah McDuell, May 4, 1742.

B.   MACFARLANE, Priscilla daughter of Daniel Macfarlane, April 15, 1744.

M.   MC GUIRK, John and Rachel Wade, December 25, 1741.

MC INTEER : MACINTEER : MACCATIER : MACANTEER : MACCANTEER

M.   MC INTEER, Sarah and Andrew Davison, November 5, 1738.

---

1 - On August 25, 1940 a handsome memorial tablet was unveiled at Lambs Creek
Episcopal Church, King George County, which reads: "To the Glory of God /
And in Memory of / Reverend Daniel Mc Donald / Born in County Antrim, Ire-
land. / Ordained in 1731. Minister of / Hanover Parish 1731-1735 and / of
Brunswick Parish 1735-1762. / Buried in Muddy Creek Churchyard / 1762.
Erected by his Descendants 1940". He married Ellen Barret who was born
April 19, 1728 in Saint Paul's Parish, daughter of Richard and Margaret Barret, and had issue, viz: (1) Theodosius, killed in the Indian Wars and not
mentioned in his father's will; (2) Daniel married Susannah Pilcher and removed to Fauquier County; (3) Anne (1744-1823) married Niel McCoull, merchant of Fredericksburg; (4) Mary married on October 25, 1768 Captain Francis Atwell of Fauquier County; (5) Helen married Edward Moor (17 -1806),
merchant of Falmouth; (6) Jane (1750-1810) married in June 1771 David Briggs
(1730-1813) of Stoney Hill, Stafford County. See Tyler's Quarterly Historical and Genealogical Magazine, Volume 28, pages 107-111.

M.   MC INTEER, Joyce and William Pattin, January 27, 1740.

M.   MACCATIAR, Alexander and Meriam Belsher, December 24, 1751. [1]

B.   MACINTEER, William son of Alexander Macinteer, November 7, 1752.

B.   MACANTEER, Gabriel son of Alexander Macanteer, May 24, 1754.

B.   MACCANTEER, Elijah son of Alexander Maccanteer, June 14, 1756.

B.   MACINTEER, Rodah daughter of Alexander and Mariam Macinteer, March [muti-
     lated], 1758 and baptized April 9, 1758.

D.   MACLOED, Katherine April 12, 1746 "a servant to John Phipps."

M.   MACMAHON, Bryan and Jane Moore, December 30, 1747.

M.   MACQUATTY, David and Mary Skaines, May 6, 1755.

B.   MACQUATTY, Nancy daughter of David and Mary Macquatty, July 10, 1755.

M.   MAC MURRY, Ann and John Donaldson, December 31, 1747.

                              M

MAC   SEE : MC - MAC PAGES 70 - 73

M.   MAHANES, Samuel and Francisina Craven, November 14, 1742.

     MAIZE   SEE : MAYS PAGE

---

1 - Alexander Mc Inteer (17 -1807) died testate in Stafford County. He mar-
    ried first, December 24, 1751 Miriam Belcher and had issue, viz: (1) Will-
    iam, born 1752, who is not mentioned in his father's will; (2) Gabriel,
    born 1754, who is not mentioned in his father's will; (3) Elijah, born
    1756, who is not mentioned in his father's will; (4) Rhoda, born 1758,
    who is mentioned as Rhoda Kendall; (5) Winifred who is mentioned as Wini-
    fred Harding; (6) Ann who is mentioned as the wife of Ewel Mason; (7) Mir-
    iam who is mentioned as Miriam Tolson and (8) Henry McInteer - said child-
    ren having received their portions of the testator's estate in his life-
    time. Alexander Mc Inteer (17 -1807) married secondly Sarah, traditional-
    ly nee Sinclair; she survived him many years, and left issue, viz: (9) Har-
    man [Herman] who was residing in Spencer County, Kentucky, in 1827; (10)
    Noah; (11) Lydia (1786-1867) married first William Patton (1785-1814) in
    1808 and secondly Jeremiah Holmes (1786-1865) in 1817; (12) Frances married
    Lewis Martin; (13) Agatha married James Patton; (14) Barsheba ("Shebia")
    married John Patton and (15) Sarah married Thornton Patton. The aforemen-
    tioned William Patton (born 1785), James Patton (born 178?), John Patton
    (born 1789) and Thornton Patton (born 1793) were sons of George Patton
    (1757-1813) and Sarah Stringfellow (1766-1848), his wife, of Stafford
    County who were married there December 24, 1784.

MALPAS : MALPHUS : MALPUS[1]

M. MALPHUS, Edward and Mary Lamb, December 28, 1740.

D. MALPAS, Edward September 15, 1743.

D. MALPUS, Mary widow of Edward Malpus, October 19, 1743.

M. MANUEL, Elizabeth and Arthur Dint, December 11, 1742.

D. MANUEL, [mutilated] March 10, 1756 at James Phillips'.

M. MARKHAM, Margaret and Taylor Chapman, September 13, 1739.

M. MARONY, Mary and Solomon Carter, May 26, 1751.

MARTIN : MARTYN

B. MARTIN, Francis son of Francis and Betty Martin, February 25, 1741.

M. MARTIN, Sarah and William Heffernon, September 29, 1741.

M. MARTIN, Thomas and Sarah Dunaway, January 22, 1742.

B. MARTIN, Jean daughter of Thomas and Sarah Martin, June 6, 1742.

B. MARTIN, Charles son of Francis and Elizabeth Martin, April 22, 1744.

M. MARTIN, Lucy and James Green, October 4, 1748.

M. MARTYN, Margaret and John Lunsford, June 6, 1756.

M. MARTIN, Sarah and Moses Fletcher, July 10, 1757.

D. MASON, Anne daughter of William and Mary Mason, August 20, 1740.

M. MASON, Mary and Thomas Butler, April 7, 1741.

B. MASON, Lewis son of William Mason, October 8, 1741.

D. MASON, Lewis son of William Mason, October 26, 1745.

D. MASON, Elizabeth November 5, 1746.

M. MASON, Margaret and Joseph Carter, November 27, 1746.

---

1 - The name is rendered MAULPIS on the court records. Edward Maulpis died
    testate September 15, 1743; his last will and Testament mentions his wife
    Mary, son John Maulpis and daughter Grace Jackson (see page 59). She was
    the widow of William Jackson who died intestate on March 16, 1749.

M. MASON, Frances and James Jones, January 8, 1747.

M. MASON, John and Mary Nelson, November 27, 1747. [1]

B. MASON, William son of John and Mary Mason, November 30, 1748.

B. MASON, John son of John and Mary Mason, February 18, 1751.

M. MASON, Mary Thomson and Samuel Selden, April 11, 1751.

M. MASON, Daniel and Elizabeth Nelson, January 30, 1753.

B. MASON, Nelson son of John and Mary Mason, August 6, 1753.

M. MASON, George and Elizabeth Duwest, October 21, 1755.

B. MASON, Sarah daughter of Daniel and Elizabeth Mason, December 16, 1753.

B. MASON, Frances daughter of George Mason, January 16, 1757.

B. MASON, Lewis son of John Mason, February 5, 1757.

M. MASSEY, Thomas and Eleanor Perender, June 26, 1745.

B. MASTERS, Mary daughter of Jared and Anne Masters, May 4, 1740.

MATHENEY : MATHENY : METHENY : METHENEY [2]

---

1 - Colonel George Mason (1628-1686) lived upon Accakeek Creek. His only
known son, Colonel George Mason (16 -1716),sold that plantation in 1694
and moved to Dogue Neck in the present county of Fairfax in which area he
and his progeny continued. In 1694 another George Mason (16 -1711) purchased land on upper Aquia Run in present Overwharton Parish and being
contemporary with Colonel George Mason (16 -1716) he is styled on the records George Mason of Aquia. He seems to have been the ancestor of the
majority of the persons mentioned in The Register of Overwharton Parish.
His son, George Mason of Aquia (16 - circa 1729/30), died testate but his
will is in lost Will Book "K" [1721-1730], page 340. He appears to have
been the father of John Mason (1722- circa 1796), also of Aquia, who married in 1747 Mary Nelson (172? - circa 1801), daughter of Henry Nelson.
Their eldest son was the well known Baptist clergyman, the Reverend William
Mason (November 30, 1748 - April 26, 1823) of Culpeper County, while their
youngest son was Colonel Enoch Mason (circa 1769 - 1828) of Clover Hill,
Stafford County. He was a prominent attorney-at-law and married April 28,
1796 Lucy Wiley Roy, a descendant of Colonel George Mason (1628-1686); they
have a number of distinguished progeny.

2 - Daniel Matheny settled in Charles County, Maryland, but early established
himself on Aquia Creek in Stafford County. Here is yet to be seen a large
tombstone said to be his, but only engraved: "D . M . / October 14, 1685."
See Matheny-Metheny Family of Virginia by W.B. Metheny, Reel 156 and The
Matheny Genealogy 998-1951 by C.M.Mathena, Reel 309, Virginia State Library.

M. MATHENEY, Mary and Edward Ponton, November 20, 1739.

M. MATHENEY, William and Sarah Jones, March 22, 1744.

D. MATHENY : "Daniel Matheny had two of his family died November 4th and 24th 1745."

M. METHENY, William and Anne Sims, September 10, 1747.

D. MATHENY, Mary January 12, 1750.

D. MATHENY, Daniel January 20, 1750.

B. MATHENY, Job son of William and Anne Matheny, February 6, 1750.

M. MATHENY, James and Lizzy Guin, December 12, 1751.

B. MATHENY, Mary daughter of James and Eliza Matheny, January 16, 1753.

B. METHENY, Mary daughter of William and Anne Metheny, April 2, 1753.

B. METHENY, William son of Thomas and Hannah Metheny, July 7, 1753.

M. MATHENY, Mary and Moses Grigsby, August 26, 1753.

B. MATHENEY, John son of James Matheney, December 20, 1754.

B. MATHENY, Anne daughter of William and Anne Matheny, March 18, 1755.

B. MATHENY, George son of Thomas and Hannah Matheny, September 8, 1755.

B. MATHENY, James son of James and Elizabeth Matheny, September 9, 1756.

MATHEWS : MATTHEWS

M. MATHEWS, Elizabeth and Timothy O'Neal, April 29, 1739.

M. MATTHEWS, Philip and Catherine Cassity, January 4, 1742.

B. MATTHEWS, [blank] daughter of Samuel and Anne Matthews, March 5, 1742.

D. MATTHEWS, John son of William Matthews, Junior, November 11, 1744, aged 6 years.

B. MATTHEWS, William, Senior, had a bastard child named Frances born at his house, December 7, 1746.

M. MATTHEWS, Sarah and James Jeffries, December 23, 1746.

M. MATTHEWS, Mary and John Waller, July 4, 1751.

B. MATTHEWS, Jean daughter of John Matthews, June 23, 1752.

M. MATTHEWS, Mary and James Turner,   March 3, 1757.

M. MATTHIS, Richard and Mary Plummer,   October 5, 1745.

MAULPIS   SEE : MALPAS : MALPHUS : MALPUS   PAGE 74

MAUZEY : MAUZY [1]

B. MAUZEY, John son of Peter and Elizabeth Mauzey,   December 17, 1739.

B. MAUZEY, Jemima daughter of John and Hester Mauzey,   March 26, 1740.

M. MAUZEY, Priscilla and William Rassan [Rosseau],   October 27, 1743.

M. MAUZEY, Henry and Ann Withers,   November 11, 1744.

B. MAUZEY, Elizabeth daughter of Peter Mauzey,   December 20, 1745.

B. MAUZEY, Peter son of Peter and Elizabeth Mauzey,   May 19, 1748.

M. MAUZY , Elizabeth and Peter Murphy,   February 9, 1752.

D. MAUZEY, George   January 10, 1754 at John Mauzey's.

M. MAYOW, Rosamund and Stephen Phips,   June 1, 1740.

MAYS : MAIZE

B. MAYS, James son of Joseph Mays,   February 1, 1752.

M. MAYS, William and Sarah Laytham,   February 9, 1752.

B. MAYS, George son of William and Sarah Mays,   February 7, 1753.

D. MAIZE, George son of William Maize,   November 14, 1753.

B. MAYS, Lydia daughter of Joseph and Sarah Mays,   February 23, 1754.

---

1 - John Mauzey (circa 1675 - circa 1718) and Henry Conyers (16 - 1733) ap-
pear on the Stafford County records circa 1700. The indications are that
John Mauzey married first a sister of Henry Conyers and had issue, viz:
(1) John Mauzey (circa 1696 - circa 1780) who married his cousin Hester
Conyers and left issue; (2) George Mauzey (circa 1698 - circa 1727); (3)
Margaret Mauzey (1702-1754) who married in 1721 Major Peter Hedgman. John
Mauzey married secondly Mary (Crosby) Mountjoy (16 -1756), daughter of
George Crosby, Gentleman, and widow of Captain Edward Mountjoy [died 1712],
and had two children, viz: (4) Peter Mauzey (circa 1714-1751) who married
in 1735 Elizabeth Sumner and died testate in Stafford County; she married
secondly in 1752 Peter Murphy; and (5) Elizabeth Mauzey who married first
William Markham and secondly Thomas Conway. Mary (Crosby) Mountjoy Mauzey
married thirdly Joseph Waugh, Gentleman. [See footnotes and citations on
pages 22, 84, and 85.]

B. MAYS, Jeany daughter of William and Sarah Mays, October 15, 1754.

B. MAYS, Joseph son of Joseph and Sarah Mays, April 18, 1756.

M. MAYS, Robert and Elizabeth Bolling, December 27, 1756.

B. MAYS, Benjamin son of William and Elizabeth Mays, September 16, 1757.

B. MAYS, George son of Joseph and Sarah Mays, January 1, 1758.

B. MERCER, Mason son of John and Catherine Mercer, July 2, 1726.[1]

D. MERCER, Mason son of John and Catherine Mercer, July 23, 1726.

B. MERCER, John son of John and Catherine Mercer, December 17, 1727.

B. MERCER, Elizabeth Mason daughter of John and Catherine Mercer, February 16, 1730.

D. MERCER, Elizabeth Mason daughter of John and Catherine Mercer, August 31, 1732.

D. MERCER, John son of John and Catherine Mercer, September 12, 1732.

B. MERCER, George son of John and Catherine Mercer, July 2, 1733.

B. MERCER, John Fenton son of John and Catherine Mercer, August 31, 1735.

B. MERCER, James son of John and Catherine Mercer, February 26, 1737.

B. MERCER, Sarah Ann daughter of John and Catherine Mercer, June 21, 1738.

B. MERCER, Mary daughter of John and Catherine Mercer, August 23, 1740.

B. MERCER, Thompson Mason son of John and Catherine Mercer, April 9, 1742.

B. MERRIMAN, Mary daughter of Adam and Elizabeth Merriman, January 19, 1741.

M. MERRINGHAM, Jane and Thomas Bettson, April 14, 1748.

METHENY   SEE : MATHENEY : MATHENY : METHENY &c. PAGES 75-76

M. MILLENER, Elizabeth and James Campbell, September 27, 1741.

M. MILLER, William and Anne Druo, March 5, 1739.

---

1 - For a detailed account of the family of John Mercer, Esquire, (1704/5-1768) of Marlborough and his wives, Catherine Mason (1707-1750) and Ann Roy (17 - 1770), see The Virginia Genealogist, Volume 4, pages 99-110, 153-162. The Register of Overwharton Parish fails to record the children of John Mercer, Esquire, who were born after 1742.

B. MILLER, Anne daughter of William and Anna Miller, December 23, 1739.

M. MILLER, Isabella and Simon Miller, October 2, 1740. [1]

M. MILLER, Simon and Isabella Miller, October 2, 1740.

D. MILLION, William son of Robert Million, December 5, 1740.

D. MILLION, Elizabeth daughter of Robert Million, December 7, 1740.

D. MILLION, Anne daughter of Robert and Grace Million, April 8, 1741.

M. MILLION, Winifred and Elias Ashby, September 4, 1745.

C. MILLION, Charky, daughter of Robert Million, December 15, 1745.

B. MILLION, William Bennit son of Robert and Grace Million, December 23,
    1747.

D. MILLION, John son of Robert Million, October [blank], 1749.

M. MILLION, Robert and Keziah Holliday, December 14, 1749. [2]

B. MILLION, Benjamin son of Robert Million, July 5, 1750.

---

1 - Captain Simon Miller (1642-1684) was a prominent inhabitant of Rappahannock
    County. His son, Simon Miller (16 -1720), died testate in Richmond County
    leaving three children, viz: (1) Eleanor Miller who married Robert Elliston
    (17 -1785) and resided in King George and Stafford counties; (2) Jane Mil-
    ler married Thomas Hord, Gentleman, (1701-1766) of King George County; and
    (3) Simon Miller (171?-1799) of King George, Stafford and Culpeper counties.
    He died in Culpeper County leaving two wills which were contested: one was
    dated 1783 and the other was dated 1798 at which time his second wife was
    deceased. By an unknown first wife he had issue, viz: (1) Simon Miller
    (17 -1806) of Culpeper County; (2) Benjamin Miller who died prior to 1783
    (when the first will was drawn) leaving issue (a) John, (b) Nelly, and (c)
    Barbary Miller; (3) Mary Miller (born 1737) married in 1755 her first cousin,
    James Hord (1736-1802) of Culpeper County; (4) Alice Miller (circa 1739-1775)
    married in 1763 John Markham (1732-1804) of Stafford County, son of William
    and Elizabeth (Mauzey) Markham. By his second wife Isabella Miller [who is
    said to have been the daughter of his uncle John Miller (16 -1743) of Essex
    County], Simon Miller (171?-1799) had issue two children, viz: (5) Eleanor
    Miller (born 1742) who married Thomas Strother and moved to Bourbon County,
    Kentucky; (6) Eliza Miller who married Captain William Richards (circa 1755-
    1817) of Culpeper County and with whom Simon Miller and his wife lived in
    their declining years.

2 - Robert and Keziah Million were among the early dissenters in Overwharton
    Parish and their names appear as subscribers to the Covenant of November
    22, 1766 to establish the Chopawamsic Baptist Church.

B. MILLION, Jemima daughter of Robert Million, November 13, 1750.

B. MILLION, Sithy daughter of Robert and Keziah Million, August 27, 1753.

B. MILLION, Sarah Ann daughter of Robert and Keziah Million, February 13, 1756.

B. MILLION, Jeany daughter of Robert and Keziah Million, April 19, 1758.

M. MILLS, Elizabeth and Edward West, October 6, 1752.

M. MILLS, Margaret and James Scoulcraft, October 14, 1753.

M. MINGS, James and Susannah Pattison, September 7, 1750.

B. MINOR, Nicholas son of James Minor, June 4, 1742.

B. MINOR, Allander daughter of John and Margaret Minor, January 10, 1743.

B. MINOR, Susannah daughter of William Minor, August 23, 1748.

B. MINOR, Amelia daughter of John Minor, July 7, 1749.

D. MINOR, John, Senior, January 12, 1751.

B. MITCHEL, Elizabeth daughter of Jedidiah Mitchel, September 18, 1743.

C. MITCHEL, John son of Jedediah and Lydia Mitchel, April 6, 1746.

B. MITCHELL, Barnaby LeGosh son of Jedediah and Lydia Mitchell, March 10, 1748.

M. MITCHELL, Samuel and Bridget Berry, January 30, 1749.

B. MITCHELL, William son of Samuel and Bridget Mitchell, January 27, 1750.

B. MITCHELL, Elizabeth daughter of Samuel and Bridget Mitchell, January 19, 1752.

D. MOBLEY, Elizabeth September 4, 1750 at Henry Robinson's.

M. MONCURE, The Reverend Mr. John, Rector of this Parish, and Frances Brown, eldest daughter of Dr. Gustavus Brown of Charles County, Maryland, June 18, 1741.

B. MONCURE, John son of the Reverend John and Frances Moncure, July 12, 1744.

D. MONCURE, John son of the Reverend John Moncure, July 13, 1744.

B. MONCURE, Frances daughter of the Reverend John and Frances Moncure, September 20, 1745.

C. MONCURE, Frances daughter of the Reverend John Moncure, September 28, 1745, by the Reverend James Scott who was her Godfather with George Mason, Gent.; Godmothers: Mrs. Anne Carter, wife of Charles Carter, Esquire, and Mrs. Sarah Scott.

B. MONCURE, John son of the Reverend John and Frances Moncure, January 22, 1747.

C. MONCURE, John son of the Reverend John Moncure, March 3, 1747, by the Reverend John Phipps. His Godfathers were: John Mercer and George Mason, Esquires; his Godmother was Elizabeth Brown, his aunt.

B. MONCURE, Anne daughter of the Reverend John and Frances Moncure, October 17, 1748.

C. MONCURE, Anne daughter of the Reverend John Moncure, December 2, 1748, by the Reverend James Scott who was her Godfather with George Mason, Esquire; Godmothers: Mary Mason and Cecilia Brown.

B. MONCURE, Jean daughter of the Reverend John Moncure, May 22, 1753; she was baptized by the Reverend James Scott on June 12, 1753 but no sponsors are mentioned. [There is a notation she died in 1823 aged 70 years.]

M. MONCURE, Frances Junior and Travers Daniel, October 7, 1762 at Clermont, by the Reverend Mister James Scott.

B. MONCURE, William son of John and Anne Moncure, September 21, 1774.

D. MONK, Gilbert January 31, 1741.

B. MONK, Priscilla daughter of Elizabeth Monk, May 7, 1742.[1]

M. MONK, Elizabeth and William Walker, May 3, 1744.

M. MONROE, Thomas and Catherine Hore, April 16, 1745.[2]

---

1 - John Waugh died November 17, 1742 and by his last will and Testament provided for his three illegitimate children by Elizabeth Monk, viz: John, Thomas, and Priscilla; he also made provisions for his concubine during the time of her good behaviour and while she remained unmarried. She married William Walker on May 3, 1744.

2 - Thomas Monroe (17 -1777), son of Captain William Monroe (169?-1760) of Westmoreland County, married Catherine Hore (172?-1778) [see page 54]. They both died intestate in Fairfax County where there are many records concerning this family. They had issue: (1) George Hore Monroe (September 3, 1747 - October 18, 1747); (2) Thomas Monroe [Jr.] born October 31, 1749, married Mildred Reagan, daughter of Michael Reagan; (3) Isabella Monroe (November 11, 1751 - 1797) married Major James Crump (17 -1800), son of Adam and Hannah (Bushrod) Crump, and moved to Montgomery County, North Carolina; (4) Lawrence Monroe (circa 1755-1806) married Jane ------ (1765-1853); (5) Catherine Monroe married Michael Keeler; (6) George Monroe; (7) Sarah Monroe who was single in 1795 and residing in Rowen County, North Carolina.

B. MONROE, George Hore son of Thomas and Catherine Monroe, September 3, 1747.

D. MONROE, George Hore son of Thomas and Catherine Monroe, October 18, 1747.

B. MONROE, Thomas son of Thomas and Catherine Monroe, October 31, 1749.

B. MONROE, Isabel[1a] daughter of Thomas and Catherine Monroe, November 11, 1751.

M. MONROE, John and Sarah Harrison, September 23, 1756.[1]

M. MONSLOW, John and Jean Waters, October 26, 1748.

D. MONSLOW, John October 3, 1751 at the house of John Waters.

D. MONTGOMERY, Sarah wife of John Montgomery, August 30, 1742.

M. MONTGOMERY, John and Mary Smith, January 16, 1744.

B. MONTGOMERY, Mary daughter of William Montgomery, August 7, 1744.

B. MONTGOMERY, Jane daughter of John Montgomery, August 20, 1746.

B. MONTGOMERY, John son of John Montgomery, April 3, 1749.

D. MONTGOMERY, John son of John and Mary Montgomery, October 22, 1749.

B. MONTGOMERY, Robert son of John and Mary Montgomery, November 13, 1750.

---

1 - Major Andrew Monroe (16 -1668) immigrated to America from Scotland about 1641 and settled in Saint Mary's County, Maryland. In 1648 he crossed the Potomac River and settled on Monroe Creek, Westmoreland County, Virginia,where he received land patents before the formation of the county. By his wife Elizabeth, traditionally nee Alexander, he had two sons, viz: (1) Andrew (1664-1714) married Eleanor Spence and (2) William (1666-1737) married Margaret Bowcock and had four sons, viz: (A) Colonel William Monroe (169?-1760) mentioned on page 81 as the father of Thomas Monroe (17 - 1777) who married Catherine Hore; (B) Andrew Monroe, Sheriff of Westmoreland County, who predeceased his father in 1735 and was the grandfather of President James Monroe (1758-1831); (C) George Monroe who died testate in Westmoreland County, 1776; and (D) Thomas Monroe who died testate in King George County, 1746, leaving five children, viz: (i) William; (ii) John; (iii) Andrew; (iv) Sarah and (v) Mary Monroe. Of these, (ii) John Monroe (circa 1736 - 1785) married Sarah Harrison (circa 1740 - 1825) and settled in Fairfax County where she had inherited land from her father, Captain William Harrison [see page 50]. They had issue: (a) William born circa 1758; (b) Spence, born 1760 [see Revolutionary Pension #S-8900], of Loudoun County, 1832; (c) Harrison born circa 1763; (d) Andrew (1765-1829) married Mary Dailey (1763-1847) and lived in Loudoun County; (e) Isabella; (f) Sarah Monroe, sole legatee named in her mother's will; and (g) George Monroe. There may have been other children. There is considerable record of John Monroe and his family in the records of Fairfax and Loudoun counties.

B.   MONTGOMERY, Elizabeth daughter of John and Mary Montgomery,   April 20, 1752.

B.   MONTGOMERY, John son of John and Mary Montgomery,   January 26, 1754.

MOORE : MORE

B.   MORE , Elizabeth daughter of Jonathan and Elizabeth More,   December 20,1740.

M.   MORE , Nathaniel and Else Nichols,   December 31, 1743.

B.   MOORE, John son of Nathaniel Moore,   August 1, 1744.

D.   MORE , Mary November 10, 1744; she was an orphan and died at John Waters'.

M.   MOORE, Nathaniel and Sarah Page,   September 11, 1745.

B.   MORE , Sarah daughter of Nathaniel and Sarah More,   November 6, 1745.

M.   MOORE, Jane and Bryan Macmahon,   December 30, 1747.

B.   MORE , Mary daughter of Nathaniel and Sarah More,   January 31, 1748.

D.   MORE , Sarah March 5, 1750 at William George's plantation.

B.   MORE , Sarah daughter of Nathaniel and Sarah More,   April 26, 1750.

M.   MORE , William and Mary Green,   November 28, 1751.

B.   MOORE, John son of Nathaniel and Sarah Moore,   September 20, 1752.

B.   MOORE, Isaac son of William and Mary Moore,   March 25, 1753.

B.   MORE , Ann daughter of Nathaniel and Sarah More,   June 8, 1754.

B.   MORE , William son of William and Mary More,   December 30, 1754.

B.   MORE , Jane daughter of Nathaniel More,   June 17, 1756.

B.   MOORE, Eliza daughter of William Moore,   December 23, 1756.

D.   MORING, James September 23, 1748 at Captain William Mountjoy's.

B.   MORRIS, [blank] daughter of Anne Morris,   November 14, 1740.

B.   MORRIS, Margaret daughter of Griffin and Elizabeth Morris, February 10, 1741.

M.   MORISS, Mary and Andrew Watson,   September 26, 1742.

B.   MORRIS, John son of Griffin and Elizabeth Morris,   January 22, 1743.

B.   MORRIS, William son of Griffin and Elizabeth Morris,   June 20, 1745.

M. MORRIS, Mary and John Smith, December 29, 1745.

D. MORRIS, James August 28, 1749 at John Smith's.

B. MORRIS, Young Griffin son of Griffin Morris, March 28, 1751.

B. MORRIS, Anthony son of Griffin and Elizabeth Morris, January 28, 1755.

M. MORTON, George and Margaret Strother, April 6, 1744.

B. MOSS, Presly son of Sylvester and Elizabeth Moss, May 24, 1746.

B. MOSS, Meredith son of Silvester and Elizabeth Moss, January 10, 1750.

B. MOSS, Triplett son of Silvester and Elizabeth Moss, August 9, 1752.

B. MOUNTJOY, Edward son of William and Phillis Mountjoy, January 1, 1736.

B. MOUNTJOY, William son of William and Phillis Mountjoy, September 28, 1737.

B. MOUNTJOY, Thomas son of William and Phillis Mountjoy, October 4, 1739.

B. MOUNTJOY, Jonathan son of Thomas and Elizabeth Mountjoy, February 28, 1741.

B. MOUNTJOY, John son of William and Phillis Mountjoy, October 25, 1741.

B. MOUNTJOY, Mary daughter of William and Phillis Mountjoy, November 6, 1743.

B. MOUNTJOY, Alvin son of William and Phillis Mountjoy, January 28, 1746.

B. MOUNTJOY, George son of William and Phillis Mountjoy, September 9, 1748.

B. MOUNTJOY, Elizabeth daughter of William and Phillis Mountjoy, May 2, 1751.

B. MOUNTJOY, Margaret daughter of William and Phillis Mountjoy, August 25, 1753.

D. MOUNTJOY, Margaret daughter of Captain William Mountjoy, March 1, 1755.

D. MOUNTJOY, George son of William and Phillis Mountjoy, June 1, 1756.

B. MOUNTJOY, George son of William and Phillis Mountjoy, September 1, 1757.

---

1 - For a detailed account of the family of Captain William Mountjoy (1711-
    1777) and Phillis Reilly, his wife, see Tyler's Quarterly Historical and
    Genealogical Magazine, Volume 26, pages 99-104. Also Dr. Daniel Morton's
    typescript, The Mortons and Their Kin, Volume 1, pages 181-182 (1920)
    [CS.71 M.89, Library of Congress], cites the Bible record of Captain Will-
    iam Mountjoy. His daughter, Elizabeth Mountjoy, married in Overwharton
    Parish on December 20, 1769 James Garrard (1747-1822); they moved to Ken-
    tucky in 1783 and he was twice governor of that state.

D. MOUSLEY, James   June 8, 1740 at Major Peter Hedgman's.

D. MOUSLEY, James   August 12, 1744,"a servant of Charles Hinson."

D. MOUSLEY, Anne   November 3, 1745 at William Mason's.

M. MUFFET, Gabriel and Mary Helms,   July 25, 1739.

M. MULLAKEN, Mary and Joseph Williams,   February 9, 1741.

M. MURDOCK, John and Margaret Strother,   October 26, 1750.

MURPHEY : MURPHY

B. MURPHY , John son of Gabriel and Mary Murphy,   September 6, 1740.

D. MURPHY , Mary   October 1, 1741 at Ed: Malpus'.

B. MURPHEY, Matthew son of John and Elizabeth Murphey,   August 17, 1742.

B. MURPHY , Peter a bastard child at William Mills', September 15, 1748.

D. MURPHY , Peter the son of Honour Carty,   December 1, 1748. [See Page 19]

M. MURPHY , Peter and Elizabeth Mauzy,   February 9, 1752. [1]

C. MURPHY , Eleanor daughter of Peter and Elizabeth Murphy,   October 29, 1752.

B. MURPHY , Ann daughter of Peter and Elizabeth Murphy,   February 27, 1755.

M. MURPHY , Isaac and Catherine Ashby,   January 1, 1756.

B. MURPHY , Lydia daughter of Isaac and Catherine Murphy,   November 15, 1756.

B. MURPHY , William   January 7, 1758.

B. MURRAY, John son of John and Mary Murray,   March 1, 1729.

B.. MURRAY, Sarah daughter of Anthony Murray,   February 24, 1739. [2]

---

1 - In July 1772 the Stafford County court directed Thomas Ludwell Lee, Esq.,
    to divide the Negroes of which Peter Murphy, deceased, died seized among
    his children, viz: (1) William Murphy, eldest son and heir at law to whom
    Peter Hansbrough acted as guardian; (2) Mary the wife of Bryan Chadwell;
    (3) John Murphy and (4) Ann Murphy, both of whom were under twenty-one
    years of age.

2 - On January 25, 1734 in Spotsylvania County, Anthony Murray obtained a mar-
    riage license to wed Mary James, daughter of John James who died testate
    in 1726. [Crozier: Virginia County Records, Spotsylvania County, Volume I,
    pages 1 and 84. (1905)]

D. MURRAY, James son of Anthony and Mary Murray, September 26, 1740.

D. MURRAY, Anthony son of Anthony and Mary Murray, October 4, 1740.

D. MURRAY, Sarah daughter of Anthony and Mary Murray, November 17, 1740.

B. MURRAY, John son of Anthony Murray, October 9, 1741.

B. MURRAY, Nancy daughter of Anthony Murray, October 8, 1743.

B. MURRAY, Lettice daughter of Anthony and Mary Murray, December 23, 1745.

B. MURRAY, Phoebe daughter of Anthony Murray, April 1, 1748.

D. MURRAY, Anthony October 5, 1750.

M. MURRAY, Margaret and John Ogilvy, October 7, 1750.

N

B. NELSON, Violetta daughter of Alexander and Margaret Nelson, January 10, 1740.

B. NELSON, Lettice daughter of Henry and Sarah Nelson, March 10, 1740.

D. NELSON, Lettice daughter of Alexander Nelson, September 25, 1740.

B. NELSON, Hannah daughter of John and Mary Nelson, October 19, 1740.

M. NELSON, John and Mary Toby, February 10, 1741.

M. NELSON, Henry and Jean Gwodkin, October 18, 1742.

B. NELSON, William son of Henry and Jean Nelson, August 14, 1743.

B. NELSON, Susannah daughter of Henry and Sarah Nelson, October 25, 1743.

M. NELSON, Alexander and Margaret Butler, February 21, 1745.

B. NELSON, Henry son of Henry and Jean Nelson, August 2, 1745.

D. NELSON, Alexander October 19, 1745.

M. NELSON, John and Sarah Whitson, December 7, 1745.

B. NELSON, William son of Alexander Nelson, February 2, 1746.

B. NELSON, Lydia daughter of John and Sarah Nelson, September 24, 1746.

B. NELSON, Frances daughter of Henry and Sarah Nelson, January 15, 1747.

B. NELSON, Jemima daughter of Henry and Jane Nelson,   January 28, 1747.

B. NELSON, John   July 18, 1747.

B. NELSON, Elizabeth   October 9, 1747.

M. NELSON, Mary and John Mason,   November 27, 1747.

M. NELSON, Margaret and John Pownall,   September 4, 1748.

D. NELSON, John   October 14, 1748 at John Pownall's.

B. NELSON, Nanny daughter of John and Sarah Nelson,   January 11, 1749.

B. NELSON, Alexander son of Alexander and Mary Nelson,   March 30, 1749.

D. NELSON, Henry   December 29, 1749.

B. NELSON, John son of Alexander Nelson,   March 5, 1751.

B. NELSON, Mary daughter of John and Sarah Nelson,   March 24, 1751.

B. NELSON, John son of Henry and Jane Nelson,   May 21, 1751.

M. NELSON, Elizabeth and Daniel Mason,   January 30, 1753.

B. NELSON, Margaret daughter of John and Sarah Nelson,   August 18, 1753.

B. NELSON, Margaret daughter of Alexander and Margaret Nelson,   January 10, 1754.

B. NELSON, Jesse son of John and Sarah Nelson,   January 22, 1756.

B. NELSON, George son of Alexander and Margaret Nelson,   December 4, 1756.

B. NELSON, Jean   January 24, 1758.

B. NELSON, Susanna daughter of John Nelson, March [mutilated], 1758.

D. NELSON, Alexander   June 20, 1758.

NEWBOLD : NUBAL

B. NUBAL, Priscilla daughter of Samuel and Hannah Nubal,   June 21, 1743.

B. NEWBOLD, William son of Samuel and Joannah Newhold,   December 12, 1745.

D. NEWBOLD, Joannah   January 16, 1746.

M. NUBAL, Sarah and Thomas Foxworthy,   December 25, 1751.

D. NEWBOLD, Ann   December 30, 1753 at Mr. Peter Daniel's.

M. NICHOLS, Else and Nathaniel More, December 31, 1743.

B. NICHOLSON, John son of John Nicholson, November 7, 1752.

B. NICKSON, Sarah Ann daughter of John and Rachel Nickson, January 30, 1752.

B. NICKSON, Patty daughter of John and Rachel Nickson, October 2, 1754.

M. NICOLSON, John and Mary Hyden, April 23, 1752.

M. NOBLE, Joshua and Hannah Blackman, September 7, 1746.

B. NOBLE, Joshua son of Joshua and Hannah Noble, August 17, 1756.

M. NOBLE, Jean and Derby Driscal, October 4, 1756.

NORMAN : NORMAND

B. NORMAND, James son of Thomas Normand, September 13, 1740.

B. NORMAND, William son of Thomas and Martha Normand, November 11, 1741.

B. NORMAN, George son of Thomas and Elizabeth Norman, June 25, 1743. [1]

B. NORMAN, Thomas son of Thomas and Elizabeth Norman, August 10, 1746.

B. NORMAN, Ann daughter of Thomas Norman, February 14, 1750.

B. NORMAN, Edward son of Thomas Norman, May 19, 1753.

M. NORTHCUTT, Elizabeth and Anthony Philips, December 26, 1743.

B. NORTHCUTT, Martha daughter of William and Margery Northcutt, August 10, 1744.

M. NORTHCUTT, Mary and Haswell Hardwick, December 25, 1750.

M. NORTHCUTT, Sarah and John Foxworthy, September 29, 1751.

---

1 - About a mile from Decaturs Store in upper Stafford County is a Norman
family cemetery. The oldest three tombstones are inscribed as follows:
"In Memory of Mrs. Elizabeth Norman who departed this life January ye 20
1771 in the 57th year of her age." "James Norman son of Thomas and Elizabeth Norman who departed this life October ye 11th A.D. 1777 in the 32[?37]
year of his age." "In Memory of Mr. Thomas Norman who departed this life
March 2nd A.D. 1780 in the 73rd year of his age."

At Valley View on upper Accakeek Creek near Ramoth Church is a lone
tombstone crudely inscribed: "Here Lyeth the Body of Mauell The Wife of
Henry Norman Who Departed this Life March 15th in the Year of our Lord
1710."

M. NORTON, Elizabeth and Charles Colston, February 1, 1739.

M. NOWLAND, Richard and Jane Wright, December 26, 1747.

M. NOWLAND, Jean and John Brown, August 24, 1755.

M. NOXAL, [?]isfield and Ann Bruing, August 1, 1757.

NUBAL   SEE : NEWBOLD : NUBAL PAGE 87

B. NUNN, Thomas son of John Nunn, January 1, 1751.

                              O

M. O'CANION, Anne and Alexander Farrow, October 5, 1753.

    O'CAEN : O'CAIN : O'CANE : OCAEN : OCAIN   : OCANE

B. O'CANE, John son of Derby and Susanna O'Cane, March 20, 1739.

M. OCAIN, Derby and Susannah Smith, December 16, 1739.

C. O'CANE, Thomas son of Derby O'Cane, May 4, 1740.

B. O'CANE, George son of Derby and Susanna O'Cane, July 14, 1742.

B. O'CAEN, Mary daughter of Derby and Susannah O'Caen, May 9, 1745.

B. OCAIN, James son of Derby and Susannah Ocain, October 4, 1747.

B. O'CAIN, Daniel son of Derby and Susannah O'Cain, April 1, 1750.

B. OCAIN, Derby son of Derby O'Cain, March 4, 1753.

B. OCAIN, Henry son of Derby and Susannah Ocain, August 4, 1755.

    O'DUNEAL : ODUNEAL : O'NEAL : ONEAL   SEE : DUNEAL PAGE 27

M. O'NEAL, Timothy and Elizabeth Mathews, April 22, 1739. [1]

B. O'DUNEAL, John son of Timothy and Elizabeth O'Duneal, October 27, 1740.

B. O'DUNEAL, Priscilla daughter of Timothy and Elizabeth O'Duneal, September 13, 1743.

---

1 - The Reverend Mr. Moncure is inconsistent in spelling some surnames. On
    April 9, 1745 Elizabeth O'Neal produced her account as administratrix of
    Timothy O'Neal, deceased, in Stafford County court. [Will Book "M", 425]

M. O'DUNEAL, Elizabeth and William Thornberry, July 10, 1746.

D. ONEAL, Elizabeth September 3, 1748.

M. ODUNEAL, James and Theodosia Conyers, October 19, 1755.

B. OGILVY, Ann daughter of John Ogilvy, April 27, 1750.

M. OGILVY, John and Margaret Murray, October 7, 1750.

B. OGILVY, Winifred daughter of John Ogilvy, July 18, 1751.

B. OGILVY, Margaret daughter of John and Margaret Ogilvy, April 5, 1754.

B. OGILVY, [mutilated] son of John and Margaret Ogilvy, July 2, 1757.

M. OLIFORD, Elizabeth and William Cooper, January 5, 1758.

B. OLIVER, Keziah daughter of John and Mary Oliver, April 5, 1754.

O'NEAL : ONEAL   SEE : O'DUNEAL &c: PAGE 89 : DUNEAL PAGE 27

M. ONSBY, Elizabeth and Carty Wells, September 10, 1738.

M. ORAM, Rachel and John Hart, March 23, 1746.

B. OSBORN, Judith daughter of William Osborn, February 2, 1751.

D. OWENDOWNNEY, John January 22, 1754 at Priscilla Hay's.

M. OWENS, Joshua and Lettice Grigsby, November 19, 1747.

B. OXFORD, Samuel son of Samuel and Mary Oxford, January 4, 1742.

P

M. PAGE, Sarah and Nathaniel Moore, September 11, 1745.[1]

PANE   SEE :   PAYNE : PANE PAGE 91

D. PANNEL, Mary October 25, 1749 at William Patton's.

---

1 - William Page, planter, died testate in Stafford County in 1716 leaving
    issue several daughters. He bequeathed 100 acres of land to his daught-
    er Grace wife of Joshua Butler during her natural life and then to his
    daughter Sarah Page. In 1743 Sarah Page broke the entail and sold the
    said 100 acres to Richard Young who in turn sold it in 1749 to Robert
    Dowling who sold it in 1766 to Ralph Hughes. In 1781 Ralph Hughes sold
    this land to John Jones of Stafford County and this deed recites the title.
    [Stafford County Book "S", page 56.]

PARENDER   SEE :   PERENDER :   PARENDER   PAGE 92

M. PARKER, Martha and Peter Bailen,   August 6, 1738.

B. PARSONS, Sarah daughter of William and Anne Parsons,   May 26, 1745.

D. PARSONS, Ann   November 26, 1748.

PATTEN :   PATTIN :   PATTON

M. PATTIN, William and Joyce McInteer,   January 27, 1740.

B. PATTEN, Margaret daughter of William and Joyce Patten,   March 10, 1741.

B. PATTIN, Jean daughter of William and Joice Pattin,   December 23, 1742.

B. PATTEN, Anne daughter of William Patten,   December 23, 1747.

D. PATTEN, Anne daughter of William Patten,   January 11, 1748.

B. PATTON, Sarah daughter of William Patton,   November 24, 1749.

B. PATTEN, John and William sons of William and Joyce Patten,   December 28, 1755.

M. PATTEN, William and Isabella Kennedy,   December 19, 1756.

PATERSON :   PATTERSON :   PATTISON

B. PATTISON, [blank] son of Charles Pattison,   November 25, 1745.

B. PATTERSON, John   May 8, 1748.

M. PATTISON, Sarah alias Conyers and Thomas Hampton,   June 1, 1749.[1]

B. PATERSON, Behethelan daughter of Mary Paterson,   April 17, 1750.

M. PATTISON, Susannah and James Mings,   September 7, 1750.

B. PATTISON, Lydia Alvin daughter of Elizabeth Pattison,   May 4, 1751.

B. PATTISON, Ruth daughter of Mary Pattison,   September 19, 1755.

PAYNE :   PANE

B. PANE, Francis son of Francis Pane,   March 18, 1748.

D. PANE, Francis son of Francis Pane,   April 15, 1748.

---

1 - See footnote on page 22.

M. PAYNE, Edward and Anne Holland Conyers, February 27, 1750. [1]

PAYTON   SEE: PEYTON PAGE 92

D. PEARSON, Frances September 20, 1740 "a servant woman of John Barber's."

D. PEARSON, Hannah November 12, 1748.

M. PEDDICOART, Jannet and Moses Rowley, May 16, 1739.

B. PEIRSON, Nanny daughter of William and Sarah Peirson, January 18, 1754.

M. PELTER, John and Judith Lunsford, February 27, 1750.

B. PELTER, Jane Lunsford daughter of John and Judith Pelter, December 11, 1753.

M. PEPPER, Mary and James Suddeth, May 13, 1738.

PERENDER : PARENDER

M. PERENDER, Eleanor and Thomas Massey, June 26, 1745.

M. PARENDER, Elizabeth and William Adie, July 25, 1754.

B. PERRY, Mary daughter of Prudence Perry, July 21, 1741.

B. PETTIGREW, James son of John and Mary Pettigrew, April 2, 1737.

B. PETTIGREW, John son of John and Mary Pettigrew, December 28, 1739.

PEYTON : PAYTON [2]

M. PAYTON, Catherine and William Scogging, February 18, 1740.

M. PAYTON, Alander and James Heffernon, May 20, 1740.

B. PEYTON, Elizabeth daughter of John and Eleanor Peyton, June 5, 1741.

B. PAYTON, William son of John Payton, July 25, 1742.

B. PEYTON, Henry son of John and Eleanor Peyton, March 9, 1743.

---

1 - See The Paynes of Virginia by Colonel Brooke Payne [1937], pages 235-238.

2 - The Reverend Mr. Moncure is quite inconsistent in spelling Peyton and Payton and for this reason these entries are grouped, however, it must not be inferred they are one family. The Reverend Mr. Horace E. Hayden in his Virginia Genealogies [1891] gives an excellent account of the Peyton family of Stafford County and this will serve to separate them from the Paytons.

B. PAYTON, Rachel daughter of John and Ureth Payton, August 22, 1743.

B. PAYTON, Charles son of John and Ureth Payton, December 1, 1746.

M. PEYTON, Anne and Thomas Harrison, July 2, 1747.

D. PEYTON, Eleanor wife of John Peyton, October 5, 1747.

D. PEYTON, Elizabeth daughter of John Peyton, May 11, 1748.

M. PEYTON, Philip and Winifred Bussell, September 15, 1748.

B. PEYTON, Valentine son of Philip and Winifred Peyton, March 19, 1749.

B. PEYTON, Jeremiah son of John and Ureth Peyton, January 29, 1750.

B. PAYTON, Nancy daughter of John and Ureth Peyton, November 13, 1751.

M. PEYTON, John and Elizabeth Waller, November 17, 1751.

B. PEYTON, John Rowzee son of John and Elizabeth Peyton, October 19, 1754.[1]

D. PEYTON, Doctor Valentine November 28, 1754.

C. PEYTON, Valentine son of John Peyton, October 20, 1756.

M. PEYTON, John and Susannah Lunsford, March 28, 1758.

PHILIPS : PHILLIPS

M. PHILIPS, James and Eliz.[a] Griffin, September 27, 1741.

B. PHILIPS, Lettice daughter of James and Elizabeth Philips, November 22, 1741.

M. PHILIPS, Anthony and Elizabeth Northcutt, December 26, 1743.

B. PHILIPS, William son of James and Elizabeth Philips, born November 1, 1744.[2]

---

1 - John Rowzee Peyton (November 17, 1754 - February 5, 1799) succeeded his father at Stony Hill and died testate in Stafford County. He married Anne Hooe (March 16, 1754 - January 1, 1837), daughter of Howson Hooe, Junior, and Mary Dade, his wife, of Prince William County. J.R. Peyton is buried at Stony Hill and his wife in Trinity Episcopal Churchyard, Staunton, Va.

2 - Colonel William Phillips (November 1, 1744 - December 30, 1797) resided at Traveller's Rest in upper Stafford County; he died there testate. He married on June 7, 1774 Elizabeth Fowke, daughter of Colonel Gerard and Elizabeth (Dinwiddie) Fowke, and left a large family. For an account of her ancestry see The Virginia Genealogist, Volume 3, pages 51-64, and for their children see their Bible record in Archives Division, Virginia State Library, #21310.

B. PHILIPS, William son of John and Mary Philips, February 2, 1745.

B. PHILIPS, Dorcas daughter of Anthony and Elizabeth Philips, March 10, 1745.

D. PHILIPS, Mary daughter of Robert and Elizabeth Philips, October 16, 1745.

B. PHILIPS, Robert son of Anthony and Elizabeth Philips, August 11, 1747.

B. PHILLIPS, Mary daughter of James Phillips, January 15, 1748.

B. PHILLIPS, Dinah daughter of Anthony and Elizabeth Phillips, February 22, 1751.

D. PHILLIPS, Dinah February 20, 1752.

M. PHILLIPS, Lettice and John Cummings, February 21, 1757. "See Sept.1741"

M. PHIPS, Stephen and Rosamund Mayow, June 1, 1740.

B. PICKART, William Stafford a mulatto son of Sarah Pickart, October 22, 1757.

D. PIKE, Marjory February 27, 1744 at Michael Pike's.

M. PILCHER, Stephen and Lucy Clarke, December 7, 1748.

B. PILCHER, Samuel son of Stephen and Elizabeth Pilcher, January 5, 1750.

D. PILCHER, Elizabeth January 23, 1750.

B. PILCHER, James son of Stephen Pilcher, February 17, 1750.

M. PILCHER, Stephen and Bridget Maconchie, December [blank], 1750.

D. PILCHER, Mary January 22, 1754 at Alexander Macanteer's.

M. PLUMMER, Mary and Richard Matthis, October 5, 1745.

B. POMPEY, Mary daughter of Will: and Sue Pompey, October 12, 1748 at George Brent's.

B. POMPEY, William son of William Pompey and Sue a slave of George Brents, November 16, 1750.

PONTON : PONTONE : PUNTON[1]

M. PONTON, Edward and Mary Matheney, November 20, 1739.

---

1 - The name is rendered PONTIN on the court records. Edward Pontin by will bequeathed one third of his estate to his wife Mary and the balance of it to his friend James Carter. [Stafford County Will Book "M", page 316, proved March 9, 1742.]

D. PUNTON, Edward   January 25, 1742.

B. PONTONE, Isabel daughter of Mary Pontone,   February 9, 1745.

M. POOLE, Sarah and John Foley,   December 11, 1744.

D. PORCH, Robert   April 5, 1747.

M. PORCH, Thomas and Rachel Limbrick,   July 22, 1748.

M. PORCH, Rachel and William Burton,   October 7, 1753.

M. PORCH, Anne and William Berry,   February 26, 1754.

D. PORTER, Thomas   February 26, 1740.[1]

M. PORTER, Howsen and John Stark,   January 1, 1746.

M. PORTER, Calvert and Elizabeth Cash,   September 21, 1749.

B. PORTER, Joseph son of Calvert and Elizabeth Porter,   October 21, 1749.

B. PORTER, Calvert son of Calvert and Elizabeth Porter,   March 1, 1752.

B. PORTER, Thomas son of Calvert and Elizabeth Porter,   January 11, 1754.

D. PORTER, John   July 14, 1754.

B. PORTER, Frances daughter of Calvert and Elizabeth Porter,   January 12, 1756.

M. PORTER, Joseph and Jemima Smith,   February 26, 1756.

B. PORTER, Charity daughter of Calvert Porter,   September 9, 1757.

POWEL : POWELL

B. POWEL, John son of Charles and Elizabeth Powel,   September 20, 1731.

B. POWEL, Peter son of Charles and Elizabeth Powel,   February 17, 1733.

B. POWELL, Elizabeth daughter of Charles and Elizabeth Powell,   April 26, 1735.

---

1 - Charles Calvert, Gentleman, (circa 1664-1733) moved from Maryland to Stafford County and married Mary Howson, daughter of Robert Howson who possessed a handsome landed estate in the Northern Neck of Virginia. They had two daughters, viz: (1) Anne wife of Thomas Porter (16 -1740) and (2) Sarah Howson wife of Nathaniel Jones (1696-1754). See Ella Foy O'Gorman Descendants of Virginia Calverts [1947], pages 64-65, 68-73.

B. POWELL, Martha daughter of Charles and Elizabeth Powell, September 26, 1736.

B. POWEL, Charles son of Charles and Elizabeth Powell, May 26, 1740.

B. POWEL, Peggy daughter of Charles and Betty Powell, April 8, 1744.

D. POWELL, Charles April 30, 1744.

M. POWELL, Elizabeth and Duke Whalbone, December 3, 1745.

B. POWEL, Richard son of Mary Powel, February 14, 1746.

B. POWELL, Renn son of Mary Powell, February 2, 1748.

D. POWELL, Mary November 21, 1750 at William Kendall's.

M. POWEL, John and Margaret Macdaniel, February 10, 1752.

B. POWEL, Jemima daughter of John and Margaret Powel, November 9, 1753.

B. POWELL, Patty daughter of John and Margaret Powell, November 11, 1755.

M. POWELL, Martha and John Goldsmith, January 19, 1756.

D. POWNALL, Elizabeth March 3, 1745.

M. POWNALL, John and Margaret Nelson, September 4, 1748.

B. POWNALL, Margaret daughter of John Pownall, November 10, 1748.

M. PRICE, William and Sarah Allenthorp, August 5, 1748.

M. PRIM, John and Margaret Welch, September 9, 1739.

C. PRIM, William son of John and Margaret Prim, July 28, 1740.

B. PRIM, Ann daughter of John and Margaret Prim, September 15, 1746.

B. PRIM, John son of John and Margaret Prim, May 17, 1750. [1]

B. PRIM, Thomas son of John and Margaret Prim, December 13, 1751.

B. PRIM, James son of John and Margaret Prim, February 9, 1754.

---

1 - John Prim(m) served as a captain in the Revolutionary War. He married
    in 1777 Elizabeth Hansbrough, born January 5, 1761, daughter of Peter
    Hansbrough (17 -1781) and Lydia Smith, his second wife. They had
    seventeen children. The Bible record of Captain John Primm is in Mrs.
    Jeannette T. Acklen's Tennessee Records, Volume 2, page 170 [1933].

D.   PRIM, [mutilated] November 9, 1755.

PRITCHET : PRITCHETT

D.   PRITCHET, Elizabeth wife of Philip Pritchet, January 29, 1739.

M.   PRITCHET, William and Jane Cook, January 26, 1742.

M.   PRITCHET, Philip and Catherine Cole, June 24, 1742.

B.   PRITCHET, Anne daughter of Philip and Catherine Pritchet, September 4, 1742.

B.   PRITCHET, Catherine daughter of Philip Pritchet, December 28, 1743.

M.   PRITCHET, Lewis and Mary Lattimore, March 31, 1744.

D.   PRITCHETT, Philip Senior, November 14, 1744.

B.   PRITCHETT, Lewis son of Lewis and Mary Pritchett, February 17, 1748.

M.   PROCTOR, Edward and Amy Weeks, February 15, 1747.

M.   PULLY, Robert and Mary Thomson, August 25, 1748.

M.   PUMPHREY, Elizabeth and Morthough Macaboy, December 27, 1747.

B.   PUNELL, Emmanuel son of Richard and Mary Punell, July 20, 1748.

PUNTON   SEE : PONTON : PONTONE : PUNTONE PAGES 94-95

M.   PYKE, Ann and Henry Hurst, March 20, 1750.

Q

D.   QUIDLEY, Stephen son of William Quidley, February 8, 1745.

R

RABLING : RABBLING

M.   RABLING, John and Elizabeth Robinson, December 29, 1748.

D.   RABBLING, John February 4, 1749 at William King's.

M.   RADCLIFFE, Eleanor and Thomas Turnum, September 13, 1746.

RAILEY : RAILLY : RAYLE : REILIEGH : REILY : RELIEGH : RYLEY

B. RYLEY, Thomas son of John and Elizabeth Ryley, July 12, 1745.

B. RAYLE, Hugh son of John Rayle, February 24, 1747.

B. RYLEY, John son of John and Elizabeth Ryley, March 11, 1749.

D. REILIEGH, Ann September 24, 1749.

B. RYLEY, Charles son of John and Elizabeth Ryley, October 11, 1750.

M. RAILLY, Thomas and Ann Waller, July 10, 1751.

B. RAILEY, Nanny daughter of Nicholas Railey, April 17, 1752.

B. RYLEY, George son of John and Elizabeth Ryley, February 28, 1753.

D. RYLEY, George son of John and Elizabeth Ryley, October 5, 1753.

B. RELIEGH, Henry son of Nicholas and Winifred Reliegh, November 21, 1753.

B. REILIEGH, Edmund son of John and Elizabeth Reiliegh, September 23, 1754.

B. RYLEY, James son of Nicholas and Winifred Ryley, January 21, 1756.

B. REILY, Mary daughter of John and Elizabeth Reily, March 20, 1757.

B. RYLEY, Betty daughter of Nicholas and Winifred Ryley, April 2, 1757.

D. RALLS, Caleb son of John Ralls, June 21, 1741.

M. RALLS, John and Margaret Williams, January 2, 1746.[1]

B. RALLS, John son of John and Margaret Ralls, March 2, 1748.

---

1 - Captain John Ralls, Junior, (17 -1763) died testate in Stafford County
before his father. He married Margaret Williams, daughter of George
Williams, founder, who died testate in Stafford County in 1750, and Jane
[Jean] Pope, his wife, daughter of Nathaniel Pope [III] (1669-1719) of
Westmoreland County and Jane Browne (16 -1752), his wife, who was one of
the three daughters of Captain Originall Browne (1648-1698) of Westmoreland County. Jane (Browne) Pope and her father, Captain Originall Browne,
both died testate in Westmoreland County. On September 26, 1748 Worden
Pope of Westmoreland County made a deed of gift to his "cuzin" [niece]
Margaret Ralls, daughter of George Williams, Founder, of Stafford County,
and Jean, his wife, of a Negro boy Ben; and on the same date Jane Pope,
widow, of Westmoreland County made a deed of gift to her grandson Nathaniel Williams, son of George Williams, Founder, of Stafford County, "by my
daughter Jane, his wife," for several Negroes.

M. RALLS, Edward and Sarah Crosby, November 24, 1748.[1]

M. RALLS, Mary Ann and Samuel Hawes, February 16, 1749.[2] [1748/9]

B. RALLS, Lydia Beck daughter of John and Margaret Ralls, October 21, 1749.

B. RALLS, Caleb son of Edward and Sarah Ralls, April 14, 1750.

D. RALLS, Sarah wife of Edward Ralls, July 24, 1751.[1]

B. RALLS, George son of John Ralls, Junior, and Margaret, his wife, October 9, 1751.

B. RALLS, Molly daughter of Henry and Isabel Ralls, December 13, 1751.

C. RALLS, Hephzeha son of John Ralls, the younger, July 1, 1753.

B. RALLS, William son of Henry and Isabel Ralls, December 14, 1754.

C. RALLS, Nathaniel Williams son of John Ralls, Junior, January 26, 1755.

D. RALLS, Hepzibah son of John Ralls, Junior, December 17, 1756.

B. RALLS, Charles son of John and Margaret Ralls, February 13, 1758.

M. RANDAL, Catherine and George Bussel, January 8, 1754.

B. RANKINS, Ann daughter of George and Sarah Rankins, January 14, 1753.

B. RANSDELL, Elizabeth daughter of Wharton and Margaret Ransdell, April 6, 1746.

B. RANSDELL, Edward son of Wharton Ransdell, June 10, 1748.

B. RANSDELL, Wharton son of Wharton and Margaret Ransdell, January 28, 1750.

---

1 - About three miles north of Stafford Court House in a body of woods is a lone tombstone quaintly inscribed: " 1751 / July 24, departed this / life, Sarah the wife of / Edward Ralls."

2 - Near Woodford in Caroline County in the Hawes family cemetery is the tombstone of Mary Ann (Ralls) Hawes: "Here Lieth the Body of Mary Ann / the daughter of John and Lidia Ralls. / She was born June 10th 1733 / was married to Samuel Hawes / February 16th 1748 and departed / this life July 29th 1750." Captain Samuel Hawes (1727-1794) was a member of the Committee of Safety during the Revolutionary War and long prominent in the affairs of Caroline County. He married secondly on June 20, 1751, Ann Walker who was born August 23, 1731, the daughter of Benjamin Walker, Gentleman, (circa 1698 - 1738) and his wife nee Anne Aylett. [See The Virginia Magazine of History and Biography, Volume 64, page 361 and references there cited]

RAPER : RAPPER

B.   RAPER, Frances daughter of Thomas and Elizabeth Raper, September 30, 1743.

D.   RAPPER, Elizabeth daughter of Frances Rapper, October 12, 1744.

B.   RAPER, John son of Elizabeth Raper, June 26, 1747.

M.   RAPER, Elizabeth and Alexander Sutor, May 8, 1757.

M.   RASSAN [RASSAU], William and Priscilla Mauzey, October 27, 1743.[1]

B.   READ, Joseph son of Robert and Dorothy Read, October 27, 1746.

M.   READ, Robert and Dorothy Connally, November 10, 1747.

B.   READ, Mary daughter of Robert and Dorothy Read, January 5, 1748.

M.   READ, John and Ann Sebastian, July 21, 1748.

M.   READ, John and Margaret Allenthorp, March 5, 1754.

M.   REAVES, George and Anne Webster, April 3, 1743.

B.   REDDISH, Jean daughter of Robert Reddish, January 8, 1741.

B.   REDMAN, Ann daughter of Patrick Redman, December 7, 1749.

B.   REDMAN, Sarah daughter of Patrick Redman, April 16, 1752.

B.   REDMAN, John son of Patrick and Elizabeth Redman, July 18, 1754.

M.   REEDS, Elizabeth and William Spilman, February 25, 1751.

REILIEGH : REILY : RELIEGH   SEE : RAILEY &c. PAGE 98

M.   REMY, John and Mary Linton, April 6, 1740.

B.   REMY, Jeremiah son of John and Mary Remy, November 10, 1740.

B.   REMY, Jacob son of William and Barbara Remy, August 27, 1741.

B.   REMY, Presly son of John and Mary Remy, December 28, 1742.

B.   REMY, Tabitha daughter of John and Mary Remy, March 8, 1745.

B.   REMY, Caleb son of John and Mary Remy, May 20, 1747.

---

1 - The groom's name is incorrectly spelt. William Rosseau died testate in
     Fauquier County, Virginia, in 1798. The name is also spelt Roussau on
     the Fauquier County court records. For a brief sketch of the family see
     The Paynes of Virginia by Colonel Brooke Payne, pages 259-260 [1937].

B.   REMY, Lydia daughter of John and Mary Remy,   July 30, 1749.

B.   REMY, Butler son of John and Mary Remy,   April 18, 1751.

B.   REMY, John son of John and Mary Remy,   November 18, 1753.

B.   REMY, Sennot son of John and Mary Remy,   February 25, 1757.

     RENNY   SEE : KENNY : KANNEY   PAGE 64

M.   RENNY, John and Elizabeth Hunter,   October 12, 1746.

M.   REYNOLDS, Peter and Esther Carr,   June 2, 1745.

M.   REYNOLDS, James and Margaret Deckon,   August 19, 1746.

M.   RHODES, Mary and Isaac Basnit,   May 18, 1745.

B.   RHODES, Sanford son of John and Martha Rhodes,   December 13, 1746.

D.   RHODES, Martha wife of John Rhodes,   April 7, 1748.

D.   RHODES, John   November 12, 1748.

M.   RHODES, Anne and Robert Fristoe,   February 23, 1752.

B.   RICE, Lydia daughter of John and Anne Rice,   November 9, 1744.

D.   RICE, John   September 2, 1749.

M.   RICHARDS, John and Mary Latham,   June 24, 1740.

B.   RICHARDS, Francis son of John and Mary Richards,   May 25, 1741.

D.   RICHARDS, Francis son of John Richards,   November 8, 1744.

M.   RICHARDS, John and Susannah Thomson Heath,   March 6, 1755.

C.   RICHARDS, Elizabeth daughter of John and Susannah Thomson Richards, January 26, 1756.

B.   RICKETTS, Sarah Ann daughter of Thomas and Sarah Ricketts,   September 21, 1747.

C.   RICKETTS, Sarah Ann daughter of Thomas and Sarah Ricketts, January 26, 1755.

B.   RIDING, Thomas son of James and Mary Riding,   April 27, 1754.

B.   RIGG, Lewis son of John and Betty Rigg,   March 17, 1757.

M.   RIGGINS, Bridget and John Flitter,   March 16, 1755.

M. RISEN, John and Hannah Chinn, October 20, 1750.

M. ROACH, Patrick and Elizabeth Wise, October 9, 1742.

M. ROACH, Thomas and Anne Cooke, December 28, 1755.

M. ROBE, Isabel and Thomas Weddell, January 3, 1748.

M. ROBERTSON, John and Rose Jones, October 15, 1747.

ROBINSON : ROBISON

M. ROBISON, Philip and Margaret Spoldin, November 26, 1738.

B. ROBINSON, John son of Benjamin and Catherine Robinson, December 22, 1740.

B. ROBINSON, Mary daughter of Christopher and Eleanor Robinson, January [blank], 1741.

M. ROBINSON, Sarah and John Kirke, June 23, 1741.

B. ROBISON, Nanny daughter of Benjamin and Catherine Robison, April 23, 1743.

M. ROBINSON, Anne and William Green, December 18, 1743.

B. ROBINSON, Christopher son of Christopher and Ellender Robinson, February 25, 1744.

D. ROBINSON, Catherine wife of Benjamin Robinson, June 19, 1744.

D. ROBINSON, Christopher Junior, December 5, 1745.

M. ROBINSON, Rebecca and William Godfrey, October 26, 1746.

B. ROBINSON, William son of Christopher and Eleanor Robinson, November 3, 1746.

B. ROBISON, Daniel the bastard son of Ann Grey, May 18, 1747.

D. ROBINSON, Mary wife of Henry Robinson, March 26, 1748.[1]

---

1 - Henry Robinson died testate in Stafford County in 1753. He married first Mary [surname unknown] who died March 26, 1748, and secondly on August 1, 1750 Winifred Bailis who survived him. By his first wife he had two sons mentioned in his will, viz: (1) Christopher Robinson who appears in The Register of Overwharton Parish, and (2) Benjamin Robinson (17 - 1785). The latter was twice married: first to Catherine [surname unknown] who died June 19, 1744 and secondly to Sarah Stacy on January 2, 1750. Benjamin Robinson died testate in Fauquier County, Virginia, in 1785; he left a large family.

D.   ROBINSON, Jane August 30, 1748.

M.   ROBINSON, Sarah and James Fernsly, November 3, 1748.

M.   ROBINSON, Joshan and John Sprayburry, November 9, 1748.

M.   ROBINSON, Elizabeth and John Rabling, December 29, 1748.

B.   ROBINSON, James son of Christopher and Ellender Robinson, April 16, 1749.

M.   ROBINSON, Benjamin and Sarah Stacy, January 2, 1750.

B.   ROBINSON, Nathaniel son of Benjamin and Sarah Robinson, April 20, 1750.

M.   ROBINSON, Henry and Winifred Bailis, August 1, 1750.

B.   ROBINSON, Caty daughter of Benjamin and Sarah Robinson, February 8, 1752.

B.   ROBINSON, George son of Benjamin and Sarah Robinson, February 7, 1754.

M.   ROBINSON, Benjamin Junior and Elizabeth Stacey, May 25, 1755.

M.   ROBINSON, Simon and Mary Jack, August 3, 1755.

B.   ROBINSON, Lishea daughter of Benjamin and Sarah Robinson, February 25, 1756.

B.   ROBINSON, [mutilated] son of Benjamin and Sarah Robinson, June 21, 1758.

B.   ROGERS, William son of Richard and Mary Rogers, October 13, 1741.

M.   ROSE, William and Sarah Grigsby, June 5, 1753.

M.   ROSE, William and Jane Grigsby, March 14, 1758.

B.   ROSS, Rebecca daughter of William and Margaret Ross, February 28, 1739.

B.   ROSS, John son of William and Margaret Ross, June 4, 1742.

D.   ROSS, John son of William and Margaret Ross, September 4, 1744.

B.   ROSS, William son of William and Margaret Ross, September 19, 1750.

D.   ROSS, William December 26, 1757.

     ROSSEAU   SEE :   RASSAN [RASSAU] PAGE 100

M.   ROSSER, Sarah and Hayward Todd, September 7, 1746.

M.   ROUND, David and Mary Turner, January 28, 1753.

ROUSSAU   SEE : RASSAN [ROSSAU]   PAGE 100

ROUT : ROUTT

B.   ROUT , Hannah daughter of Peter and Martha Rout,   January 31, 1740.[1]

B.   ROUTT, John son of Peter and Martha Routt,   December 17, 1742.

B.   ROUT , James son of Peter and Martha Rout,   July 29, 1745.

D.   ROUT , Betty daughter of Peter Rout,   June 27, 1749.

M.   ROUTT, William and Winifred Byram,   November 27, 1753.

B.   ROUT , Peter son of William and Winifred Rout,   October 22, 1754.

B.   ROUTT, William son of William and Winifred Routt,   May 29, 1756.

M.   ROWLEY, Moses and Jannet Peddicoart,   May 16, 1739.[2]

B.   ROWLEY, Moses a bastard son of a servant woman of Moses Rowley's,
     October 25, 1743.

C.   ROWLEY, Moses a bastard at Potomack Church,   September 16, 1744.

B.   ROWLLS, Jesse son of Henry and Isabell Rowlls,   January 28, 1757.

D.   RUNNILS, Frank   March 10, 1751.

M.   RUSH, Benjamin and Alice Grigsby,   April 1, 1744.[3]

---

1 - Peter Routt (17 -1765) came of a family long seated in Northumberland
    County; his wife Martha is mentioned as a daughter in the will of Mrs.
    Martha Booth which was proved at Northumberland County court in 1757.
    Peter Routt died testate in Stafford County. His daughter Hannah Routt
    (January 31, 1740 - October 9, 1774) married John Withers (December 15,
    1738 - June 12, 1818) and had seven children. She died in Stafford Coun-
    ty and John Withers married secondly Dilly Allen and moved to Jessamine
    County, Kentucky. The family Bible record of John Withers is preserved.

2 - Moses Rowley (1719 - 18) lived in Stafford and King George counties.
    He married Jannet successively the widow of Joseph Sumner, Junior, who
    died in 1734 and of John Peddicoart [Peddicoat, Peddycoat], who died in
    1736. There are a considerable number of Rowley records in Stafford and
    King George counties.

3 - Benjamin Rush (February 3, 1717 - May 23, 1801) is said to have been mar-
    ried three times; it appears Alice Grigsby was his second wife. He died
    testate in Chatham County, North Carolina. He was the son of Benjamin
    Rush of Westmoreland, King George, and Prince William counties, Virginia,
    whose will was proved at January Court, 1767 in Bute County, North Caro-
    linia.

M. RUSSELL, James and Martha Hill, February 24, 1754.

B. RUSSELL, Thomas son of James and Martha Russell, November 15, 1754.

B. RUSSELL, Anna daughter of James and Martha Russell, April 11, 1757.

D. RYAN, William son of Michael and Winifred Ryan, December 4, 1745.

B. RYAN, Daniel son of Michael and Winifred Ryan, September 2, 1747.

D. RYAN, Daniel son of Michael and Winifred Ryan, March 7, 1748.

B. RYAN, George son of Michael and Winifred Ryan, October 4, 1756.

D. RYAN, Michael October 10, 1757.

    RYLEY   SEE : RAILEY : RAILLY &c. PAGE 98

S

B. SANDERSON, William son of John and Jean Sanderson, June 7, 1747.

B. SANDERSON, John son of John and Jean Sanderson, August 2, 1749.

B. SANDERSON, Thomas son of John Sanderson, May 2, 1751.

B. SANDERSON, Sarah daughter of John Sanderson, February 21, 1753.

B. SAUNDERSON, Jenny daughter of John and Jean Saunderson, December 15, 1754.

M. SAVAGE, Eleanor and John Hogg, December 19, 1744.

M. SAYAS, Richard and Anne Castello, September 30, 1746.

B. SAYAS, William son of Richard Sayas, March 10, 1747.

M. SCOGGING, William and Catherine Payton, February 18, 1740.

B. SCOTT, Helen daughter of James and Sarah Scott, June 7, 1739.[1]

B. SCOTT, Alexander son of James and Sarah Scott, July 10, 1740.

B. SCOTT, Sarah daughter of the Reverend James Scott, January 22, 1741.

B. SCOTT, James son of the Reverend James and Sarah Scott, January 8, 1742.

---

1 - There is an excellent account of the family of the Reverend James Scott
    in Hayden's Virginia Genealogies, pages 585-668 [1891].

B.   SCOTT, Christian daughter of James and Sarah Scott,   March 4, 1745.

SCOULCRAFT : SCOOLCRAFT

M.   SCOULCRAFT, James and Margaret Mills,   October 14, 1753.

B.   SCOOLCRAFT, Mary daughter of James and Margaret Scoolcraft,   March 16, 1754.

M.   SEBASTIAN, Ann and John Read,   July 21, 1748.

M.   SEBASTIAN, William and Sarah Kelly,   June 11, 1751.

D.   SEKRE, William an orphan at George Arsbury's, September 21, 1746.

M.   SELDEN, Samuel and Mary Thomson Mason,   April 11, 1751.[1]

B.   SELDEN, Miles Carey son of Samuel and Mary Selden,   November 24, 1751.

B.   SELDEN, Samuel son of Samuel and Mary Thomson Selden,   March 23, 1753.

D.   SELDEN, Samuel son of Samuel Selden,   April 19, 1753.

B.   SELDEN, Mary Mason daughter of Samuel and Mary Thomson Selden,   October [blank], 1754.

B.   SELDEN, Samuel son of Samuel and Mary Thomson Selden,   April 30, 1756.

D.   SELDEN, Mary wife of Samuel Selden,   January 5, 1758.

B.   SELMAN, William son of Benjamin and Anne Selman,   November 19, 1753.

B.   SHADBORN, Frances Ann daughter of Jane Shadborn,   April 23, 1752.

M.   SHAMLIN, Martha and John Gunn,   September 30, 1753.

M.   SHAW, John and Mary Waters,   June 12, 1743.

D.   SHAW, Mary, a mulatto,   April 9, 1746.

---

1 - Colonel Samuel Selden (1725-1790) inherited from his ancestors, who were residents of Elizabeth City County, a valuable tract of land on Potomac Creek called Salvington. When a young man he seated the plantation and married first in 1751 Mary Thomson Mason (1731-1758), daughter of Colonel George Mason (1690-1735). His second wife was his first wife's first half-cousin, Sarah Ann Mason Mercer (June 21, 1738 - July 26, 1806), daughter of John Mercer, Esquire, (1704-1768) of Marlbrough and his first wife nee Catherine Mason (1707-1750). Colonel Samuel Selden died at Salvington and his last will and Testament was admitted to probate at Stafford Court. His widow died there and the estate passed to her son Wilson Cary Selden (1772 - 1822). The handsome mansion house was destroyed during the Civil War.

D. SHORT, Jean wife of John Short,   December 9, 1741.[1]

SHUMATE : SHOEMAKE

B. SHOEMAKE, Spencer son of William and Ann Shoemake, November 26, 1753.

B. SHUMATE, William son of William and Ann Shumate, August 11, 1756.

B. SHUMATE, Lettice daughter of William and Ann Shumate, November 5, 1757.

M. SILMAN, Ann and [mutilated], May 7, 1758.

SILVY : SYLVA : SYLVIE

M. SYLVA, John and Bridget Cooper, July 1, 1750.

B. SYLVIE, Nancy daughter of John Sylvie, October 22, 1750.

B. SILVY, Suky daughter of John and Bridget Silvy, February 20, 1754.

B. SILVY, Phebe daughter of John and Bridget Silvy, March 10, 1756.

B. SIMMONDS, Jemima daughter of George and Elizabeth Simmonds, March 17, 1743.

M. SIMMONS, Keziah and William Bruing, February 4, 1753.

SIMPSON : SIMSON[2]

D. SIMPSON, Mary January 15, 1739.

B. SIMPSON, Million daughter of William and Diana Simpson, May 5, 1740.

M. SIMPSON, John and Silent Johnston, August 17, 1740.

M. SIMPSON, Alexander and Catherine Fant, July 17, 1743.

M. SIMPSON, Elizabeth and John Whitcomb, November 24, 1743.

---

1 - There is a sketch of the Short family of Stafford and King George counties in Tyler's Quarterly Historical and Genealogical Magazine, Volume 32, pages 208 - 225.

2 - John Simson [Simpson], a Scotchman, settled on Aquia Creek. He received land grants there as well as on Great Hunting Creek. It appears he gave rise to a large family. His eldest son was John Simpson (1680-1756); he died testate in Stafford County. There is some account of this family in Tyler's Quarterly Historical and Genealogical Magazine, Volume 21, pages 54 - 61. Near Aquia Creek is an ancient tombstone: "Heare lyes ye body of Elizabeth / Simson the daughter of John / Simson. Departed this life / March ye 14, 1698. Borne July the 27, 1695."

B.   SIMPSON, Priscilla daughter of George and Margaret Simpson,   September 26, 1744.

B.   SIMSON, Elizabeth daughter of Alexander and Catherine Simson,   January 14, 1746.

C.   SIMPSON, Nancy October 12, 1746.

B.   SIMPSON, Mary daughter of Alexander Simpson,   December 10, 1747.

B.   SIMSON, Susannah daughter of George and Margaret Simson,   January 28, 1748. [She was Christened as Susannah Simpson on March 13, 1748].

B.   SIMPSON, Jane daughter of John and Elizabeth Simpson,   January 27, 1750.

B.   SIMPSON, Sarah daughter of Alexander Simpson,   December 13, 1750.

M.   SIMSON, Elizabeth and David Bradley,   April 17, 1755.

B.   SIMPSON, Franky daughter of Alexander and Catherine Simpson,   November 13, 1755.

M.   SIMPSON, William and Lettice Lunsford,   January 18, 1756.

B.   SIMPSON, Sarah daughter of William and Lettice Simpson,   June 25, 1758.

SIMS : SIMMS

M.   SIMS, Anne and William Metheny,   September 10, 1747.

M.   SIMMS, Richard and Betty Bridwell,   October 15, 1750.

B.   SIMS, James son of Richard Sims,   April 16, 1753.

M.   SINCLAIR, Sarah and Robert Cockley,   September 21, 1740.

B.   SINCLAIR, George son of George and Winifred Sinclair,   November 7, 1740.

M.   SINCLAIR, Margaret and Francis Tennel,   November 9, 1740.

D.   SINCLAIR, George son of George and Winifred Sinclair,   January 12, 1741.

B.   SINCLAIR, Winifred daughter of George and Winifred Sinclair,   October 5, 1742.

D.   SINCLAIR, Winifred wife of George Sinclair,   October 22, 1742.

D.   SINCLAIR, Clementina daughter of George Sinclair,   July 21, 1743.

M.   SINCLAIR, Patience and William Young,   July 22, 1744.

D.   SINCLAIR, George January 12, 1751 at Hannah Bailis.

M. SINCLAIR, Elizabeth and Charles Jones, April 21, 1751.

M. SKAINES, Mary and David Macquatty, May 6, 1755.

M. SLAUGHTER, Robert and Susannah Harrison, December 11, 1750.

M. SMITH, Elizabeth and Charles Cornish, December 17, 1738.

M. SMITH, Susannah and Derby O'Cain, December 16, 1739.

B. SMITH, Withers and George sons of Nathaniel and Elizabeth Smith, June 13, 1740. [1]

D. SMITH, William son of Henry and Sarah Smith, September 25, 1740. [2]

B. SMITH, Henry son of Henry and Sarah Smith, February 3, 1741.

M. SMITH, Mary and William Cammel, July 25, 1742.

B. SMITH, William son of Henry and Sarah Smith, October 28, 1742.

D. SMITH, Temple son of Nathaniel Smith, January 24, 1743.

M. SMITH, Susannah and John Cotton, February 17, 1743.

B. SMITH, Anne daughter of Robert and Phillis Smith, May 21, 1743.

M. SMITH, Mary and John Montgomery, January 16, 1744.

B. SMITH, Temple son of Nathaniel Smith, April 6, 1745.

B. SMITH, Susannah daughter of Robert and Phillis Smith, April 16, 1745.

B. SMITH, George son of Henry and Sarah Smith, October 19, 1745.

---

1 - Nathaniel Smith, planter, of Stafford County, made a deed of gift to his nine children on December 20, 1752 for various chattels. They are named in this instrument as follows: Clator, Nathaniel, Benjamin, Susannah (wife of John Cotton of Fairfax County), George, Withers, Temple, Sarah and Jemima Smith. Of these Withers [Weathers] Smith died in Bourbon County, Kentucky, leaving issue several children, and there are records of some of the others in the counties of northern Virginia and Kentucky.

2 - Henry Smith married Sarah Crosby, daughter of Daniel Crosby, and had issue: (1) Lydia married 1752 Peter Hansbrough; (2) Margaret married 1754 Joseph Jeffries; (3) Mary married 1758 James Hardage Lane; (4) William, died 1740; (5) Henry (1741-1801) [see page 59]; (6) William born 1742; (7) George born 1745, lived in Loudoun County; (8) General Daniel (1748-1818) who died in Sumner County, Tennessee; (9) Sarah, twin of Daniel, died shortly after birth; (10) Enoch (1750-1825) moved to Kentucky; (11) Sarah, born 1752, married Mr. Kerr; (12) Thomas born 1754; and (13) Joseph Smith, born 1756, married Ann Browne [see page 111] and lived in the area of his ancestors.

M. SMITH, John and Mary Morris, December 29, 1745.

B. SMITH, Martha daughter of Robert Smith, November 3, 1747.

B. SMITH, Christian daughter of John and Catherine Smith, December 22, 1747.

M. SMITH, John and Elizabeth Hornbuckle, December 31, 1747.

B. SMITH, Daniel son of Henry and Sarah Smith, October 17, 1748.

B. SMITH, Sarah daughter of Henry and Sarah Smith, October 19, 1748.

C. SMITH, Daniel and Sarah children of Henry Smith, October 24, 1748.

D. SMITH, Sarah daughter of Henry Smith, October 29, 1748.

D. SMITH, Thomas a servant of John Foley's, October 7, 1748.

M. SMITH, Catherine and Joshua Kendall, April 4, 1749.

M. SMITH, William and Betty Barbee, January 1, 1750.

B. SMITH, Seth daughter of Robert and Phillis Smith, January 10, 1750.

B. SMITH, Enoch son of Henry and Sarah Smith, June 21, 1750.

B. SMITH, Sarah daughter of Henry and Sarah Smith, January 21, 1752.

B. SMITH, Nathaniel son of Robert and Phillis Smith, March 19, 1752.

D. SMITH, Elizabeth wife of Nathaniel Smith, April 25, 1752.

M. SMITH, Lydia and Peter Hansbrough, May 27, 1752.

D. SMITH, Elizabeth daughter of Nathaniel Smith, July 20, 1752.

M. SMITH, Richard and Susanna Davis, November 17, 1752.

M. SMITH, Mary and Michael Dial, November 19, 1752.

D. SMITH, Ann wife of Thomas Smith, "aged 108 years," July 20, 1753.

D. SMITH, John September 23, 1753.

B. SMITH, Sarah daughter of Parker and Catherine Smith, February 28, 1754.

B. SMITH, Thomas son of Henry and Sarah Smith, October 4, 1754.

M. SMITH, Margaret and Joseph Jeffries, October 24, 1754.

D. SMITH, John December 4, 1754

B. SMITH, Susanna daughter of Richard and Elizabeth Smith, January 20, 1755.

M. SMITH, Rosamund and William Hammet, May 6, 1755.

C. SMITH,[mutilated] Bannister Smith and Susanna Bannister Smith, July 6, 1755.

B. SMITH, Ann daughter of John Smith, July 24, 1755.

M. SMITH, Thomas and Mary Ann Williams, February 21, 1756.

M. SMITH, Jemima and Joseph Porter, February 26, 1756.[1]

B. SMITH, Joseph son of Henry and Sarah Smith, June 6, 1756.[2]

M. SMITH, Phillis and John Green, December 19, 1756.

B. SMITH, William son of Thomas and Mary Ann Smith, January 24, 1757.

M. SMITH, John and Elizabeth Welit, December 7, 1757.

B. SMITH, Sarah daughter of John Smith, January 8, 1758.

M. SMITH, Mary and James Hardage Lane, January 12, 1758.

M. SPILMAN, William and Elizabeth Reeds, February 25, 1751.

---

1 - Jemima Smith married first in 1756 Joseph Porter (1727 - circa 1775);
    his will is in lost Stafford County Will Book "N" (1767-1783), page 301.
    He was the great-great-grandson of two distinguished colonial governors
    of Maryland, viz: the Honorable Leonard Calvert (circa 1610 - 1647) and
    the Honorable William Stone (circa 1603 - 1660). She married secondly
    Mr. Edrington, widower, and thirdly Hawkins Stone (1748 - 1810), widower,
    son of Barton Stone (17 - 1786) who moved from Charles County, Mary-
    land, to Stafford County about 1779, Hawkins Stone was also a great-great-
    grandson of Governor William Stone. Jemima had issue by her first marriage
    only and among was Sarah Porter (1769 - 1816) who married first William
    Barton Stone (1757 - 1793), son of Barton Stone and Sarah Speake, his wife,
    and secondly John Catesby Edrington, Senior, (1775 - 1820), son of the
    above mentioned Mr. Edrington and his first wife. Thus the first husband
    of Sarah Porter was the younger brother of her mother's third husband, and
    her second husband was the son of her mother's second husband, and to fur-
    ther complicate the genealogical siutation her son Captain John Catesby
    Edrington, Junior, (1800 - 1879) married Elizabeth Hawkins Stone (1810 -
    1891), daughter of the aforementioned Hawkins Stone (1748 - 1810) and his
    third wife Elizabeth Burroughs, daughter of Captain George Burroughs.

2 - Joseph Smith married Ann Browne, born August 2, 1765, daughter of Joseph
    Browne (1732 - 1806) who died testate in Stafford County. In 1785 Joseph
    Smith received a deed of gift from his aged father Henry Smith and his
    father-in-law Joseph Browne; both are of record at Stafford court.

B. SPILMAN, Thomas son of William and Elizabeth Spilman, November 29, 1751.

M. SPILMAN, Jeremiah and Bridget Edwards, January 16, 1755.

B. SPINKS, Enoch son of John and Rosamond Spinks, November 10, 1742.

SPOLDIN : SPOLDING

M. SPOLDIN, Margaret and Philip Robison, November 26, 1738.

B. SPOLDIN, Francis son of Thomas and Elizabeth Spoldin, January 7, 1744.

B. SPOLDING, Sarah daughter of Thomas and Elizabeth Spolding, March 4, 1750.

B. SPOLDIN, Elizabeth daughter of Thomas and Elizabeth Spoldin, May 2, 1752.

SPOORE : SPORE

B. SPORE, Sranooko a Negro male child to Anne Spore, June 29, 174_2_.

B. SPORE, Immoridda a Negro female child to Anne Spore, July 22, 174_2_.

D. SPOORE, Anne January 29, 1746.

SPRAYBURRY : SPRABURY : SPREDBERRY

M. SPRAYBURRY, John and Joshan Robinson, November 9, 1748.

B. SPRABURY, James son of John and Joshan Sprabury, June 14, 1749.[1]

B. SPREDBERRY, John son of John and Joshan Spredberry, January 18, 1755.

STACEY : STACY

M. STACEY, Simon and Judith Tolson, August 22, 1741.

B. STACEY, Sarah daughter of Simon and Judith Stacey, August 20, 1742.

B. STACY , Katherine daughter of Elizabeth Stacy, March 9, 1743.

B. STACEY, Benjamin son of Simon and Judith Stacey, April 7, 1744.

M. STACY , Catherine and William Hill, September 17, 1745.

B. STACY , Sith daughter of Simon Stacy, June 30, 1746.

---

1 - Henry Robinson, mentioned in footnote on page 102, by his last will and
    Testament of 1753 mentioned James Spreybra, son of John Spreybra. James
    Spreybra [Sprayburry] was probably a grandson of the testator. The evid-
    ence is strong that Henry Robinson had more children than the two sons
    mentioned in his last will and Testament which is of record at Stafford
    court.

B. STACY , Silvia daughter of John Stacy, Junior,   December 6, 1748.

B. STACY , Mary daughter of Simon and Judy Stacy,   February 19, 1749.

M. STACY , Sarah and Benjamin Robinson,   January 2, 1750.

B. STACEY, Peggy daughter of John and Elizabeth Stacey,   September 14, 1750.

D. STACEY, Dorothy wife of John Stacey, Senior,   February 5, 1751.

B. STACEY, Sinai daughter of Simon Stacey,   March 1, 1751.

M. STACEY, Elizabeth and William Howard,   May 29, 1751.

B. STACY , Suky daughter of John and Elizabeth Stacy,   July 10, 1754.

M. STACEY, Elizabeth and Benjamin Robinson, Junior,   May 25, 1755.

M. STACEY, Peter and Ruth Crosewel,   May 25, 1755.

B. STACEY, Shadrack son of John and Elizabeth Stacey,   August 20, 1756.

M. STACEY, Sarah and [mutilated]her Edwards,   May 6, 1757.

M. STANLY, Marjory and Edmond Webster,   November 20, 1741.

    STARK : STARKE

B. STARK, Sarah daughter of James and Elizabeth Stark,   August 23, 1731.

B. STARK, Jean daughter of James and Elizabeth Stark,   February 22, 1734.

B. STARK, Anne daughter of James and Elizabeth Stark,   February 9, 1736.

B. STARK, Benjamin son of James and Elizabeth Stark,   September 27, 1738.

B. STARK, Daniel son of James and Elizabeth Stark,   May 30, 1744.[1]

M. STARK, John and Howsen Porter,   January 1, 1746.

B. STARK, Isabella daughter of James and Elizabeth Stark,   June 25, 1746.

B. STARK, Mary daughter of James and Catherine Stark,   June 12, 1746.

B. STARK, Ann daughter of John and Howson Stark,   October 26, 1746.

M. STARK, Jeremiah and Tabitha Lowry,   January 29, 1747.

B. STARK, James son of James and Catherine Stark,   December 21, 1747.

B. STARK, Lydia daughter of James Stark,   June 30, 1748.

---

1 - On May 12, 1815 Daniel Stark, aged 71 years, wrote his last will and Testa-
    ment; it was proved on April 8, 1817 at Spotsylvania County, Va., court.

B. STARK, John son of Jeremiah and Tabitha Stark, November 6, 1748.

B. STARK, Elizabeth daughter of John and Howson Stark, August 16, 1749.

B. STARK, Sarah Ann daughter of James and Catherine Stark, November 25, 1749.

B. STARK, Sarah daughter of John and Howson Stark, January 29, 1752.

B. STARK, Jeremiah son of James Stark, June 11, 1752.

B. STARK, Mary daughter of Jeremiah and Tabitha Stark, May 19, 1753.

D. STARK, James April 12, 1754. [1]

---

1 - John Stark, a Scotchman, immigrated to America and settled in Londonderry, New Hampshire, in 1710. His second son, James Stark (1695-1754), married there Elizabeth Thornton and moved to Stafford County about 1720 with their children; the names of their six children born in Stafford County appear in The Register of Overwharton Parish. James Stark died testate in Stafford County in 1754; of his fourteen children I will mention his three sons who gave rise to large families in Stafford, Fauquier, Culpeper and Prince William counties and whose descendants are widely dispursed, viz: (1) John Stark (1717-1781) died testate in Stafford County. He married first in 1746 Howson Porter (circa 1730-1755), daughter of Thomas and Ann (Calvert) Porter, and their only son, Captain William Stark(e) (1754-1838) married Mary Kendall [see page 63]. John Stark married secondly in 1756 Hannah Eaves and from a Book of Psalms and Hymns we have the names of their children, viz: (i) James, born February 7, 1757; (ii) Thomas born May 6, 1759; (iii) John born December 15, 1761; (iv) Mary born December 6, 1762; (v) John born September 10, 1765; (vi) Susannah born April 16, 1768; (vii) Joseph born April 19, 1771. (2) James Stark, Junior, (1719-1761) married Catherine (surname unknown). In giving her consent on April 23, 1765 for the marriage of her daughter Sarah Ann Stark to Edmund Hoomes (17 -1805) of Fauquier County, Catherine Stark, widow, says of her husband: "he went to Carolinea and there has been ded fore years com the 6 of May." James and Catherine Stark had a large family. Of their sons, James (1747-1829) died testate in Fauquier County; Jeremiah (1749-1824) died testate in Abbeville County, South Carolina; Henry died intestate in Stafford County [see page 63]; and William died in Fauquier County in 1807. (3) Jeremiah Stark (1723-circa 1804) married Tabitha Lowry in 1747; he died testate in Stafford County and on July 23, 1805 John Stark (1747-1814), as executor of his deceased father, conveyed 130 acres of land on Aquia Run which he had purchased from William Shumate on May 11, 1762. John Stark (1747-1814) married on January 4, 1769 in King George County, Sarah English (1749-1820) and moved to Sumner County, Tennessee, where they both died. Their son John Stark married Margaret Prim, daughter of Captain John and Elizabeth (Hansbrough) Prim, also natives of Stafford County. For the Bible records of John Stark and his wife Sarah English see Mrs. Jeannette T. Acklen's Tennessee Records, Volume 2, pages 169 and 175. There are many records of the Stark(e) family in Stafford and adjoining counties and should not be confused with the Storke family.

B. STARKE, William son of John and Howson Starke,   December 14, 1754.

D. STARKE, Howson wife of John Starke,   April 11, 1755.

M. STARK, John and Hannah Eaves,   May 29, 1756.

B. STARK, James son of John and Hannah Stark,   February 7, 1757.

D. STEPHENS, Mary January 18, 1750 at the house of Edward Ralls.

M. STEWARD, James and Mary Gorman,   June 20, 1751.

B. STONE, Josias son of Josias and Mary Stone,   June 17, 1747.

B. STONE, Betty daughter of Josias and Mary Stone,   April 14, 1749.

B. STONE, Valentine son of Josiah Stone,   February 14, 1751.

B. STONE, Mary daughter of Josias Stone,   April 28, 1753.

B. STONE, Philadelphia daughter of Josias and Mary Stone,   September 22, 1755.

M. STRINGFELLOW, Benjamin and Mary Foley,   June 15, 1743.

M. STRINGFELLOW, Mary and William Bouchard,   November 12, 1751.

B. STRONG, John son of Nathaniel and Mary Strong,   June 22, 1740.

M. STROTHER, Elizabeth and John Frogg,   November 9, 1738.

M. STROTHER, Margaret and George Morton,   April 6, 1744.

M. STROTHER, Anne and Francis Tyler,   May 17, 1744.

M. STROTHER, Margaret and John Murdock,   October 26, 1750.

M. STROTHER, Alice and Robert Washington,   December 16, 1756.

M. STUART, James and Mary Dunaway,   February 12, 1740.

B. STUART, William son of James and Mary Stuart,   January [blank], 1741.

---

1 - William Strother, Gentleman, (circa 1696-1733) died possessed of Ferry
    Farm, King George [now Stafford] County; his widow, nee Margaret Watts,
    married Captain John Grant and moved to Overwharton Parish with her six
    daughters, viz: (1) Alice married Henry Tyler; (2) Elizabeth married
    Captain John Frogg; (3) Agatha married John Madison (17 -1784) of Augus-
    ta and Botetourt counties; (4) Margaret (September 3, 1726 - October __,
    1822) married first George Morton and secondly October 18, 1749 the Hon.
    Gabriel Jones (May 17, 1724 - October 18, 1806); (5) Anne married Francis
    Tyler and (6) Jane (circa 1731-1820) married January 26, 1749, Thomas
    Lewis (1718-1790) of Augusta County, Virginia.

D.   STUART, William October 13, 1742 at Mr. Scott's.

B.   STUART, James son of James and Mary Stuart, October 26, 1742.

M.   STURDY, Margaret and Parish Garner, January 21, 1742.

D.   STURDY, Elizabeth daughter of Robert and Elizabeth Sturdy, November 20, 1742.

D.   STURDY, Robert November 3, 1749.

M.   STURDY, William and Phillis Jones, December 17, 1752.

M.   STURDY, Joanna and Rowley Lunsford, June 16, 1754.

     SUDDETH : SUDDUTH : SUTHARD : SADURTH

M.   SUDDETH, James and Mary Pepper, May 13, 1738.

D.   SUDDETH, Thompson son of James and Elizabeth Suddeth, February 28, 1741.

M.   SUTHARD, Benjamim and Silent Jefferys, January 19, 1744.

M.   SUDDUTH, Mary and Edmund Boling, May 4, 1744.

M.   SUDDETH, Lawrence and Dorothy West, April 18, 1745.

M.   SUDDETH, Henry and Mary Latham, June 25, 1745.

M.   SUDDETH, Sarah and Thomas Griffin, July 18, 1745.

B.   SUDDETH, Ann daughter of Benjamin and Silent Suddeth, July 19, 1745.

B.   SUDDETH, Elizabeth daughter of Lawrence and Dorothy Suddeth, November 3, 1745.

B.   SUDDETH, John son of Henry and Mary Suddeth, March 14, 1746.

B.   SUDDETH, Ann daughter of Benjamin Suddeth, July 17, 1746.

M.   SUDDETH, Anne and James Dillon, July 24, 1746.

B.   SUDDETH, James son of Benjamin and Silent Suddeth, December 13, 1746.

B.   SUDDETH, Margaret daughter of Benjamin and Silent Suddeth, January 12, 1748.

B.   SUDDETH, Grace daughter of Lawrence and Dorothy Suddeth, September 23, 1749.

B.   SUDDETH, Catherine daughter of Benjamin Suddeth, March 27, 1750.

D. SUDDETH, Catherine daughter of Benjamin Suddeth, April 11, 1750.

B. SUDDETH, William son of Benjamin and Silent Suddeth, March 7, 1751.

B. SUDDETH, Lawrence son of James and Hannah Suddeth, February 21, 1752.

B. SUDDETH, Susannah daughter of Benjamin and Mary Suddeth, April 25, 1753.

B. SUDDETH, Elizabeth daughter of James Suddeth, May 20, 1753.

B. SUDDETH, Moses son of Joseph and Jemima Suddeth, July 28, 1753.

B. SUDDETH, Mary daughter of James and Hannah Suddeth, June 7, 1754.

B. SADURTH, Sarah daughter of Joseph Sadurth, March 21, 1756.

B. SUDDETH, Jane daughter of James and Hannah Suddeth, May 18, 1756.

B. SUDDETH, Priscilla daughter of James and Hannah Suddeth, September 1, 1757.

M. SUITOR, Alexander and Margaret Isaac, July 21, 1745.

M. SUTOR, Alexander and Elizabeth Raper, May 8, 1757.

M. SULLIVAN, Sarah and George Hinson, February 4, 1753.

M. SULLIVANT, Mary and Peter Going, May 28, 1745.

M. SUMMERS, Elizabeth and John Taylor, November 8, 1755.

M. SUTHERLAND, Doctor John and Susannah Brent, September 15, 1756.

SYLVA : SYLVIE   SEE : SILVY : SYLVA : SYLVIE PAGE 107

T

M. TAYLOR, Catherine and William Chimp, January 31, 1739.

B. TAYLOR, Elizabeth daughter of Henry Taylor, July 25, 1740.

B. TAYLOR, Ann daughter of Henry Taylor, June 10, 1743.

B. TAYLOR, John son of John and Eleanor Taylor, December 1, 1745.

M. TAYLOR, John and Elizabeth Summers, November 8, 1755.

B. TAYLOR, Philadelphia, daughter of John Taylor, February 2, 1757.

M. TAYLOR, Alexander and Hannah Brooke, February 24, 1757.

M. TENNEL, Francis and Margaret Sinclair, November 9, 1740.

B. TENNEL, Joseph son of Francis and Margaret Tennel, February 18, 1742.

D. THOM, Robert   December 11, 1751.

THOMPSON : THOMSON

M. THOMPSON, Robert and Catherine Tomlinson, September 12, 1742.

M. THOMSON, Mary and Robert Pully, August 25, 1748.

B. THOMSON, John Clement son of Jean Thomson, February 13, 1753.

M. THOMSON, Jane and Feanly Macoy, July 18, 1757.

M. THORNBERRY, William and Elizabeth O'Duneal, July 10, 1746.

B. THORNBERRY, Anne daughter of William and Elizabeth Thornberry, April 9, 1747.

M. THRELKELD, Henry and Mary Hinson, November 3, 1748.

M. TICER, William and Aggy Hutt, December 15, 1754.

B. TIMBER, Priscilla mulatto daughter of Sarah Timber, March 19, 1756.

D. TISER, Samuel May 9, 1750 at Morris Lynaugh's.

M. TOBY, Mary and John Nelson, February 10, 1741.

B. TOBY, [blank] daughter of John Toby, Junior, March 3, 1749.

B. TOBY, Thomas son of John and Elizabeth Toby, January 20, 1751.

D. TOBY, John November 3, 1751.

B. TOBY, John son of John Toby, July 3, 1753.

D. TOBY, John son of John Toby, February 3, 1754.

D. TOBY, Thomas the son of John Toby, April 24, 1754.

B. TOBY, Mary daughter of John and Elizabeth Toby, July 28, 1755.

M. TODD, Hayward and Sarah Rosser, September 7, 1746.[1]

---

1 - Hayward Todd (17 -1755), son of Richard and Lucy (Ellit) Todd of Saint
    Paul's Parish, died testate in Stafford County leaving five children, viz:
    (1) Samuel, born 1747, moved to Kentucky in 1794; (2) Richard (1748-1824)
    of Spotsylvania County; (3) Hester, born 1750; (4) Lucy, born 1751 and (5)
    Hayward, born 1755.

B.   TODD, Nanny daughter of William and Margaret Todd,   October 13, 1752.

M.   TODD, William and Margaret Cocklen,   October 23, 1752.

M.   TOLSON, Judith and Simon Stacy,   August 22, 1741.

D.   TOLSON, Mary wife of Benjamin Tolson,   June 24, 1748.

M.   TOLSON, Benjamin Junior and Hannah Maccollough,   December 31, 1751.

M.   TOLSON, Benjamin and Elizabeth Dunnaway,   February 25, 1752.

B.   TOLSON, Mary daughter of Benjamin and Hannah Tolson,   February 19, 1753.

M.   TOLSON, Mary Ann and Isaac Dunnaway,   May 25, 1754.

B.   TOLSON, Peggy daughter of Benjamin and Hannah Tolson,   August 15, 1755.

B.   TOLSON, Nanny daughter of Benjamin and Hannah Tolson,   December 4, 1757.

B.   TOMISON, Richard and William sons of Simon and Barbara Tomison,   August 21, 1743.

B.   TOMISON, Jane daughter of Simon and Barbara Tomison,   November 17, 1745.

B.   TOMISON, Elizabeth daughter of Simon and Barbara Tomison,   July 8, 1748.

B.   TOMISON, James son of Simon and Barbara Tomison,   July 8, 1748.

D.   TOMISON, Elizabeth daughter of Simon Tomison,   September 8, 1748.

D.   TOMISON, Jean   September 14, 1748.

D.   TOMISON, Barbara wife of Simon Tomison,   August 19, 1751.

M.   TOMLINSON, Catherine and Robert Thompson,   September 12, 1742.

M.   TONGATE, Jeremiah and Elizabeth Evans,   March 3, 1751.

B.   TOUNGATE, Hannah   January 9, 1750 in Prince William County.

D.   TRAVERS, Rawleigh   October 15, 1749.

M.   TRAVERSE, Sarah and Peter Daniel,   July 15, 1736.

D.   TREWICK, Eleanor daughter of Robert Trewick,   May 19, 1740, aged 8 years.

B.   TREWICK, Elizabeth daughter of Robert and Margary Trawick,   December 24, 1740.

B.   TREWICK, Eleanor daughter of Robert and Margaret Trewick,   January 24, 1743.

B.   TURNER, Margaret daughter of Henry and Mary Turner,   June [blank], 1733.

B.   TURNER, Betty daughter of Henry and Mary Turner,   May 28, 1736.

B.   TURNER, Alexander son of Edward and Jean Turner,   July 25, 1741.

B.   TURNER, Hannah daughter of Henry Turner,   October 30, 1742.

B.   TURNER, Sarah daughter of Henry Turner,   November 13, 1744.

D.   TURNER, Sarah December 25, 1744.

D.   TURNER, William September 25, 1745.

D.   TURNER, Lawrence December 22, 1749 at Peter Byram's.

M.   TURNER, Mary and David Round,   January 28, 1753.

M.   TURNER, Betty and Henry Dawson,   December 15, 1754.

M.   TURNER, James and Mary Matthews,   March 3, 1757.

B.   TURNHAM, John son of Thomas and Eleanor Turnham,   May 3, 1749.

M.   TURNUM, Thomas and Eleanor Radcliffe,   September 13, 1746.

M.   TYLER, Margaret and William Waugh,   September 10, 1738.

B.   TYLER, John son of Henry and Else Tyler,   April 17, 1743.

M.   TYLER, Francis and Anne Strother, May 17, 1744.[1]

C.   TYLER, Harry son of Henry and Else Tyler,   August 18, 1746.

C.   TYLER, Anna daughter of Henry and Else Tyler,   January 30, 1749.

C.   TYLER, Mary daughter of Henry and Alice Tyler,   March 20, 1751.

---

1 - Francis Tyler came to Stafford County from York County after his brother
Captain Henry Tyler had established himself there as clerk of Stafford
court, 1736. These two brothers married sisters, daughters of William
and Margaret (Watts) Strother [see page 115]. On February 24, 1748 John
Spotswood, Gentleman, eldest son of Governor Alexander Spotswood, gave to
Francis Tyler of Orange County a general power of attorney to be his agent
and collect his rents in Orange County. In 1748 Francis Tyler received a
patent for 400 acres of land in Culpeper County and in 1752 his wife Anne
joined him in conveying it to Anthony Strother. They had five children,
viz: (1) William who d.s.p., 1805, in Columbia County, Georgia; (2) Francis
who d.s.p.; (3) Margaret, unmarried in 1806 in Columbia County, Georgia;
(4) Henry Tyler of Oglethorpe County, Georgia, 1806; and (5) Alice married
Joseph Allen of Fauquier County; this family also moved to Georgia shortly
after 1800.

U

V

B.   VANT, Franky daughter of James and Margaret Vant,   May 15, 1758.

B.   VASPER, James a mulatto son of Ann Vasper, October 22, 1732; he was bound
     apprentice to Mrs. Elizabeth Cooke.

B.   VOUCHEART, John son of William Voucheart,   October 21, 1752.

W

M.   WADE, Rachel and John McGuirk,   December 25, 1741.

M.   WALKER, William and Elizabeth Monk,   May 3, 1744.

B.   WALKER, Elizabeth daughter of William and Elizabeth Walker,   April 3, 1747.

B.   WALKER, Mary daughter of William and Elizabeth Walker,   January 9, 1750.

B.   WALKER, Margaret daughter of William and Elizabeth Walker,   May 1, 1752.

D.   WALL, Margaret   April 7, 1757, "a poor Parishoner."

B.   WALLER, Hannah daughter of George and Elizabeth Waller,   October 11, 1739.[1]

B.   WALLER, William son of Edward and Anne Waller,   November 26, 1740.

B.   WALLER, Margaret daughter of Charles and Elizabeth Waller,   November 27,
     1741.

B.   WALLER, John son of Edward and Ann Waller,   April 7, 1742.

B.   WALLER, Margaret daughter of George Waller,   July 27, 1744.

---

1 - William Waller came to Virginia in 1650 and with Gerrard Masters patented
    800 acres on Hope Creek in Stafford County in 1669. His son and heir Will-
    iam Waller (circa 1673-1703) married Elizabeth Allen and died testate in
    Stafford County; his youngest son was George Waller, Gentleman, (1703-circa
    1768) of Spring Hill, who married his cousin Elizabeth Allen. At Spring Hill
    are two tombstones: "Here lies the body of Enoch Waller, son of George and
    Elizabeth Waller, who died November 1738 aged 11 months." "Here also lies
    the body of Hannah, the daughter of George and Elizabeth Waller, who died
    the 13th of June 1744, aged 4 years." The last will and Testament of
    George Waller of Spring Hill was recorded in lost Stafford County Will Book
    "N" [1767-1783], page 30. George and Elizabeth (Allen) Waller were surviv-
    ed by nine children.

B. WALLER, Charles son of Edward and Anne Waller,   January 27, 1746.

B. WALLER, Jeany daughter of George and Elizabeth Waller,   July 28, 1746.[1]

B. WALLER, Edward son of Edward Waller,   February 29, 1748.

D. WALLER, Anne wife of Edward Waller,   February 29, 1748.

D. WALLER, John son of Edward Waller,   June 6, 1748.

D. WALLER, Susannah   October 18, 1748.[2]

D. WALLER, Charles   December 4, 1749.

M. WALLER, John and Mary Matthews,   July 4, 1751.

M. WALLER, Ann and Thomas Railly,   July 10, 1751.

M. WALLER, Elizabeth and John Peyton,   November 17, 1751.

B. WALLER, William son of John and Mary Waller,   December 24, 1751.

---

1 - George Waller, Gentleman, (1703-circa 1768) of Spring Hill and Elizabeth
Allen, his wife, were survived by nine children, viz: (1) Colonel George
Waller (1734-1814), married Ann Winston Carr (1735-1839), moved to Henry
County, Virginia - they were the great-great-grandparents of the Honorable
Sam Rayburn, Speaker of the House of Representatives; (2) Barsheba Waller
(17 -1815) d.s.p.; (3) Mary Waller [see page 52]; (4) Allen Waller (17 -
1777) d.s.p.; (5) Mariam Waller married Paul Hoye and on May 18, 1780 while
residing in Montgomery County, Maryland, they deeded to her sister Jane
Waller her interest in certain land devised to her by her late father; (6)
Margaret Waller (1744-177?) married William Waller (1740-1817) of Concord
as his second wife and had an only child Margaret Ursula Waller, born October 16, 1771 who married Richard Morton; (7) Jane Waller (1746-1815) who
married Captain John Markham as his third wife; (8) Elizabeth Waller who
married George Norman and (9) Theodosia Waller (1753-1829) married Elias
Hore [see page 55]. For the wills of Barsheba Waller, Allen Waller and
Jane (Waller) Markham see Tyler's Quarterly Historical and Genealogical
Magazine, Volume 31, pages 263-267. The will of Captain John Markham
(1732-1804) may be found in the same quarterly, Volume 31, pages 180-187.

2 - Charles Waller of Gloucester and Essex counties died possessed of land on
Aquia Creek in Stafford County. By his will, proved in 1725 at Essex County court, he bequeathed this land to his sons Charles (17 -1749) and Edward (1706-1753) and with their widowed mother nee Susannah Forrest (1678-
1748) they moved to Stafford County; the last wills and Testaments of all
three remain of record there. The tombstones of Susannah Waller (1678-1748),
Edward Waller (1706-1753) and other members of the family are at Concord.
Edward Waller married Ann Tandy and Charles Waller married Elizabeth Rowzee,
both in Essex County before their removal to Stafford County, and their progeny to the present day are communicants in Overwharton Parish.

C. WALLER, Theodosia daughter of George Waller, April 1, 1753.

M. WALLER, Mary and Edward Herndon, April 15, 1753.

B. WALLER, Sarah daughter of John and Mary Waller, June 12, 1753.

D. WALLER, Edward November [blank], 1754 "suddenly."

M. WALLER, Mary and George Dabney, September 11, 1754.

D. WALLER, Milly daughter of Charles Waller, January 7, 1755.

B. WALLER, Edward son of John and Mary Waller, December 10, 1755.[1]

B. WALLER, John son of John and Mary Waller, December 27, 1757.[1]

M. WALLER, Sukey and James Withers, December 7, 1757.[2]

M. WANT, Sarah and William Corbin, August 2, 1744.

M. WARNER, Margaret and James Dillon, November 6, 1742.[3]

B. WASHINGTON, William son of Bailey and Catherine Washington, February 28, 1752.

B. WASHINGTON, Bailey son of Bailey Washington, December 12, 1753.

---

1 - William Waller (circa 1673-1703) left two sons, viz: (1) William Waller who married his cousin Sarah Allen, daughter of William Allen (circa 1675-1741), and (2) George Waller of Spring Hill mentioned on pages 121 and 122. These two brothers, whose wives were sisters, have many descendants. John Waller (1732-1784), son of William and Sarah (Allen) Waller, married in 1751 Mary Matthews; they had three sons who early settled in Kentucky and left numerous progeny, viz: (i) Edward (1755-1791) who died testate in Bourbon County, Kentucky; (ii) John (1757-1823) who died testate in Pendleton County, Kentucky; and (iii) Doctor Thomas (1774-1823) who married in Bourbon County, Kentucky, in 1800 Elizabeth McFarland, and moved to Portsmouth, Ohio.

2 - Susannah Waller, daughter of Charles and Elizabeth (Rowzee) Waller, married James Withers, son of John Withers (1714-1794) and Hannah Allen, his wife, daughter of William Allen (circa 1675-1741); they had nine children. His sister, Ursula Withers (1750-1815) was the third wife of William Waller (1740-1817) of Concord, where their tombstones now are; they were the parents of Withers Waller (1785-1827) of Clifton, Stafford County, Virginia. The first wife of William Waller of Concord was Elizabeth Allen, daughter of William and Bridget (Withers) Allen; his second Margaret Waller [see page 122] and his third Ursula Withers, above mentioned. He left issue by each.

3- She was the widow of John Warner who died testate in 1742; see page 61.

B. WASHINGTON, John son of Bailey and Catherine Washington, May 5, 1756.

M. WASHINGTON, Robert and Alice Strother, December 16, 1756.

B. WASHINGTON, Elizabeth daughter of Bailey and Catherine Washington, March 16, 1758.[1] [She married William Storke (1753-1822) and left issue.]

M. WATERS, Thomas and Catherine Hays, September 28, 1738.

B. WATERS, Margaret daughter of Edward and Catherine Waters, January 25, 1739.

B. WATERS, Philomen son of Thomas Waters, March 22, 1739.

B. WATERS, James son of Thomas Waters, Junior, and Mary, his wife, October 25, 1739.[2]

B. WATERS, Ann daughter of Edward and Catherine Waters, February 25, 1742.

M. WATERS, John and Elizabeth Higgerson, June 5, 1743.

M. WATERS, Mary and John Shaw, June 12, 1743.

D. WATERS, Edward February 22, 1745.

B. WATERS, Diana daughter of Thomas and Mary Waters, November 5, 1747.

D. WATERS, Diana daughters of Thomas Walters, May 27, 1748.

M. WATERS, Jean and John Monslow, October 26, 1748.

M. WATERS, William and Jean Cash, April 6, 1751.

M. WATERS, Mary and John Fitzpatrick, February 12, 1752.

B. WATERS, Jean daughter of Charles and Hannah Waters, June 28, 1753.[3]

---

1 - Bailey Washington (1731-1807) married on January 12, 1749 in Saint Paul's Parish,Catherine Storke (1722-1804). Their first two children were born there and the last four in Overwharton Parish as above recorded. Their son, Colonel William Washington (1752-1810), distinguished himself in the Revolutionary War, while their son Bailey Washington (1753-1814) continued upon his father's plantation on Aquia Creek and left a large family. The plantation of Colonel Bailey Washington was called Windsor Forest.

2 - In March 1756 James Waters, with the consent of his mother Mary Fitzpatrick, bound himself apprentice to William Copein, mason or bricklayer, of Dettingen Parish, Prince William County, until he arrived to the age of 21 years. William Copein at this time was building Aquia Church.

3 - John Rhodes in his last will and Testament proved at Stafford County court in 1748 mentions his daughter Hannah Waters.

B. WATERS, James son of William and Jane Waters, May 26, 1754.

M. WATERS, Mark and Ann Harding, July 20, 1756.

M. WATERS, Virgin and Richard Fristoe, February 28, 1757.

B. WATERS, Peter son of Charles Waters, March 8, 1757.

M. WATSON, Andrew and Mary Moriss [Morris], September 26, 1742.

B. WATSON, John son of Elizabeth Watson, January 27, 1743.

D. WATSON, Francis July 1, 1743 "a servant to John Minor."

M. WAUGH, William and Margaret Tyler, September 10, 1738. [1]

B. WAUGH, Tyler son of William and Margaret Waugh, February 29, 1739.

B. WAUGH, Elizabeth daughter of Joseph and Million Waugh, March 31, 1740.

M. WAUGH, Mary and Alexander Doniphan, June 17, 1740.

M. WAUGH, James and Betty French, August 22, 1740.

D. WAUGH, Elizabeth daughter of Joseph Waugh, September 26, 1740.

B. WAUGH, John son of James and Betty Waugh, October 20, 1741.

B. WAUGH, Priscilla daughter of William and Margaret Waugh, October 22, 1741.

D. WAUGH, John November 17, 1742.

B. WAUGH, Travers son of Joseph and Million Waugh, January 24, 1743.

B. WAUGH, Sarah daughter of James and Betty Waugh, May 27, 1744.

B. WAUGH, James son of James and Elizabeth Waugh, February 4, 1746.

D. WAUGH, James son of James and Betty Waugh, September 3, 1746.

B. WAUGH, Betty daughter of James and Betty Waugh, September 4, 1747.

D. WAUGH, Joseph September 4, 1747.

---

1 - Margaret Tyler was the only child of John Tyler of Brunswick Parish, King
George County, who died testate in 1756 and directed he be "decently buried in Falmouth churchyard without much noise or funeral." William Waugh
died in 1748 and his widow married secondly Daniel Royalty [Rayathy] of
Overwharton Parish. The last will and Testament of John Tyler mentioned
his five grandchildren Tyler, William, Thomas, Priscilla and Million Waugh;
he also decreed that Daniel Rayathy, the "wicked husband" of his daughter
Margaret, should not enjoy any part of his estate.

D. WAUGH, Betty daughter of James Waugh, September 14, 1747.

M. WAUGH, Solomon and Betty Chinn, April 13, 1748.

B. WAUGH, James son of James and Betty Waugh, September 26, 1748.

B. WAUGH, Micajah son of Solomon and Elizabeth Waugh, January 9, 1749.

D. WAUGH, Captain James May 9, 1750.

M. WAUGH, Betty and Andrew Edwards, May 7, 1751.

B. WAUGH, Grace daughter of Solomon and Betty Waugh, July 21, 1751.

D. WAUGH, David March 22, 1753 at Priscilla Hay's.

WEATHERS[1]   SEE : WITHERS

B. WEATHERS, Susannah daughter of John and Judy Weathers, February 17, 1748.

D. WEATHERS, Susannah daughter of John and Juda Weathers, October 9, 1748.

B. WEATHERS, Nancy daughter of John and Judith Weathers, July 1, 1749.

B. WEATHERS, Ann daughter of Thomas and Anne Weathers, December 10, 1749.

D. WEATHERS, Samuel January 30, 1750.

B. WEATHERS, Joel son of Thomas and Anne Weathers, February 7, 1752.

B. WEATHERS, John son of John and Judith Weathers, March 14, 1752.

B. WEATHERS, Sarah daughter of John and Judith Weathers, March 25, 1754.

B. WEATHERS, Mary Ann daughter of Thomas and Anne Weathers, April 19, 1756.

B. WEATHERS, Leanna daughter of John and Judith Weathers, January 15, 1757.

B. WEATHERS, Jean and Anne daughters of Thomas and Anne Weathers, October 13, 1757.

D. WEATHERS, Anne wife of Thomas Weathers, October 13, 1757.

M. WEBSTER, Edmund and Marjory Stanly, November 20, 1741.

M. WEBSTER, Anne and George Reaves, April 3, 1743.

---

1 - The Weathers family is not identical with the Withers family. They came
    to Stafford County from the Lancaster County and Middlesex County area.
    Elizabeth Blufard, the mother of Thomas Weathers, died August 13, 1750.

M. WEBSTER, Barbara and William Groves, February 2, 1749.

M. WEDDELL, Thomas and Isabel Robe, January 3, 1748.

M. WEEKS, Amy and Edward Proctor, February 15, 1747.

M. WELCH, Margaret and John Prim, September 9, 1739.

M. WELIT, Elizabeth and John Smith, December 7, 1757.

M. WELLS, Carty and Elizabeth Onsby, September 10, 1738.

B. WELLS, Sarah daughter of Carty and Elizabeth Wells, October 10, 1739.

B. WELLS, Charles son of Charles and Mary Wells, January 10, 1740.

D. WELLS, Sarah daughter of Carty Wells, April 13, 1741.

B. WELLS, Isabel daughter of Carty and Elizabeth Wells, October 31, 1741.

B. WELLS, John son of Charles and Mary Wells, July 3, 1742.

B. WELLS, George son of Carty and Elizabeth Wells, November 18, 1743.

B. WELLS, Haydon son of Charles Wells, September 9, 1744.

B. WELLS, Carty son of Carty and Elizabeth Wells, February 22, 1746.

B. WELLS, Eleanor daughter of Charles Wells, April 19, 1747.

B. WELLS, Eleanor daughter of Carty Wells, February 21, 1750.

B. WELLS, Benjamin son of Charles and Mary Wells, August 22, 1751.

---

1 - On November 12, 1759 Townshend Dade conveyed to Baldwin Dade 300 acres of land in Saint Paul's Parish, Stafford County, reciting that it was the same which had been purchased by him of Samuel, Charles and Carty Wells by deeds of record at Stafford County court; unfortunately these deeds are among the missing records. However it appears these men were brothers, sons of Samuel and Eleanor Wells of Saint Paul's Parish. They appear on the registers of Saint Paul's and Overwharton Parish, and on the Stafford County and Prince William County records. Charles Wells (17 -1765) married on December 10, 1733 Mary Edwards; he died testate in Prince William County. This family is closely associated on the records with Haydon [Haden, Hayden] Edwards (1716-1803) of Stafford, Prince William, and Fairfax counties and Bourbon County, Kentucky, and it appears he was a brother of Mary (Edwards) Wells. Carty Wells, Senior, (17 -1781) died testate in Stafford County; his will was recorded in lost Will Book "N", page 450. His son, Carty Wells, Junior, moved to Shelby County, Kentucky, about 1797 with several of his children but his daughter Lydia, wife of Thomas Fristoe [see page 37] remained in Stafford County, Virginia.

B. WEST, James son of John West, September 26, 1742.

B. WEST, Caty daughter of Thomas and Catherine West, March 12, 1743.

M. WEST, Dorothy and Lawrence Suddeth, April 18, 1745.

B. WEST, James son of Thomas and Catherine West, February 10, 1746.

M. WEST, Edward and Elizabeth Mills, October 6, 1752.

B. WEST, William Mills son of Edward and Elizabeth West, March 29, 1755.

M. WEYTON, Susannah and James Williamson, November 4, 1756.

M. WHALBONE, Duke and Elizabeth Powell, December 3, 1745.

B. WHALEBONE, Thomas son of Duke and Elizabeth Whalebone, September 4, 1746.

B. WHALEBONE, Nanny daughter of Duke and Elizabeth Whalebone, October 5, 1749.

M. WHEALY, James and Hannah Higgerson, July 8, 1739.

D. WHEELER, John August 5, 1746.[1]

M. WHEELER, Eleanor and William Edwards, February 12, 1756.[2]

M. WHEELER, Martha and William Howard, April 25, 1756.

---

1 - Henry Allday (1630-1670) came to Potomac River, Virginia, in 1656 on the
ketch, the Sea Horse of London on which John Washington (1634-1677) was
also a seaman. During a storm the vessel sank and both men settled in
Westmoreland County. Henry Allday married Grace, who is thought to have
been the daughter of Francis Grey [Gray] as he made Grace Allday a deed
of gift on January 5, 1661 shortly after her marriage. They had an only
child, Mary Allday (circa 1665-ante 1720), who was thrice married and left
issue by each husband, viz: first to Edward Wheeler who died testate in
1692; secondly to Evan Price, Senior, and thirdly to Daniel Field (circa-
1662/3-1720) who survived her and died testate in Westmoreland County. Her
eldest son was John Wheeler (1684-1746); he settled on Potomac Creek upon
lands inherited from his father. He married Diana (surname unknown) and
their only child Mary Wheeler married George James, Gentleman.[See page 59]

2 - A descendant of this couple sent me the following data: William Edwards was
born in Virginia, 1728; died November 9, 1813. He married February 12, 1756
Eleanor Wheeler who was born in Maryland, 1730; died June 9, 1811 on the
Potomac River. Issue: (1) William, born May 11, 1757, married Elizabeth
Combs, and moved to Clark County, Kentucky; (2) John (September 27, 1759-
August 3, 1838) [see Revolutionary Pension #R-3257 for his Bible record];
(3) Richard (June 25, 1762- 1783); (4) George Rumney born January 11, 1763;
(5) Theresa, born November 25, 1773;(6) Thomas Wheeler Edwards born October
27, 1776 and moved to Kentucky about 1800.

M. WHITCOMB, John and Elizabeth Simpson, November 24, 1743.

B. WHITCOMB, Mary daughter of John Whitcomb, August 29, 1744.

D. WHITCOMB, Richard February 7, 1746.

B. WHITCOMB, Margaret daughter of John and Elizabeth Whitcomb, August 16, 1749.

D. WHITCOMB, Mary April 23, 1751 at Richard Wine's.

B. WHITCOME, Eliza daughter of John Whitcome, February 26, 1752.

M. WHITE, George and Anne Doniphan, August 4, 1743.

B. WHITE, Mary daughter of George and Anne White, September 9, 1747.

D. WHITE, Rosamond February 19, 1748.

M. WHITE, Joseph and Elizabeth Gill, January 31, 1749.

B. WHITE, Alice daughter of Joseph and Elizabeth White, December 18, 1749.

B. WHITE, Alexander son of George and Anne White, August 11, 1750.

B. WHITE, Thomas son of Joseph and Betty White, March 30, 1752.

B. WHITE, Anne daughter of George and Anne White, January 14, 1754.

D. WHITE, Alice daughter of Joseph and Elizabeth White, August 17, 1754.

D. WHITE, Ann December 13, 1757 at Edward Templeman's.

B. WHITECOTTON, Mary daughter of George and Bridget Whitecotton, January 20, 1739.

B. WHITECOTTON, Lettice and Jean daughters of Sarah Whitecotton, November 14, 1741.

D. WHITECOTTON, George March 23, 1744.

M. WHITECOTTON, Bridget and William McConchie, November 10, 1747.

B. WHITECOTTON, Axton son of Husband Foot Whitecotton, February 3, 1748.[1]

---

1 - Major Lewis Burwell (1621-1653) claimed John Axton as a headright in a land patent issued to him in 1648. Before Stafford County was formed he settled on the south side of Potomac Creek and the small branch now called Beaver Dam Creek was known as Axton's Creek in colonial times. He received a patent for 600 acres of land in this area in 1668 and in 1707 Mealy White-cotton, the son and heir of his daughter Anne Axton, sold 200 acres of this land to John Gowry (16 -1722) of Potomac Creek, Stafford County, Virginia.

D. WHITING, Cherebub June 9, 1750 at Richard Fristoe, Senior's.

B. WHITSON, William son of William and Margaret Whitson, March 7, 1740.

M. WHITSON, Margaret and Nicholas George, December 25, 1740.

B. WHITSON, William son of Samuel and Nan Whitson, January 29, 1742.

B. WHITSON, Charles son of William and Margaret Whitson, March 5, 1742.

B. WHITSON, James son of William and Margaret Whitson, February 10, 1744.

B. WHITSON, Mary daughter of Samuel and Ann Whitson, April 19, 1744.

M. WHITSON, Elizabeth and George Green, December 23, 1744.

D. WHITSON, Margaret January 25, 1745.

M. WHITSON, Mary and William George, November 1, 1745.

M. WHITSON, Sarah and John Nelson, December 7, 1745.

B. WHITSON, [blank] daughter of Samuel and Ann Whitson, June 17, 1746.

B. WHITSON, Jesse son of William and Margaret Whitson, May 8, 1750.

M. WHITSON, Elizabeth and Benjamin Macollough, December 19, 1751.

WIGGINTON : WIGGONTON

M. WIGGONTON, Peter and Winifred Eaves, October 13, 1746.

B. WIGGONTON, Anne daughter of Peter and Winifred Wiggonton, June 25, 1747.

D. WIGGINTON, Anne November 22, 1747.

B. WIGGONTON, William son of Peter and Winifred Wiggonton, May 29, 1749.

---

1 - There are records of the Whitson family in both Westmoreland and Stafford
    counties. Joseph Whitson received a land patent for 300 acres of land on
    the north side of Aquia Creek on October 1, 1694. He died testate in 1696
    and devised this property to three of his children and of these there is
    considerable genealogical detail recited in Stafford County Deed Book "J",
    pages 413 and 491, in two deeds dated April 8, 1727 and October 11, 1727.

2 - William Wigginton was an early settler on Aquia Creek. On July 9, 1697
    his wife and three of his children were murdered by a band of Indians who
    came to his house from Maryland. There are many records of the family in
    Westmoreland, Stafford, Prince William, Loudoun &c: counties. William Wig-
    ginton (16 -1733) and his son Henry Wigginton (17 -1736) both died testate
    in Stafford County; the latter was the father of Peter Wigginton, above men-
    tioned.

M. WIGGONTON, Jane and Moses Bland, January 14, 1750.

M. WIGGINTON, Henry and Margaret Bridwell, November 12, 1750.

B. WIGGONTON, Peter son of Peter and Winney Wiggonton, September 17, 1752.

D. WIGGENTON, James son of Peter and Winey Wiggenton, February 10, 1755.[1]

B. WIGGONTON, James son of Peter and Winifred Wiggonton, April 2, 1755.[1]

M. WIGGONTON, James and Sarah Botts, February 9, 1756.

B. WIGGONTON, Nancy daughter of James and Sarah Wiggonton, November 8, 1756.

B. WIGGONTON, James son of Peter and Winny Wiggonton, February 24, 1757.

WILKERSON : WILKINSON : WILKISON

M. WILKISON, William and Sarah Heffernut, August 21, 1740.

B. WILKINSON, John son of William Wilkinson, July 6, 1741.

D. WILKERSON, John son of William Wilkerson, March 10, 1745.

B. WILLIAMS, Nathaniel son of George and Jean Williams, October 5, 1730.

B. WILLIAMS, Margaret daughter of George and Jean Williams, April 17, 1732.

B. WILLIAMS, Benjamin son of George and Jean Williams, June 14, 1734.

B. WILLIAMS, George son of George and Jean Williams, August 21, 1736.

B. WILLIAMS, John Pope son of George and Jean Williams, July 27, 1739.

D. WILLIAMS, Mary June 20, 1740 at Edward Turner's.

M. WILLIAMS, Joseph and Mary Mullaken, February 9, 1741.

B. WILLIAMS, Jesse son of George and Jean Williams, December 21, 1741.

B. WILLIAMS, George son of Joseph Williams, January 19, 1742.

B. WILLIAMS, Charles son of George and Jane Williams, May 1, 1745. [2]

---

1 - It appears likely that these two dates are reversed.

2 - On May 25, 1761 Jane Williams of Stafford County apprenticed her son Charles Williams, born May 1, 1745, to Elijah Wickliffe, bricklayer, of Prince William County. In 1777 Charles Williams is styled Captain on the Prince William County records. He married Ann ("Nancy") Edwards, daughter of Hayden Edwards (1716-1803) and Penelope Sanford, his wife; they removed to Bourbon County, Kentucky, where he died testate in 1812. He was known in Kentucky as General Charles Williams.

M. WILLIAMS, Margaret and John Ralls, January 2, 1746.

B. WILLIAMS, William Waller son of Jean Williams, January 26, 1749.

D. WILLIAMS, George February 12, 1750.[1]

M. WILLIAMS, Elizabeth and John Gill, March 3, 1754.

M. WILLIAMS, Mary Ann and Thomas Smith, February 21, 1756.

M. WILLIAMSON, James and Susannah Weyton, November 4, 1756.

M. WILSON, John and Anne Asberry, August 16, 1748.

C. WILSON, George June 12, 1749, a foundling male child.

D. WILSON, Ann December 31, 1749 at John Peyton's.

D. WILSON, Mary March 9, 1750 at William Lunsford's.

B. WILSON, Spencer son of John and Ann Wilson, August 30, 1750.

M. WILSON, John and Sarah Brookes, February 7, 1752.

B. WILSON, Nanny daughter of John Wilson, February 25, 1752.

B. WILSON, Hannah daughter of John Wilson, June 16, 1753.

B. WILSON, John son of John and Ann Wilson, March 25, 1755.

B. WILSON, Else daughter of John and Ann Wilson, May 16, 1757.

M. WINE, Richard and Anne Harvie, July 23, 1738.

B. WINE, Mary daughter of Richard and Anne Wine, October 1, 1740.

B. WINE, Benjamin son of Richard and Anne Wine, December 19, 1742.

---

1 - George Williams appears in Stafford County in 1726 as a witness to deeds;
the records describe him as a founder. About this time Captain Augustine
Washington and several business associates began operations at the Accakeek Iron Works in Stafford County with John England, Iron Master, formerly with the Principio Iron Works in Maryland, as superintendent. George
Williams acquired a plantation in Overwharton Parish and by his last will
and Testament dated January 31, 1750 [which was proved April 10, 1750] he
mentions the cash due to him from the Accakeek Iron Mining Company. He
married Jane [Jean] Pope whose parentage may be found on page 98; the
births of all their children are recorded in The Register of Overwharton
Parish. George Williams appears to have been previously married as by
will he bequeathed to his son John Williams in England one shilling and
no more. From Captain John Lee he purchased land on Chopawamsic Creek in
Stafford County and also died possessed of a landed estate in Prince William County as well as a very handsome personal estate.

B. WINE, Richard son of Richard and Ann Wine, February 14, 1745.

B. WINE, [blank] two children of Richard Wine, September 2, 1747.

D. WINE, [blank] one of the children of Richard Wine, September 28, 1747, who was born September 2, 1747.

B. WINE, Peggy daughter of Richard and Ann Wine, December 2, 1749.

M. WINGFIELD, Owen and Mary Hurst, November 9, 1748.

B. WINLOCK, Elizabeth daughter of Joseph and Margaret Winlock, April 12, 1752. [1]

B. WINLOCK, Sarah daughter of Joseph and Margaret Winlock, February 10, 1755.

B. WINLOCK, Joseph son of Joseph and Margaret Winlock, May 11, 1758. [2]

B. WIOT, Edmund son of Daniel and Susannah Wiot, October 1, 1740.

B. WIOT, William son of Edmund and Sarah Wiot, November 20, 1741.

B. WISE, John son of John and Mary Wise, October 6, 1742.

M. WISE, Elizabeth and Patrick Roach, October 9, 1742.

B. WISE, Samuel son of John Wise, July 15, 1746.

B. WITHERS, Elizabeth daughter of John and Hannah Withers, February 8, 1741.

B. WITHERS, Margaret daughter of John and Hannah Withers, February 8, 1743.

M. WITHERS, Bridget and William Allen, February 15, 1743.

D. WITHERS, Wilmoth August 21, 1744 at William Matthews'.

M. WITHERS, Ann and Henry Mauzey, November 11, 1744.

B. WITHERS, Mary daughter of John and Hannah Withers, January 22, 1745.

---

1 - Joseph Winlock was the son and heir of Jane (Harrison) Winlock English who was the daughter of Thomas Harrison (16 -1726) of Overwharton Parish. In 1777 Joseph Winlock and Margaret, his wife, of Stafford County conveyed his interest in certain land then in King George County which descended to him from his maternal aunt Catherine Harrison, wife of Colonel William Rowley, who died without issue.

2- Joseph Winlock (1758-1831) moved to Kentucky and was prominent. He married Effie Stephenson (1770-1851) on January 14, 1787. General Joseph Winlock died in Shelby County, Kentucky.

D. WITHERS, James June 3, 1746 "in the 66th year of his age." [1]

B. WITHERS, William son of John and Hannah Withers, March 21, 1747.

M. WITHERS, Keene and Elizabeth Cave, December 21, 1747. [2]

C. WITHERS, Ann daughter of Cain and Betty Withers, December 4, 1748. [3]

B. WITHERS, Thomas son of John and Hannah Withers, January 15, 1749.

B. WITHERS, James son of Keene Withers, May 9, 1752.

B. WITHERS, George son of John and Hannah Withers, February 2, 1753.

B. WITHERS, William son of Keene and Elizabeth Withers, February 20, 1754.

B. WITHERS, Hannah daughter of John and Hannah Withers, September 8, 1754.

B. WITHERS, John son of Cain Withers, February 23, 1756.

B. WITHERS, Ann daughter of John and Hannah Withers, November 9, 1756.

M. WITHERS, James and Sukey Waller, December 7, 1757.

M. WITHERS, Elizabeth and Andrew Edwards, January 19, 1758.

B. WOOD, Archibald son of John and Tabitha Wood, April 15, 1741.

B. WOOD, Ann daughter of Thomas and Margaret Wood, September 18, 1745.

B. WOOD, Lizzy daughter of Thomas and Margaret Wood, March 8, 1748.

D. WOOD, Lizzy daughter of Thomas and Margaret Wood, November 13, 1748.

---

1 - See page 32 for the titles of two genealogies of the Withers family.

2 - Keene Withers (1728-1756) was the son of James Withers (1680-1746) and
    Elizabeth Keene, his wife; the name is incorrently rendered Cain Withers.
    His wife, nee Elizabeth Cave, was the daughter of William Cave and Ann
    Travers, his wife, daughter of Giles Travers, Gentleman, (16 -1717) an
    early settler on Potomac Creek. She married secondly in 1758 Andrew
    Edwards (1725-1788), widower, and thirdly Thomas Walker.

3 - Anne Withers was born November 8, 1748 and married on November 15, 1767
    Captain Thomas Mountjoy who was born October 4, 1739 [see page 84]. Their
    only child was Mary Mountjoy who married on March 1, 1786 Robert Baylor
    Morton, son of George Morton (1717-1766) of King George County and Lucy
    Baylor, his wife. Robert Baylor and Mary (Mountjoy) Morton had seven
    children. For Bible records of the Mountjoy and Morton families and con-
    siderable genealogical data see Doctor Daniel Morton's typescript in
    three volumes in the Library of Congress: The Mortons and Their Kin, CS.
    71 M.89. Volume I [1908], page 79 and Volume I [1920], pages 181-182.

D. WOOD, Thomas   February 8, 1750.

B. WOOD, Elizabeth daughter of Thomas and Margaret Wood,   April 29, 1750.

B. WOODWARD, Jenny daughter of William and Hannah Woodward,   August 11, 1755.

M. WORRAL, Charles and Mary Hall,   November 16, 1751.

M. WREN, James and Catherine Brent,   March 27, 1753.[1]

C. WREN, James son of James and Catherine Wren,   December 21, 1755.

B. WRIGHT, John son of William and Rosamond Wright,   August 3, 1735.[2]

---

1 - Her birth is recorded on page 11; see The Descendants of Hugh Brent and Some Allied Families, page 59 [1936], by Chester Horton Brent.

2 - On October 14, 1700 at Stafford County court before John Washington, Gentleman Justice, Dade Massey, aged 21, and William Garner, aged 20, deposed that on October 10, 1700 they were at the house of Captain Richard Fossaker in Saint Paul's Parish where Richard Wright lay upon his death bed and he said it was his will that Mary Ellis have his son William and Gilbert Alsop have his son Richard and that Alsop should administer upon his estate. Gilbert Alsop acted as Wright's administrator and returned an inventory of it on April 8, 1701. William Wright (circa 1700-1789) married Rosamond [Rosanna], surname unknown, and the births of their five children are of record in The Register of Overwharton Parish. After her death on March 16, 1753, William Wright married Mary Brent on October 18, 1753; she predeceased him. In his old age he moved to Fredericksburg and the Virginia Herald of October 15, 1789 announced his death: "DIED: On Monday last, Mr. William Wright, aged 89 years." His last will and Testament remains of record. The children of William and Rosamond [Rosanna] Wright were: I. John (August 3,1735-May 11,1791) married on June 4, 1755 Rosamond Grant (June 10, 1733-June 10,1799), daughter of Captain John Grant (circa 1704-June 25,1762) and Margaret Bronough (17 -March 11, 1756),his first wife, of King George County. John Wright was inspector of tobacco at the time of his death in Spotsylvania County; by will he bequeathed property in Spotsylvania and Culpeper [later Madison] counties. His children were: (i) Margaret (1756-1818) married 1771 James Fulton; (ii) Rosanna (1758-post 1808); (iii) Elizabeth (1760-1779) married Charles Metcalf; (iv) William (1762-18) married Ann Lowens; (v) John (1767-1819) of Mine Run, Orange County, died testate. He married first 1789 Susanna Goodrich Lightfoot Grasty (November 23,1769-August 31,1796) and secondly 1801 Polly Shavers, widow. (vi) Winfield (circa 1770-18) married 1795 Judith Tinsley (February 28,1774-   ), daughter of Edward Tinsley of Madison County. II. Betsy, born September 10, 1737, married Mr. Porter; III. Constant, born September 7, 1739 married Mr. Cooper; IV. Winfield (March 22,1742-March 14,1772) married Margaret Grant (174?-April 19,1772), sister of his brother's wife, and had issue, viz: (i) William Grant, born September 10,1763; (ii) Lucy, born March 2, 1765; and (iii) John born July 15, 1769. V. Mary Wright, born February 10, 1746, married Mr. Peck. William Wright (circa 1700-1789) by will mentioned his above named five children

B. WRIGHT, Betty daughter of William and Rosamond Wright, September 10, 1737.

B. WRIGHT, Constant daughter of William and Rosamond Wright, September 7, 1739.

B. WRIGHT, Winfield child of William and Rose Wright, March 22, 1742.

B. WRIGHT, Mary daughter of William and Rosamond Wright, February 10, 1746.

M. WRIGHT, Jane and Richard Nowland, December 26, 1747.

D. WRIGHT, Rosanna wife of William Wright, March 16, 1753.

M. WRIGHT, William and Mary Brent, October 18, 1753.

Y

M. YATES, Elizabeth and [mutilated] Knight, February 4, 1758.

M. YELTON, James and Isabell Hinson, November 13, 1743.

B. YELTON, Charles son of James and Isabel Yelton, November 1, 1746.

B. YELTON, James son of James and Isabel Yelton, July 15, 1749.

B. YELTON, Ann daughter of James and Isabel Yelton, April 18, 1752.

B. YELTON, Mary daughter of James and Isabel Yelton, July 26, 1755.

M. YOUNG, Margaret and John Humphreys, Junior, September 23, 1738.

M. YOUNG, William and Patience Sinclair, July 22, 1744.

B. YOUNG, Robert son of William and Patience Young, May 30, 1745.

D. YOUNG, Robert son of William Young, October [blank], 1745.

M. YOUNG, Richard and Elizabeth Green, December 27, 1746.

B. YOUNG, Sarah daughter of William and Patience Young, April 17, 1747.

D. YOUNG, John   March 11, 1752 at William Kirk's house.

Z

F I N I S

SECTION II

NEGRO SLAVE OWNERS

IN

OVERWHARTON PARISH

SECTION II

NEGRO SLAVE OWNERS IN OVERWHARTON PARISH

THE REGISTER abounds with recordings of the births and baptisms of Negro slaves.
This seems to have been required in order that their owners could be taxed when
the slaves came to proper age to be tithables. Below are listed the names of the
slave owners; the date following a name indicates the first year that person had
a slave born or baptized in Overwharton Parish. Consistent with the rest of the
register, the recordings relative to Negro slaves are very sparse prior to 1738.

ADIE, Hugh	1740		CALMES, Marquis	1740	
ALLEN, William	1743		CARTER, Charles Esq:	1737	
			Charles	1740	
BAILIS, Hannah	1748		Colonel Charles	1754	
Hannah Estate	1751		George Esq:	1741	
			James	1741	
BALL, Edward	1740		John	1745	
			Joseph	1748	
BARBEE [BARBY], Thomas	1740		Landon Esq:	1743	
			Mary	1742	
BLACK, William	1746				
			CAVE, Ann	1742	
BLACKBURN, William	1741		William	1740	
BOOTH, Hannah	1755		CHAMBERS, Daniel	1749	
Martha	1751				
			CHAPMAN, Taylor Estate	1750	
BOTTS, Seth	1749				
			COOKE, Elizabeth	1744	
BRENT, Benjamin Estate	1755		Hannah	1748	
Charles & Hannah	1732		Million	1742	
George & Catherine	1738		Travers	1744	
Mary	1751				
Susanna	1751		COMBS, Joseph	1732	
William	1751				
			DANIEL, Peter Gent:	1739	
BROWN, John	1756				
			DENT, Thomas	1749	
BURGES, Garner	1755				
			DONIPHAN, Alexander	1755	
BUTLER, Mary	1744		Mott	1752	
Thomas	1741				
BYRAM [BYROM], Peter	1742		EDRINGTON, William	1745	

EDWARDS, Andrew	1756
EUSTACE, Isaac	1753
FITZHUGH, Captain Henry	1740
John Estate	1740
John	1752
Thomas	1755
Col. William	1749
FOWKE, Captain Chandler	1744
FRENCH, Hugh Estate	1742
Margaret	1743
Mason	1756
Rachel	1745
GEORGE, Nicholas	1741
William	1754
GOUGH, Thomas	1743
GRANT, John & Margaret	1738
John	1741
John Junior	1741
GREGG, Mathew	1749
GRIGSBY, James	1742
William	1741
HANSBROUGH, James	1755
Peter	1747
HARDING, George	1751
HARRISON, Isabella	1748
Capt. William	1740
HAY, Priscilla	1741
HEDGMAN, Peter	1743
Major Peter	1750
HINSON, Charles	1741
HOGG, John	1745
HOLDBROOKE, Janet	1745
HOOE, John	1739

HORTON, John	1757
William	1753
HUGHES, John	1744
HURST, Jane	1750
John	1735
HYDEN, William	1745
JACKSON, John	1743
JAMES, George	1749
JEFFRIES, Alexander	1755
George	1754
James	1747
JONES, Brereton	1742
KIRK, Ann	1750
LEE, Captain John	1741
Colonel Philip	1752
Thomas Esq:	1744
Colonel Thomas	1747
Thomas Ludwell	1754
LOURY, William	1740
LYNAUGH, Morris	1749
MACHEN, Henry	1740
MASON, Mrs. Ann	1740
Mary	1740
MATTHEWS, William Junior	1752
MAUZEY, John	1740
John Senior	1745
Peter	1745
MERCER, John & Catherine	1735
MONCURE, Rev. John	1730
[See comment in Preface]	
MONROE, Thomas	1744
MOUNTJOY, William	1739

MURRAY, Anthony & Mary	1740	STROTHER, Benjamin		1741
NELSON, Henry	1745	STUART, Rev. David		1741
		James		1742
PEARSON, Mrs. Hannah	1744	Rev. William		1756
PEYTON, John	1742	SUDDETH, Laurence		1745
PONTON, Edward & Mary	1740	TOMISON, Simon		1750
POPE, Worden	1742	TRAVERS, Raleigh		1743
PORCH, Richard	1748	TYLER, Henry		1743
PORTER, Ann	1746	WAINWRIGHT, John		1737
RALLS, John	1740	WALLER, Edward		1745
		George		1746
RALLS, John Junior	1752	Sarah		1742
RANSDELL, Edward	1752	WASHINGTON, Bailey		1751
Wharton	1746			
		WAUGH, Goury		1748
ROBINSON, Benjamin	1757	James		1740
		Captain James		1746
ROUT, Peter	1753	John		1758
		Joseph Estate		1751
SCOTT, Christian	1745	Joseph & Traves		1755
Helen	1741	Million		1748
[See Note in Preface]				
Rev. James	1740	WELLS, Carty		1748
SEDDON, Thomas	1742	WEST, John		1741
SELDEN, Samuel	1746	WHEELER, Diana [Dinah]		1747
		John		1745
SIMPSON, John	1740			
		WHITSON, William		1750
SINCLAIR, Alexander	1741			
		WIGGINTON, James		1754
SMITH, Henry	1754			
Nathaniel	1741	WILLIAMS, George & Jean		1739
		Mrs. Jane		1752
SPOORE, Mrs. Anne	1744			
		WINGFIELD, Owen		1749
STARK, James & Elizabeth	1733			
Jeremiah	1747	WITHERS, Elizabeth		1746
John	1753	John		1748
		Keene [Cain]		1752
STEWARD, William	1755			

SECTION III

A QUIT RENT ROLL FOR 1723

SECTION III

A QUIT RENT ROLL FOR 1723

THE QUIT RENT system in Virginia was most complex and cannot be dealt with here. The agents of the Proprietors of the Northern Neck of Virginia appointed subordinate agents or collectors in the various counties to collect the quit rents and many of them appear to have conducted that business very haphazardly. It was a source of constant complaint and dissatisfaction. Finally, after the death of Colonel Robert Carter in 1732, who had been sole agent of Lord Fairfax for the preceeding ten years, the Proprietor sent his first cousin, William Fairfax, Gentleman, to Virginia to inquire into his business there. In May 1735 the Proprietor himself, Thomas, Sixth Lord Fairfax, came to Virginia to personally attend to his complicated business and this resulted in a detailed survey of his Northern Neck domain in 1737.

Very few quit rent rolls have been preserved. This one for Stafford County, in The Virginia State Library, is by no means complete. Neither is the rent roll up to date; I will cite a few examples to illustrate this fact. In 1723 Colonel William Fitzhugh (circa 1685-1713) had been dead ten years. Richard Hews [Hues] died testate in Northumberland County in 1714 and bequeathed this land in Stafford County to his step-son, John Johnson. The latter had also died testate in 1721 and bequeathed the land to his half-sister, Mary Ball (circa 1708-1789) [who married Captain Augustine Washington on March 6, 1731] and in whose name it should have been listed in 1723. By her last will and Testament Mrs. Mary (Ball) Washington bequeathed this 600 acres on Accakeek Creek to her son, General George Washington and some few years later he gave it to his nephew, Robert Lewis, Esq., who sold it. Major Lawrence Washington (1659-1698) by will bequeathed to his only daughter Mildred Washington "all my land in Stafford County, lying upon Hunting Creek ... by estimation 2,500 acres to her and her heirs forever." Mildred married John Lewis (169?-1718) and shortly after his death, Colonel Roger Gregory of King and Queen County and thus this land should have been in the name of Mildred Gregory on the 1723 quit rent roll. In 1726 Colonel and Mrs. Gregory conveyed this property to her brother, Captain Augustine Washington and the Mount Vernon mansion stands upon this tract.

Space will not permit further discussion of the imprefections of the quit rent roll for 1723. It appears to be the earliest quit rent roll for Stafford County which has been preserved and is presented in an attempt to supplement the sparse recordings in the early years of The Register of Overwharton Parish.

The ancestry of James Carter (1684-1743),who compiled this rent roll, is to be found in Mr. Chester Horton Brent's excellent work, The Descendants of Hugh Brent and Some Allied Families, page 60 [1936] and in Doctor Joseph Lyon Miller's work, The Descendants of Captain Thomas Carter [1912]. The manuscript was originally sent to Colonel Robert Carter (1663-1732) in Lancaster County, Virginia.

Stafford County rent roll for the year 1723 Returned by James Carter, July ye 18th 1724.

PERSONS NAMES	NUMBER OF ACRES	PROPERTY ALTERED; AMOUNTS PAID; WHY NOT PAID AND GENERAL REMARKS
A		
John Adams	361	Sold Henry Washington 300 acres.
William Allen	1,175	Paid 283 lbs. Tobacco.
David Anderson	300	Lawfully demanded
Francis Awbrey	421	Lives in Westmoreland County.
Robert Alexander	4,675	Paid £ 4.13.6
Isaac Allerton	1,052	Reputed to belong to Han: Lee.
Wansford Arrington	2,178	Lawfully demanded
John Allen	150	Paid 36 lbs. Tobacco.
John Allen and William Hackney	1,013	Paid 122 lbs. Tobacco in part; due 122 lbs. Tobacco.
B		
[Mutilated - several lines lost]		
James Bland	320	[mutilated]
John Bland	125	[mutilated]
James Butler	550	Paid 132 lbs. Tobacco.
Daniel Bourn	350	Paid 84 lbs. Tobacco. Thomas Kitchen's orphans land.
Richard Byram	200	Pays in King George County
Thomas Barton	500	Paid 240 lbs. Tobacco; Paid 2 years.
Robert Brent's orphans	5,810	Paid 3, 899 lbs. Tobacco in part for 3 years; due 353 lbs. Tobacco.
Jane Brent, widow	2,143	Land unknown
Alexander Beach	400	Can't hear of him.
Captain Briscoe	1,500	Can't hear of him.
William Brent's orphans	6,752	Paid 1, 620 lbs. Tobacco.
Joshua Butler	100	Not demanded.
Ann Brent, widow	637	
Major William Buckner	800	
[Mutilated - several lines lost]		
- - - man's orphans	203	Land unknown.
Peter Byram	190	Paid 48 lbs. Tobacco.
John Brown	200	
William Benitt	291	Paid 150 lbs. Tobacco. Paid 2 years and sold part to Col. Mason.
Thomas Barbee	260	Paid 124 Lbs. Tobacco; paid 2 years.
John Berryman's orphans	840	Paid 202 lbs. Tobacco. Pays for but 840 acres.
John Baker	100	Lawfully demanded.

PERSONS NAMES	NUMBER OF ACRES	PROPERTY ALTERED; AMOUNTS PAID; WHY NOT PAID AND GENERAL REMARKS
John Ball	670	Paid 162 lbs. Tobacco.
[mutilated] Brahine, Clk.	1,689	Taken away by Col. Lee's survey.
[mutilated] Bradford	230	Paid 156 lbs. Tobacco. Paid 3 years.
Maurice Biven	100	Paid 48 lbs. Tobacco. Paid 2 years. 120 acres recorded in Brent Town.
Thomas Botts	198	Paid 48 lbs. Tobacco.
Widow Bland	200	Can't hear of her.
Widow Broadwater	1,350	Paid 324 lbs. Tobacco.

C

[Mutilated - several lines lost]

Crawford	?	Paid 3 years
David McGill	2,200	Paid 528 lbs. Tobacco
Dennis Conyers	840	Paid 202 lbs. Tobacco
Captain Henry Conyers	1,975	Paid 948 lbs. Tobacco. Paid 2 years. and John Mauzey's land included
Sarah Colbert	109	Not demanded
Benjamin Coleclough	100	Paid 24 lbs.Tobacco. Sold part to John Allen
Thomas Chapman	150	Can't hear of him
George Calvert	417	Promised payment
John Calvert	100	Paid 72 lbs. Tobacco. Paid 3 years.
Francis Coffer	520	In dispute with Colonel Mason
John Chadwell	300	Paid 244 lbs. Tobacco. Paid 2 years.
George Crosby, Sr.	222	Paid 153 lbs. Tobacco

[Mutilated - several lines lost]

Alexander Cummings	50	Paid 24 lbs. Tobacco. Paid 2 years.
Idem in King George County	220	Paid 108 lbs.Tobacco. Paid 2 years.
Ralph Cotten	460	Promised payment
James Cordoner	450	In dispute
John Catlett	358	Promised payment
Sarah Conway	1,350	Promised payment
John Cornwall	170	Can't hear of him
Jo.S Chapman	795	No such land to be found
Thomas Carpenter	346	No such land to be found
Jo.S Chapman	150	Paid 108 lbs. Tobacco. Paid 3 years.
Char: Corbin	300	Part of James Butler's land. Lives in Westmoreland County
Marquis Calmeus	700	Part of Stephen Fuller's land
John Champ	200	Paid 192 lbs. Tobacco. Paid 4 years.
Jo.S Combs	243	Paid 59 lbs. Tobacco. Land that was Michael Judd's.
John Creel	100	Part of William Spiller's land.

PERSONS NAMES	NUMBER OF ACRES	PROPERTY ALTERED; AMOUNTS PAID; WHY NOT PAID AND GENERAL REMARKS
D		
Mich.ª Dermott	636	Paid 153 lbs. Tobacco.
[Mutilated - several lines lost]		
Samuel Durham	100	
Mattix Derrick	600	Paid 192 lbs. Tobacco.
Robert Duncomb	230	Land in King George County
William Darrell's orphans	1,414	Paid 339 lbs. Tobacco.
Samuel Demovell	404	Westmoreland County land - unseated.
William O'Daniel	300	Paid 72 lbs. Tobacco.
Richard Davis	476	Not demanded
E		
George Eskridge	2,298	Refuseth payment
Thomas Ellzey	518	
Thomas Edge	150	
Nathaniel Elkins	75	Paid 36 lbs. Tobacco. Paid 2 years.
Richard Elkins	75	Paid 72 lbs. Tobacco. Paid 4 years.
Thomas Eaves	50	Paid 12 lbs. Tobacco.
John Elzey	150	
F		
Daniel French	550	Paid 132 lbs. Tobacco.
Idem	903	Paid 216 lbs. Tobacco. Part of Mott Doniphan's land.
Gerrard Fowkes	1,032	Paid £ 1.0.8
Richard Foote	405	Paid 97 lbs. Tobacco.
James Fletcher	100	Paid 24 lbs. Tobacco.
Abraham Farrow	2,550	Paid 757 lbs. Tobacco; 145 lbs. in balance for 1722.
Daniel Field	100	Paid 24 lbs. Tobacco.
Bryan Fowley's orphans	150	Not demanded
Stephen Fuller	944	Lawfully demanded and sold part.
Henry Filkins	50	Refuseth. Sold part to sundry persons.
James French	100	Paid 96 lbs. Tobacco. Paid 4 years. Part of Henry Filkin's land.
James Fulk	200	Lives in Northumberland County.
Colonel William Fitzhugh	17,630	Paid 5,016 lbs. Tobacco. Due 242 lbs. Tobacco. 600 acres paid in King George County for 1722.
[mutilated] Fitzhugh	3,375	Paid £ 3.7.6

[Mutilated - several lines lost; probably Fitzhugh entries as the family held considerable more land than is listed above.]

PERSONS NAMES	NUMBER OF ACRES	PROPERTY ALTERED; AMOUNTS PAID; WHY NOT PAID AND GENERAL REMARKS
G		
[Mutilated - several lines lost]		
John Grigsby	940	Paid 224 lbs. Tobacco.
James Gregg	600	Promised payment.
Thomas Garner	2,000	Paid 480 lbs. Tobacco.
John Goslin	400	Paid 233 lbs. Tobacco. Paid 2 years, and 41 lbs. Tobacco for 1721.
Major Gwin	800	Lawfully demanded.
Patrick Grady	150	
Jo.^{s} Guess	386	Not demanded.
Walter Griffin	426	Not demanded.
Jacob Gibson	100	Paid 72 lbs. Tobacco. Paid 3 years.
Jeremiah Greenham	316	Lives in Lancaster County.
William Goin	266	Taken away by Colonel Lee's survey.
[Mutilated - several lines lost]		
H		
Thomas Hopper's heir	60	Paid 28 lbs. Tobacco. Paid 2 years.
Blageane Hopper	248	Paid 14 lbs. Tobacco and ye rest paid in King George County.
Charles Harrison	190	Land Unknown.
Widow Heabeard	450	Paid 216 lbs. Tobacco. Paid 2 years.
John Hudman	100	Can't hear of him.
John Higgison	100	Promised payment.
Richard Hews	600	Northumberland County - unseated.
John Hall	500	Paid 360 lbs. Tobacco. Paid 3 years.
Colonel Rice Hooe	4,200	Paid £ 4.4.1
William Harrison	3,302	Paid 500 lbs. Tobacco ye rest in dispute with Colonel Lee.
Nathaniel Hedgman	450	Paid 216 lbs. Tobacco. Paid 2 years.
Elias Hore	896	Paid 216 lbs. Tobacco.
John Hancock	650	Promised payment.
Charles Hinson	190	Paid 48 lbs. Tobacco.
Widow Hawley	565	Lawfully demanded.
William Hawley	520	Paid 125 lbs. Tobacco.
[Mutilated - several lines lost]		
Richard Higgins	400	Paid 96 lbs. Tobacco.
Robert Hedges	600	Paid 144 lbs. Tobacco.
Captain Thomas Harrison	1,629	Paid 781 lbs. Tobacco.
Burr Harrison	200	Paid 96 lbs. Tobacco. Paid 2 years. Part of Captain Harrison's land.

PERSONS NAMES	NUMBER OF ACRES	PROPERTY ALTERED; AMOUNTS PAID; WHY NOT PAID AND GENERAL REMARKS
John Herryford	315	Paid 62 lbs. Tobacco in part; due 13 lbs. Tobacco.
Widow Hewitt	1,200	Paid 980 lbs. Tobacco in part for 4 years; due 172 lbs. Tobacco.
Thomas Harrison	350	Paid 84 lbs. Tobacco.
Captain Thomas Hooper	1,060	Paid 254 lbs. Tobacco.
Idem in King George County	1,260	Paid 304 lbs. Tobacco.

J

Thomas James	330	Paid 80 lbs. Tobacco. 100 acres sold to Robert Carter, Esqr
Samuel Jackson	460	Lawfully demanded.
Margery Janeways	150	
Sir Jeofrey Jeofreys	14,114	

[Mutilated - several lines lost]

Jackson's orphans	469	John Peake has ye orphans.
Thomas Jackson	460	Can't hear of him.
Emanuel Jones	2,200	of Gloucester County.
Richard Johnson for Wheeler's heirs	125	

K

Mathew Keen	400	Paid 96 lbs. Tobacco.
Keeife	230	Not demanded.
Widow Kneaton	300	Paid 72 lbs. Tobacco.
Jo^s King	220	
Wilford Kelly	50	Paid 12 lbs. Tobacco.
Isaac Kent	150	Paid 2 years but for 150 acres.
Kent	173	Paid 143 lbs. Tobacco. Paid 4 years.

[Mutilated - several lines lost]

L

[Mutilated]   Lord

[Mutilated - several lines lost]

Colonel Thomas Lee	3,663	Not demanded.
Maurice Lynah	646	
Moses Lynton	79	Paid 57 lbs. Tobacco. Paid 3 years.
John Lynton	1,050	Lawfully demanded.
Thomas Longman	630	Can't hear of him.

PERSONS NAMES	NUMBER OF ACRES	PROPERTY ALTERED; AMOUNTS PAID; WHY NOT PAID AND GENERAL REMARKS
Mildred Lewis	2,500	Paid 1,068 lbs. Tobacco in part for 4 years. Due 280 lbs. Tobacco.
William Lock	400	Land unknown.
Hancock Lee's orphans	3,235	Not demanded.
Richard Lee	235	Not demanded.
Thomas Leatchman's orphans	316	Not demanded.
John Lewis	[?]	Paid 133 lbs. Tobacco. Land y^t was Thomas Sandiford's.
[Mutilated] Lomax	[?]	Part of Joseph Waugh's land.

M

Colonel George Mason	18,807	Paid 4,514 lbs. Tobacco.
French Mason	1,455	Paid 256 lbs. Tobacco - in part. Due 281 lbs. Tobacco.
Dade Massey	1,200	Paid 288 lbs. Tobacco.
John Marr	100	Not demanded.
James Millykin	200	Paid 96 lbs. Tobacco. Paid 2 years.
Thomas Mathews	300	Heirs in England. Wheeller holds 600 acres.
Benjamin Massey	200	Paid 48 lbs. Tobacco.
John Mountjoy	100	
Widow Martin	50	Promised payment.
George Mason	150	
Daniel Matheny	662	Paid 164 lbs. Tobacco.
Captain Daniel McCartey	6,898	Paid 941 lbs. Tobacco - in part.
William McCartey	150	Paid 36 lbs. Tobacco.
John Meely	150	Paid 144 lbs. Tobacco. Paid 4 years.
Mathew Moss	350	
Thomas Morris	1,280	

[Mutilated - several lines lost]

N

William Newton	270	Lives in Westmoreland County.
Benjamin Newton	200	Paid 48 lbs. Tobacco.
Widow Norman	150	Lawfully demanded.
Henry Norman	175	Paid 34 lbs. Tobacco - in part. Due 8 lbs. Tobacco.
Rosewal Neile	300	Paid 144 lbs. Tobacco. Paid 2 years.
Philip Nowland	250	Paid 60 lbs. Tobacco. Land y^t was Nicholas Carrell's.
William Normand's orphans	400	Can't hear of them.
Widow Nowland	100	Can't hear of her.

PERSONS NAMES	NUMBER OF ACRES	PROPERTY ALTERED; AMOUNTS PAID; WHY NOT PAID AND GENERAL REMARKS
O		
William Overhall	100	Paid 24 lbs. Tobacco.
Thomas Owsley	600	
Daniel and John Orea	400	
P		
Thomas Paise	438	Paid 420 lbs. Tobacco. Paid 4 years.
Idem	408	Holds no such land.
Humphrey Pope	266	Westmoreland County; not demanded.
George Prockter	150	Lawfully demanded.
Magery Page	438	Paid 105 lbs. Tobacco.
John Page	400	Paid 192 lbs. Tobacco. Paid 2 years.
William Perkins	176	Not demanded.
John Pratt	175	Paid three years.
William Purlow	150	Part of Henry Filkins' land. Refuseth.
John Peake	1,600	Paid 384 lbs. Tobacco.
Philip Payton	100	
William Payton	150	Paid 36 lbs. Tobacco.
John Payton	100	Paid 24 lbs. Tobacco.
[?] Payton	100	

[Mutilated - several lines lost]

R		
Lewis Renoe	581	Paid 317 lbs. Tobacco. Paid 2 years. Paid 36 lbs. Tobacco for 1721.
Richard Rowley	275	Pays in King George County.
Richard Rosser	150	Pays in King George County.
William Ridoles orphan's	106	Land unknown.
John Rout	143	Land unknown.
Thomas Robinson	150	Land unknown.
Captain James Rankins	320	Heirs in England.
Colonel William Robinson	2,276	Paid 546 lbs. Tobacco.
Richard Rout	200	Can't hear of him.
Richard Rowley	283	Can't hear of him.
[?] Russel	[?]	Not demanded.

[Mutilated - three lines lost]

S		
William Smith	150	Pays in King George County.
Absolum Spicer	83	Pays in King George County.
Joseph Sumner	2,200	Paid 386 lbs. Tobacco - in part. Due 94 lbs. Tobacco.

PERSONS NAMES	NUMBER OF ACRES	PROPERTY ALTERED; AMOUNTS PAID; WHY NOT PAID AND GENERAL REMARKS
John Scott	200	
Francis Spencer	2,500	Pays in Westmoreland County.
Widow Stribling	66	
Benjamin Stribling	33	
Thomas Simpson	1,050	Paid 252 lbs. Tobacco; holds but 1050 acres.
Thomas Sharp	100	Paid 24 lbs. Tobacco.
William Sewell	50	Lawfully demanded.
Smallwood's Heirs	150	Lawfully demanded.
William Struttfield	1,034	Land unknown.
Thomas Simmons	600	Paid 96 lbs. Tobacco - in part. Due 48 lbs. Tobacco.
Mary Sheild	200	

[Mutilated - several lines lost]

Samuel Seldon	1,500	
ye Rev^d. Alexander Scott	2,836	Paid 680 lbs. Tobacco.
Idem	450	Paid 108 lbs. Tobacco.
Thomas Seddon	429	Paid 155 lbs. Tobacco.
Robert Singleton	750	Lives in Gloucester County.
Peter Smith	1,160	Lives in Westmoreland County.
John Spry's heirs	395	Lives in Northumberland County.
Patrick Spence	230	No patent for this land.
John Sutton	100	Can't hear of him.
John De la Shoemake	200	Not demanded.
John Smith	100	Paid 24 lbs. Tobacco. Part of Thomas Brooks' land.
John Stone of King George Co.	150	Part of James Butler's land.

T

Giles Tillitt	400	Paid 96 lbs. Tobacco.
Rawleigh Travers	3,525	Paid 362 lbs. Tobacco - in part. Due 484 lbs. Tobacco.
Richard Tullis	200	Paid Mr. Thos. Berry in Northumberland.
Samuel Todd	100	Promised payment.
Daniel Tebbs	116	Lives in Westmoreland County.
Anthony Thornton	350	Paid £ 0.7.0
Thomas Timmons	243	Paid 60 lbs. Tobacco.
Charles Tyler	749	10 acres overcharged. Promised.
Owen Thomas	443	Paid in part 54 lbs. Tobacco.
John Todd for Hillburn's heirs	290	Now John Peake's.
Idem	236	Holds no such land.
[?] Todd	405	Refuseth.

[Mutilated - several lines lost]

PERSONS NAMES	NUMBER OF ACRES	PROPERTY ALTERED; AMOUNTS PAID; WHY NOT PAID AND GENERAL REMARKS
V		
Elias Vickers	100	Not demanded.
Maurice Veale	266	Paid 266 lbs. Tobacco. Paid 4 years.
John Veale	266	Lives in Westmoreland County.
W		
William Williams	170	Land unknown.
Thomas Walker	382	Lives in Westmoreland County.
[Mutilated - several lines lost]		
Captain William Woodbridge	500	Lives in Richmond County.
John Washington	1,100	Paid 262 lbs. Tobacco.
Joshua Whitson	100	Can't hear of him.
John Waugh's orphans	6,163	Paid 5,916 lbs. Tobacco. Paid 4 years.
Widow Ann West	350	Can't hear of her.
William Wigginton	89	Paid 21 lbs. Tobacco.
Henry Wigginton	100	Paid 24 lbs. Tobacco.
Francis Wadington	300	Lawfully demanded.
John Wood	2,360	Heirs live in Maryland.
John Wheeler	1,701	Paid 408 lbs. Tobacco. Part of Thomas Mathews' land.
James Withers	1,766	Paid 422 lbs. Tobacco. 100 acres of Joseph Waugh's land.
William Whitson	400	Paid 96 lbs. Tobacco.
Thomas Whitledge	922	Paid 220 lbs. Tobacco.
David Waugh	1,500	Lawfully demanded.
Henry Washington	300	Paid 72 lbs. Tobacco.
[Mutilated - several lines lost]		
Thomas Watts	100	Paid 24 lbs. Tobacco.
Augustine Washington	300	
Idem	248	Part of Michael Dermott's.
Richard Watts	1,208	Belongs to John Chilton, Westmoreland County.
Y		
Bryan Young	369	Paid 90 lbs. Tobacco.
William Young	330	Lives in Westmoreland County.

****
**

Total number of acres	301,969

SECTION IV

TENDERS OF TOBACCO

IN

OVERWHARTON PARISH

1724

TENDERS OF TOBACCO IN OVERWHARTON PARISH

IN ORDER TO "improve the Staple of Tobacco" the House of Burgesses in May 1723 passed The Tobacco Act; this legislation was to be effective April 1, 1724. This law provided that all laboring persons may tend 6,000 tobacco plants and no more, and that male persons between the ages of 10 and 16 years may tend 3,000 tobacco plants. Liberty was given to housekeepers to tend 10,000 tobacco plants. Persons interested in The Tobacco Acts of 1723 and 1729 will find them in The Virginia Magazine of History and Biography, Volume 20, pages 158-178.

The Tobacco Act of 1723 caused two lists of tobacco tenders in Overwharton Parish to be compiled. While there may have been others these two, preserved in The Virginia State Library, are the only ones known to this compiler. They are helpful in bridging the gap left by the destruction of many of the Stafford County records and the sparse recordings for the early years covered by The Register of Overwharton Parish. The names of all Negroes have been omitted.

* * *

"A List of the Tithables Allow'd to Tend Tobacco and Quantity of Plants in the Precincts Between Aquia and Quantico [Creeks] Viz."

NAMES	TITH-ABLES	PLANTS	NAMES	TITH-ABLES	PLANTS
Thomas Masters)	2	13,000	Walter Humphrys)	2	1,800
James Gorman)			Hugh Evans)		
Garret Masters 13#			William Hand 10#		
Henry Wigington)			Alexander Nelson		3,500
William Kirk)	3	6,000			
George Clemmons)			Samuel Whitson		1,500
William Wigington 14#					
Henry Wigington 11#			James Fletcher)		
			William Fletcher)	4	14,254
Edward Pontone)			Moses Fletcher)		
Denis Lee)	3	10,700	Joseph Whitson)		
Charles Coale)			Michael Morne 15#		
Thomas Grubbs 14#			Aaron Fletcher 14#		
A Negro 14#					
			William Mason)	3	300
			2 Negroes)		

- This character means years of age, viz: Garret Masters 13 years of age.

NAMES	TITH-ABLES	PLANTS	NAMES	TITH-ABLES	PLANTS
Amos Chadburn)	2	9,000	James Starke)	3	18,000
William Chadburn)			2 Negroes)		
Tobias Wood		6,500	George Grant)	4	11,860
			3 Negroes)		
John Wigington		9,700			
			James Cork		8,818
Joseph Macully		5,000			
			Thomas Burke		9,550
Michael Judd)					
Michael Judd, Jun.ʳ)			At William Fenwick		
William Judd)	5	20,000	2 Negroes)	2	11,000
Benjamin Macully)					
William White)			At Bunch Roe		
Isaac Judd 10#			5 Negroes)	6	21,500
At Mr. Alexander			John Holms)		
Scott's Quarter			Thomas Holms)		
Edward Waters)			James Holms)	5	12,710
Scott Anderer)	5	29,975	Christopher Holms)		
3 Negroes)			Gabriel Lavey)		
			[?] Holmes 14#		
Joseph Combs)			Edmund Holmes 11#		
James Ceed)					
Sofias Rogers)	6	36,000	Thomas Snow	1	2,812
Patrick Barraway)					
2 Negroes)			At Francis Hamersly)		
			Michael Mosey)	6	26,858
At Mr. John FitzHugh's Quarter			4 Negroes)		
James Quidle)			A Negro boy 12#		
Alice Parker)	7	30,270			
William Travis)			At Mrs. Susanna Brent		
4 Negroes)			Martin Lions)-	7	17,245
			6 Negroes)		
Henry Young		1,500	A Negro Boy 12#		
At Capt. Hoare			Bryan Chamlin)	2	16,658
Henry Jones)			William Chamlin)		
Christopher Bigam)	7	30,000	Bryan Chamlin Jun.ʳ 14#		
5 Negroes)			Aaron Chamlin 12#		
At Mr. Cooke			William Bethell	1	2,880
John Skanes)			Edward Bethell 14#		
Robert Smith)	6	30,420	[?] Bethell 10#		
4 Negroes)					
Negro boy 12#			Benjamin George	1	3,000

NAMES	TITH-ABLES	PLANTS	NAMES	TITH-ABLES	PLANTS
Thomas Whitledge)			At Morrice Bevans		9,208
Thomas Whitledge Jr.)			on Acco^t Tho. Barton		21,773
William Whitledge)	6	34,537			
William Anderson)			William Spiller)		
2 Negroes)			John Spiller)	4	17,210
John Whitledge			Warington Spiller)		
			William Grubs)		
Mathew Kelly)	1	980			
			William Spiller,Junr	1	6,000
At Captain Thomas Harrison					
Thomas Harrison Jr.)			William Howell)	1	8,455
Nat Jacobs)					
Thomas Quin)	*	44,929	Charles Gwatkins)		
2 Negroes)			John Chadburn)	4	25,700
William Kelly)			William Whitesides)		
Jacob White) Boys			William Parsons)		
2 Negro boys)			A Negro boy		
Morrice Bevans)			[Mutilated] Moss)	2	16,000
Patrick Lynch)	4	24,000	James Steward)		
William Fearnsby)					
James Maglaughlin)			Thomas Barton,Junr)	1	3,500
James Hagard)	1	11,554	James French)	1	10,315
James Hagard Jr. 14#			William Dolehy 15#		
Richard Hagard 12#					
William Hagard 11#			William Thorne)	1	16,000
			Daniel Orea 14#		
John Young)	2	6,905	John Orea 11#		
James Humstead)					
			William Purler)	1	7,950
William Adams)	2	11,020			
George Adams)			William Triplet)	5	26,898
			4 Negroes)		
John Adams, Senr)					
Richard Adams)	3	15,812	Lewis Renoe)		
Daniel Adams)			Thomas Renoe)	3	21,594
George Burn 15#			Henry Moffet)		
			Lewis Renoe, Junr)		
John Nelson)	1	600	Francis Renoe) Nonage		
William Slaid 13#			Gabriel Moffet)		
Thomas Barton)			At Lewis Tacquet		
Valentine Barton)	3	12,565	James Gainer	*	11,310
Bur Barton)			Lewis Tacquet, Junr 15#		
James Barton 13#			John Tacquet 12#		

* Number of tithables not entered

NAMES	TITH-ABLES	PLANTS	NAMES	TITH-ABLES	PLANTS
Philemon Waters)	*	12,312	Michael Dearman)	*	12,878
William Rice)			Michael Dearman Jr. 13#		
Phil Waters, Junr 13#			William Miller 13#		
Thomas Waters 10#					
			Daniel Blackman)	*	3,000
Edward Askins	*	7,517			
			James Pendrgrass)	*	5,210
John Catlet)	*	16,000			
John Catlet, Junr)			John Jackson)	*	4,109
			John McMillion)		
William Simson)	2	12,000			
Moses Gess)			Henry Justice)	*	7,660
William Simson,Junr			John Justice 12#		
William Gess					
			Robert Ashby	*	2,586
At Edward Feagins					
3 Negroes)	3	18,000	Samuel Timmons)	*	2,860
Edward Shute at home		1,400	Edward Grimes)	*	15,568
at Edward Feagins		3,950	Charles Grimes 12#		
		5,350	John Grimes 10#		
Thomas Ashby	1		Roger Day)	*	3,895
at Thomas Drummon on					
his account		2,245	Abraham Griffin)	*	1,872
			Edward Wood 11#		
Thomas Drummon)	*	14,510			
Samuel Drummon)			Marquiss Calamees)	*	3,925
James Drummon 12#					
			Henry Hardin)		
James Mullikin)	1	3,000	Zenony Willson)	*	10,035
			William Jenkinson)		
Mathew Gess)	1	380	John Leechman 15#		
			Henry Hardin Jr. 10#		
John Shumate)	1	7,372			
Samuel Shumate 14#			George Williams)	*	1,867
Daniel Shumate 12#			Geo. Williams, Junr 14#		
William Hogin)	1	4,018	John Greston)	*	3,523
John Shumate, Junr)	1	4,120	At Col. Mason's Quarter in		
			ye fork of Aquia Run		
Mathew Simmons)	*	2,300	John Moore)	*	7,041
			3 Negroes)		
Thomas Simmons)	*	3,450			
			John Hall)	*	4,543

* Number of tithables not entered

NAMES	TITH-ABLES	PLANTS	NAMES	TITH-ABLES	PLANTS
Abraham Bridwell) William Bridwell) John Bridwell 13#	*	7,084	Edward Cumberford) John McKenterse) Moses Congrove) A Negro) James Cotten 13#	*	18,711
Edward Berry) John Conly)	*	9,051	Mary Purler) Patrick Mugier) John Chapman Purler	*	15,914
Richard Frister) Richard Frister Jr. 10#	*	1,018	Joseph Chapman)	*	6,823
Abraham Bridwell,Jr.)	*	7,925	John Parker at Joseph Chapman's		2,595
Benjamin Bullett) Philemon Dermot) James Burne)	3	17,259	Thomas Smith at home at Joseph Chapman Richard Parker 13#		2,010 4,331 6,341
William Bennet) John Lowden) Mason Bennet 13# W.m Bennet,Jun.r 11#	2	12,705	Leonard Knight) Christopher Knight) Isaac Knight) Epraim Knight)	*	8,270
Robert Hedges at home At John Farrow		2,178 379 2,557	William Murphy) Thomas Murphy) James Leatherland 10#	*	13,308
Abraham Farrow) Anderson Poore) William Downing) A Negro	*	24,000	John Hall) John Hall, Jun.r 15# Edward Hall	*	16,000
William Farrow) 2 Negroes) John Hogins 13#	*	12,026	Henry Nellson) Alexander Simson 10#	*	10,460
Mr. Abraham Farrow) Richard Pierson) William Rouse) 2 Negroes 10# & 16#	*	6,229	Ralph Cotten)	*	4,126
John Maddin)	*	1,776	Richard Higgins) John Hedges 12#	*	1,875
William Graves) John Gibbons) Mathew Graves 10#	*	[blank]	At John Shelton's Quarter Murphy Brand) 4 Negroes) 1 Negro boy	*	12,437
			John Higerson)	*	3,830

* Number of tithables not entered

NAMES	TITH-ABLES	PLANTS	NAMES	TITH-ABLES	PLANTS
Burr Harrison) Michael McCormick) A Negro	*	11,042	Peter Battue)	*	1,600
John Malt) Richard Davis) Thomas Davis)	*	2,981	Henry Filkin)	*	6,500

[Signed]   Henry Filkin

Henry Young

Copy Test

Geo: Mason

Cl:Cur:

* * *

"A List of Tobacco Tenders from the South Side of Potomack [Creek] To ye Lower End of Overwarton Parish" [1]

TOBACCO TENDERS	TOBACCO PLANTS	TOBACCO TENDERS	TOBACCO PLANTS
John Chadwell) John Chadwell, Junr) James Chadwell) George Chadwell) William Chadwell #) Joseph Chadwell #)	31,279	William McCarty)	10,000
John McDaniel) Edward Grady) John McDaniel #)	12,388	Garret Farrell)	6,661
		Catherin Smith)	2,689
		James Bates)	717
John Travis) Nathaniel Morgan) Owen Sullivant) Thomas Hardman) 6 Negroes	21,102	John Gregsby) Thomas Gregsby) William Gregsby)	15,593
		Benjamin Gregsby)	[mutilated]
		James Gregsby)	8,225

* No. of tithables not entered
1- On this list no definite ages are given. Names followed by this character [#]
   are in a separate column indicating they are between 10 and 16 years of age.

TOBACCO TENDERS		TOBACCO PLANTS	TOBACCO TENDERS		TOBACCO PLANTS
William Gregsby	)		Vivion Limbrick	)	5,188
Owen Daily	)				
John Hum	)	22,780	Ann Grant	)	1,546
William Walker	#)				
William Gregsby	#)		Mealy Whitecotton	)	
			Husband Whitecotton #	)	10,416
Charles Gregsby	)		Timothy Carty	#)	
James Gregsby	)	8,312			
John Macduel	#)		Alexander Jeffrys	)	9,085
Charles Gregsby	#)				
			John Waugh	)	1,314
Joseph Hall	)	4,938	1 Negro	)	
Richard Duggins	)	6,581	John Boring	)	9,534
Capt. Chandler Fowlke	)		Thomas James	)	
Edward Sweeting	)		John James	#)	23,882
John Cooper	)	43,848	Joseph James	#)	
6 Negroes	)		2 Negroes	)	
2 Boys	#)		Alexander Sinkler	)	
			William Stone	)	
Joseph Chambers	)		Wayman Sinkler	#)	24,000
Patrick Johnson	)	38,988	John Sinkler	#)	
6 Negroes	)		1 Negro	)	
3 Boys	#)				
			Thomas Botts	)	
David Waugh	)	876	Thomas Botts	#)	15,770
			John Botts	#)	
Mary Smith	)	46	Seth Botts	#)	
James Mullin	)	2,069	John Taylor	)	
			Robert Lynes	)	20,076
Lewis Elzey's Quarter			William Chilton	)	
William Cave	)		1 Negro	)	
3 Negroes	)	9,157			
2 Negro Boys	#)		John Pattison	)	7,469
Joseph Waugh's Quarter			Robert Sturdy	)	2,605
John Smith	)				
Joseph Waugh	#)	19,469	Edward Henson	)	
4 Negroes	)		Joseph Henson	)	15,377
1 Negro Boy	#)		James Henson	#)	
James Gregg	)		James Jones	)	7,007
Thomas Gregg	)	2,072			
James Gregg, Junr	)		Richard Johnson	)	9,675

TOBACCO TENDERS		TOBACCO PLANTS
Capt. Henry Fitzhugh's Quarter		
5 Negroes	)	28,797
John Wheeler	)	19,274
	)	
James Taylor	)	
2 Negroes	)	
George Clark	)	2,867
Thomas Jenkins	)	2,031
Henry Suddarth	)	154
Philip Payton	)	5,981
Patrick Grady	)	8, 698
John Payton	#)	
Snowdal Horton	)	9,377
John Courtney	)	
Luke Scanlen	)	13,618
1 Negro	)	
Charles Payton	)	2,871
John Lamb	)	
John Elzey	)	50
Negro Robin	)	
Margaret Warrington	)	6,593
2 Negroes	)	
Charles Blisford	)	12,570
Thomas McCarty	#)	
Joseph Sumner	)	
James Daniel	)	50,638
Andrew Baily	)	
7 Negroes	)	
John Chandler	)	
George Downing	)	15,379
Richard Whitson	)	
Richard Whitcomb	)	10,000 Cut 1,485

TOBACCO TENDERS		TOBACCO PLANTS
John Simson	)	
John Robertson	)	
John Simson	#)	32,805
John Dogen	#)	
Lenn Stanton	#)	
Charles Webster	)	12,099
Edward Webster	#)	
John Foley	)	
John Canzy	)	
John Brown	)	27,000 Cut
John Foley	#)	1,485
James Foley	#)	
1 Negro	#)	
Richard Foley	)	
Henry Foley	#)	10,499
John May	#)	
Thomas Fletcher	)	10,359
James Fletcher	#)	
Joseph Philips	)	5,471
Randall Holebrook	)	
Alexander Robertson	)	20,828
2 Negroes	)	
Richard Wintn [Winty]	)	6,363
Jacob Jacobs	)	7,953
Thomas Harrison	)	
3 Negroes	)	27,000 Cut
1 Negro Boy	#)	923
Timothy O'Doneal	)	12,244
John O'Doneal	#)	
Francis Watts	)	2,871
James Kemp	)	
Motoone Lewis	)	890
William Mathews	)	
Samuel Mathews	#)	
James Mathews	#)	18,535
Benjamin Mathews	#)	

TOBACCO TENDERS			TOBACCO PLANTS	TOBACCO TENDERS			TOBACCO PLANTS
Thomas Barby		)	5,471	Joseph Waugh's Quarter			
James Norris	#	)		John Smith		)	3,629
James Withers		)	22,751	George Clark		)	10,735
4 Negroes		)		John Clark	#	)	
William Smith		)	7,427	Francis Spaldin		)	5,667
				John Spaldin		)	
John Scott		)					
Joseph Simmons		)		Edward Wayman		)	8,019
Francis Kelly		)	19,151	William Limbrick		)	
Charles Simmons	#	)					
1 Negro		)		Daniel McHeasant [?]		)	
				Joseph Watts		)	23,921
George Henry		)		Alexander Carson		)	
Oliver King		)	6,138	1 Negro		)	
George County		)					
				William Cave		)	1,882
				1 Negro		)	

Charles Payton

and   Counters

Joshua   Davis

Copy Test

Geo: Mason
Cl:Cur:

* * *

Neither of the above lists of Tenders of Tobacco in Overwharton Parish are dated.
The dates of both, however, are firmly fixed as 1724 mainly by the Tobacco Act of
May 1723 which was to be effective April 1, 1724.   Several persons who are listed with a definitely stated age later make depositions which confirm 1724 as the
true date of these lists. John Orea [Oriar], aged 11 years [page 159] made a deposition in Prince William County court on March 21, 1796 and stated he was 83
years of age.
Colonel George Mason (1690-1735) who certified these copies was clerk of Stafford
Court (1719-November 11, 1724). He suceeded his brother-in-law, Thomas Fitzhugh,
Gentleman, (circa 1689-1719) upon his death and was succeeded by Catesby Cocke
who served until March 11, 1731 when he became clerk of the newly formed county
of Prince William.

SECTION V

A HISTORICAL SKETCH

OF

OVERWHARTON PARISH

SECTION V

A HISTORICAL SKETCH

THE FIRST ENGLISHMEN to view the lands which were to become Overwharton Parish were a party under the command of Captain John Smith; they left Jamestown in the summer of 1608 and explored the Potomac River from its mouth to the falls. They found the Northern Neck peninsula occupied by Algonquin Indians in all respects similiar to those previously encountered on the James and forming part of the same Powhatan confederacy. Their principal town, Patowmacke ("the place where the tribute is brought"), from which the great river took its final English name, was on the estuary still called Potomac Creek. The peninsula itself was patented by Colonel Giles Brent (circa 1600-1672) and called Potomac Neck and later Peale's Neck after Captain Malachi Peale (16 -1698) who was living there in 1691 when fifty acres of land in Potomac Neck were appropriated as the public port town for Stafford County and designated to be called Marlborough.

For fifteen years after Smith's explorations, the Jamestown colony kept in touch, almost in alliance, with the Indians of the Potomac River in order to trade for their corn, and thus the town of Patowmacke [Potomac] became the scene of some of the most vivid of the early adventures of the colony. Here young Captain Henry Spelman, an Englishman of gentle birth lived several years with the Indians, mastered their language, and has left us an interesting account of his experiences there. It was also at Potomac Town that Captain Samuel Argall kidnapped the Indian Princess Pocahontas and carried her to Jamestown where she met and married John Rolfe. In 1622 Captain Raleigh Croshaw erected a fort on Potomac Neck and devised statesmanlike plans for the conquest of the country by setting the Indians at logger heads among themselves. With Ralph Hamer, Captain Croshaw made an alliance with Japasaw, Prince of the Passapantanzy Tribe and brother of the King of the Potomacs, against Opechancanough which Captain Isaac Madison violated in a sudden reflex of the passions aroused by the massacre at Jamestown on Good Friday 1622. Captain Madison and his garrison at Potomac Neck feared treachery and became alarmed for their safety. They captured the King of the Potomacs, his son and four of his great men, slew thirty or forty of the men, women and children of the town and escaped to Jamestown, taking his prisoners with him and forcing the village of Potomac to ransom them with corn. Although George Sandys, Esq., Treasurer of Virginia 1621-1625, subsequently renewed the treaty with the Potomacs, Madison's unhappy outrage had definitely ended all confidence in Jamestown by the Potomac tribes and the outpost so early established at Potomac Neck was withdrawn.

When Maryland was founded in 1634 by a settlement at Saint Mary's on the Potomac River, Virginia had not extended her settlements north of the York River. That estuary was, indeed, recognized as a political boundry as late as October 1646 in the treaty of peace and amity made with the Powhatan nation after the death of Opechancanough. The Northern Neck of Virginia was thus Indian territory and practically outside the jurisdiction of Virginia during all the early years of

Saint Mary's. The interesting fact is that the history of the settlement of the
Northern Neck of Virginia begins in relation to Maryland rather than to Virginia.
Although the date is a bit uncertain, as early as 1644 a band of white men, hostile
to, but keenly interested in Maryland, were living among the Chicacoan tribe on
Coan River in the present county of Northumberland across the Potomac River from
Saint Mary's. These men were Protestants and former residents of Kent Island,
Maryland, during the occupancy of Colonel William Claiborne (1600-1676) of Virginia, who had, after a bitter struggle, surrendered the island to the powerful Catholic, Lord Baltimore, in 1637. They had settled in Saint Mary's County, but becom-
ing involved in Ingle's Rebellion there took refuge across the Potomac River to
escape the tyranny of Governor Leonard Calvert, brother of Lord Baltimore and governor of Maryland, who was very hostile to these Protestants. The entire story is
most interestingly told by Mr. Nathaniel Claiborne Hale in his masterly biography
of Colonel William Claiborne entitled Virginia Venturer [1951]. Among these early
Marylanders who "fled by night to the house of Mr. John Mottrom at Chicacoan were
Major Andrew Monroe [ancestor of President James Monroe (1758-1831)], Thomas Sturman, John Sturman, Francis Gray, and Thomas Youell; all of these men ultimately
became prominent citizens of Westmoreland County, Virginia.

After Ingle's Rebellion these men at Chicacoan were joined by a number of
recalcitrant Marylanders, and there being no court of record in the Northern Neck
of Virginia at the time, the most we learn of them is thru the Maryland records.
Remote from Jamestown and intent on "self-determination," these pioneers did not
for several years acknowledge any government; indeed, Captain Edward Hill [founder
of the Shirley family on James River] wrote letters from Chicacoan which spoke of
"returning to Virginia"! Under such conditions, Coan, as the name was soon abbre-
viated, became a nuisance to both Maryland and Virginia, and eventually and neces-
sarily had to be disciplined by the Virginia government. For this purpose the entire Northern Neck of Virginia was, in 1648, erected into the county of Northumberland.

However, before the county of Northumberland was created, a gentleman of
Catholic faith, weary of the bickerings of the Puritans in Maryland and of his own
dissatisfactions with the Calvert regime, crossed the Potomac River and settled on
the peninsula at the conflux of Aquia Creek with Potomac River, commonly called
since 1647 Brent's Point; this was the first permanent settlement in Overwharton
Parish. Colonel Giles Brent (circa 1600-1672), "first citizen" of Stafford County,
was the son of Sir Richard Brent (1573-1652), Lord of Stoke and Admington, in Gloucestershire. He had settled in Maryland in 1637 and married there Princess Kitta-
maquad, only child of the Emperor of the Piscataway Indians, who was given the
Christian name of Mary by Father Andrew White, S.J., upon her baptism in 1642. Upon
the death of his father-in-law and in right of his wife, Colonel Brent lay claim to
a large portion of Maryland which had been granted in 1632 by King Charles I of Eng
land to the Honorable Cecil Calvert (1605-1675), Second Lord Baltimore. Brent fell
into contentious but futile dispute over his Maryland land claims with Lord Baltimore and his brother the Honorable Leonard Calvert (circa 1610-1647), founder and
first governor of Maryland, and took his departure with his Indian bride, yet in
her teens, from that province late in 1647. He called his new home in Virginia
Peace and a bit later he moved a short distance up Aquia Creek and established another plantation which he called Retirement; he died there in 1672. He was followed
to Virginia from Maryland in 1651 by his two spinster sisters Mary Brent (circa

1600-1658) and Margaret Brent (1601-1671), both of whom left last wills and Testaments of record as did their brother Colonel Giles Brent. Mistress Margaret Brent was active in political affairs in Maryland and in 1648 demanded a vote in the Maryland General Assembly, on the grounds that she was the sole executrix of the late Honorable Leonard Calvert, Governor of Maryland. She appeared before the Maryland courts and her name is sometimes rendered in those records, Margaret Brent, Gentleman! She was the first woman suffragist in America and after her removal to Virginia lived at Peace. Giles, Margaret and Mary Brent received large land patents in Virginia and Mistress Margaret Brent was the first patentee of the lands upon which the present cities of Alexandria and Fredericksburg were to rise according to Chester Horton Brent in The Descendants of Coll? Giles Brent, Capt George Brent and Robert Brent, Gent: [1946].

While Colonel Giles Brent called his plantation in Virginia Peace, ironically it was not a place of complete tranquility. When Lord Baltimore learned of the removal of his former lieutenant governor across the Potomac River, he issued instructions in 1651 to Governor William Stone of Maryland to issue land patents in the Northern Neck, including "that place where Mr. Giles Brent now resides and called by him Peace," and sent into Virginia settlers with grants that bore his great seal. On March 16, 1654 Captain Gyles Brent appeared at the quarterly court held at Jamestown and requested that action be taken to protect the residents of the Northern Neck from the encroachments of Lord Baltimore and the ensuing investigation put an end to these troubles and nothing further was heard of it.

On March 23, 1662 Captain Giles Brent exhibited a charge of high treason and murder to the Grand Assembly sitting at Jamestown against Wahanganoche, King of the Potomac Indians, but the charges were dismissed by Governor Francis Moryson and the committee appointed to inquire into the differences between the English and the Indians on Potomac River. They decreed that Captain Giles Brent, Colonel Gerrard Fowke, Mr. John Lord and Captain George Mason had done the King of Potomacs many injustices, injuries and affronts and they were ordered to pay him various tributes and give bond "for their good behaviour especially towards the said Wahanganocke and his and all other Indians." They were also declared "incapable of holding any office civil or military in this countrey." However, this was a period of extremist action by those both in and out of office. Certainly later records show that their standing in the colony was not impaired. The trouble seems to have been caused by the murder of several Englishmen by the Indians, quarrels over land bounds, and other dissatisfactions. At the same court Wahanganoche, King of the Potomac Indians, acknowledged before the committee appointed for the Indian business, his sale of land to Henry Meese and Peter Ashton.

In regard to the trial at Jamestown, Colonel John Catlett (16 -1670) of Rappahannock County has left us some first hand information in his letter of April 1, 1664 to his cousin, Mr. Thomas Catlett in Kent, England. He describes the King of Potomacs as "one of an emperious spirit and very subtitle" and says that to the astonishment of all he was cleared and sent home with a reward. "But no sooner dismiss'd than Almighty God the Impartial Judge Sumoned ye notorious villaine to his great tribunal, to answer for those many murders comitted by him upon the English and others of his owne nation, for hee was arrested by death in his way home." Thus the last King of the great Potomac tribe died enroute to his native habitat in what was soon to become the new county of Stafford and shortly thereafter all the Potomac Indians seem to have vanished.

Within Overwharton Parish, in the ancient Roman Catholic cemetery on Aquia Creek, are buried the early members of the Brent family as well as many later members of the Brent and other Roman Catholic families who inhabited that area in the Seventeenth and Eighteenth Centuries.

Peace, established by Colonel Giles Brent in 1647, was some seventy miles up the Potomac River from the Chicacoan settlement and contemporary writers inform us that "all stopped by his home for refreshments and information." Captain George Brent (circa 1640-1697), nephew of Colonel Giles Brent, was sent from England to his uncle "to learn how to live," says a gentleman who knew him, and he established that well known seat called Woodstock on upper Aquia Creek and gave rise to a numerous progeny.

The outpost established in 1647 at Brent's point by Colonel Giles Brent in what was to be called in succession Potomac Parish, the upper Parish, Stafford Parish and finally about 1700 Overwharton Parish, greatly furthered the settlement of this entire region and this area was peopled considerably more rapidly than the opposite side of the Northern Neck on the Rappahannock River. Major John Taliaferro (1687-1744) of Spotsylvania County and his brother-in-law Francis Thornton, Gentleman, (1682-1758) of Caroline County, who resided on opposite sides of Snow Creek at its conflux with Rappahannock River, stated in depositions in 1736 that about 1707 they recollected the uppermost plantation on the North side of the Rappahannock River [now in Stafford County] was about three miles below the falls. The plantation to which these gentlemen refer is Little Falls Farm, originally a thousand acre tract which was seated by Alexander Swan of Lancaster County and by him sold in 1695 to John Newton late of Kingston upon Hull, Yorkshire, England, who had settled in Westmoreland County. Little Falls Farm was entailed male by the last will and Testament of John Newton (16 -1697) and descended to Major William Newton (circa 1720-1789) who died there. From the Newtons John Hobby had a lease of fifty acres on Little Falls Run; here he lived while he acted in the double capacity of sexton of Falmouth Church and schoolmaster. George Washington, residing at Ferry Farm a short distance up the Rappahannock River from Little Falls Farm, attended Master John Hobby's school in Falmouth.

While Colonel Giles Brent and his Roman Catholic followers were the first settlers in what was to become Overwharton Parish, Stafford County, their faith precluded any ecclesiastical connections with the parish. However, members of the Brent family were officers in the colonial militia, and the half-breed Colonel Giles Brent (1652-1679), who spoke the Indian language fluently, was much engaged in Indian warfare. Colonel Brent married his first cousin Mary Brent, sister of Colonel George Brent of Woodstock who was Attorney-General of Virginia in 1686 and represented Stafford County in the House of Burgesses in 1688.

The settlement upon Aquia Creek made by the Brents and their followers was destined to become the hub of an ever expanding community. Events in England in 1649-1650 gave rise to a great migration to Virginia and many of these emigrants during the Commonwealth settled in what was to become Stafford County. There they were joined from across the Potomac by a steady stream of settlers from Maryland and land patents issued in great numbers for large acreages. The several large navigable creeks which flow into the Potomac River were great assets and the river itself, wide and beautiful, made communication relatively easy for the colonial period.

Among these cavaliers who settled in Stafford County was Colonel George Mason
(1628-1686), a native of Staffordshire, England; it was doubtless thru his influence that the county of Stafford was so named. Colonel Mason received patents for
large acreages and lived on Accakeek Creek not far from Brooke. His son and heir,
Colonel George Mason (16 -1716) in 1694 sold "all that plantation commonly called
Accakeek being the late mansion house of Colonel George Mason, deceased," but re-
serving "the tomb of the said Colonel George Mason and the burying place in which
it stands." He moved to what is now Dogue Neck in Fairfax County, then called
Doags Island, and in 1704 paid quit rents on "my home seat of Doags Island" and
about 8,000 acres of land in Stafford County. Like his father, the first George
Mason, the son was actively engaged in surpressing the Indians in the upper regions
of Stafford County. He was thrice married and had a large family; he was the grandfather of the Honorable George Mason (1725-1792) of Gunston Hall, author of the
Bill of Rights.

Another early settler in Overwharton Parish before the organization of the
county and who indirectly left his mark there was Colonel Henry Meese (16 -1682),
a native of the Parish of Overwoorten in Oxfordshire. Unlike his contemporary,
Colonel George Mason who founded an aristocratic family, his name has long since
been forgotten by most persons. On November 19, 1665 he was sworn lieutenant colonel of the Stafford County militia and on the same day took the oath as a justice
of the peace. Colonel Meese was the first representative of Stafford County in the
House of Burgesses, 1666, and was appointed to the Council on March 14, 1679. He
resided on the south side of Potomac Creek and called his plantation Overwarton
after the parish of his birth. On December 12, 1681 he was replaced on the Council,
having returned to England. He shortly wrote his last will and Testament in which
document he describes himself as "Henry Meese of London, Merchant, and Citizen and
Draper of London." This document was offered for probate on April 5, 1682 at the
Prerogative Court of Canterbury in London and he bequeathed all his "plantations,
lands, stock and appurtenances wheresoever scituate being in Virginia, Maryland, or
elsewhere, equally to be divided between my four children Henry, John, Anne and
Frances Meese," and further vested his wife and executrix Anne Meese with the authority to sell and dispose of the said properties for the benefit of his four infant
children.

Overwarton, the plantation of Colonel Henry Meese in Stafford County, came into possession of the Reverend John Waugh (1630-1706), the fiery minister of Staf -
ford Parish and thus the upper parish of colonial Stafford County derived its name.
In various records, however, during the first half of the Eighteenth Century the
name is spelt Overwarton, Overwarten and Overwharton.

When Westmoreland County on the Potomac River was formed in 1653, the uppermost parish thereof was called Potomac and extended from the junction of Machodoc
Creek with the Potomac River up the Potomac River to the falls and backward into
the forest to include all that land which was drained by the great Potomac River.
In 1664 Stafford County was formed and included all that region just described as
Potomac Parish and shortly the various records indicate that Potomac Parish was
divided into two parishes which were called "the upper Parish" and "the lower Parish" and the dividing line between them was Passapatanzy Creek. Probably by no
official act, but as time went on, the upper Parish came to be known as Stafford
Parish and the lower Parish as Chotank Parish and they were so designated in 1680.

At the first court of record held for Stafford County on May 27, 1664 the following gentlemen justices were present: Lieutenant Colonel Robert Williams, Captain John Alexander, Mr. Richard Heabeard, Mr. Roger Perfitt and Mr. Richard Fossaker. At the same time Colonel John Dodman was sworn clerk upon presenting his letter of appointment by Sir William Berkeley, governor of Virginia, under the hand of the Honorable Philip Ludwell, secretary of Virginia. On September 7, 1664 William Green and Vincent Young were sworn church wardens of Potomac Parish.

On December 6, 1666 before Colonel John Dodman, Colonel Henry Meese, Colonel George Mason, Mr. Hugh Dowding, Mr. Richard Heabeard and Mr. Robert Osbourne, gentlemen justices of Stafford County court, the following men were nominated vestrymen in Potomac Parish: Captain John Alexander, Mr. Robert Howson, Mr. Richard Fossaker, Mr. Richard Heabeard, Mr. Robert Osbourne, Mr. John Heabeard, Mr. William Heabeard, Mr. Vincent Young, William Greene, John Withers, Thomas Humphrey and Thomas Grigg. At the same time Mr Robert Osbourne and Mr. John Withers were nominated church wardens in Potomac Parish.

At a court held for Stafford County on April 3, 1667 it was ordered "that the Minister preach in three particular places in this county, viz: at the Southwest side of Aquia, at the Court House, and at Choatank at the house belonging to Mr. Robert Townsend: to officiate every Sabbath day in one of these places until further order." The first two named places were in the upper part of the newly formed county of Stafford while the house of Mr. Robert Townshend (1640-1675) stood upon his plantation, Albion, in the lower part of the county [now Saint Paul's Parish] and where his tombstone is yet to be seen. This court order gives some idea of the manner in which the settlement of Stafford County had progressed at this period.

At a court held for Stafford County on October 28, 1667 it was ordered that "whereas there is noe certain place in the upper precincts of this County for the Reading of Divine Service, the Court Doth Order that John Withers, Church warden for these precincts, agree for a house to Read in at the most convenient place."

The loss of all the Seventeenth Century parish records and of the majority of the Stafford County court records of the same period renders the historian's task difficult. From the surviving fragments it appears the first minister of Potomac Parish was the Reverend Morgan Godwyn. He entered Oxford on June 27, 1662, aged 21, received his B.A. degree from Christ Church College there on March 16, 1665 and came to Virginia shortly thereafter. He served as minister of Marston Parish in York County for a year or so and then took charge of Potomac Parish about 1667 and served as its minister until about 1670. During his tenure in Stafford County he engaged in a bitter contest in the courts with his vestry, or members of it, which finally went up by appeal to the General Court at Jamestown.

While the details are scant, it appears in January 1668, Colonel John Dodman, a vestryman of Potomac Parish and one of the leading citizens of Stafford County, secured a judgment in Stafford County court against the Reverend Mr. Morgan Godwyn and under that judgment the sheriff seized the parson's books and other property and gave it all to Colonel Dodman. The Reverend Mr. Godwyn appealed the case to the General Court of Virginia and the matter came up for trial in 1670. The judgment of Stafford County court was reversed and the Reverend Mr. Godwyn was exoner-

ated; Colonel Dodman was ordered to return the books and other property which had
been seized. Godwyn also brought suit against the sheriff, Major George Mason,
and won a judgment against him. Cross suits brought by Godwyn and a Mr. Massey,
another resident of Stafford County who seems to have been involved in the proceedings, were both dismissed and each plaintiff ordered to pay his own costs.
The final action of the General Court was to order the dismissal of the original
suits brought by Colonel Dodman against the Reverend Mr. Godwyn and Colonel Dodman
in open court apologized for the statements he had made about Mr. Godwyn. After
these unhappy events the Reverend Mr. Godwyn returned to England and he was succeeded by the Reverend Mr. John Waugh (1630-1706) who held the charge until 1700.

The first list I have found of the public officers of Stafford County after
the Reverend Mr. John Waugh was curate of Stafford Parish is in 1680

CIVIL OFFICERS

Colonel George Mason	Major Andrew Gilson	Mr. Anthony Buckner
Mr. James Ashton	Mr. Malachi Peale	Mr. Edward Thomason
Captain Robert Massey	Dr. William Banks	Mr. Martin Scarlett
Mr. Mathew Thompson		Mr. Vincent Young

MILITARY OFFICERS

Colonel George Mason	Major Andrew Gilson
Lieutenant Colonel Cadwalader Jones	Captain Robert Massey

The Reverend Mr. John Waugh was a man of education and parts, but a natural
agitator. He constantly quarrelled with his neighbors and the local authorities,
but he seems to have had a strong hold on the majority of his parishoners. His
cloth did not deter him from active participation in politics. He aligned himself
with Captain Martin Scarlett (16 -1695) against Colonel William Fitzhugh (1651-
1701) and preached Whig doctrine in opposition to the Tory influence among the local
gentry. In religion, as might be expected, he was what was called at the time "of
enthusiastic principles," meaning evangelicanism mingled with puritanism and he
courted popularity. From the pulpit the sermons of the Reverend Mr. Waugh caused
a tumult and the entire county was stirred to a frenzy in 1689 by his general thun-
der against the Catholics and even more dangerous thesis that there "being no King
in England, there was no Government here," and the people should remain in arms in
their own defence. Finally, by order of the Council, the ring leaders in the Stafford County uprising were arrested, Parson Waugh was forbade to preach, and George
Mason removed from command of the Stafford County militia. Parson Waugh was eventually brought before the General Court at Jamestown and there "made a publick and
humble acknowledgment, by a set form drawn up by the Court and ordered to be recorded ... with a hearty penitence for his former faults and promised obedience for the
future, which he sincerely prays for the accomplishment of and for the sake of his
Coat to do so."

In 1674 the Reverend Mr. Waugh's license to perform marriages was suspended
by Sir William Berkeley, governor of Virginia, for joining in marriage Mathew
Steele and Restitute Whetstone "contrary to y[e] wholesome laws of this country."
Parson Waugh pleaded to the governor that he was "a poor man, sorry for my former
offences" and prayed to be restored to his parish and his fine remitted as it will
be "y[e] undoing of your petitioner's wife and family." It appears from an order

in Westmoreland County court dated October 10, 1674, that the Parson's license to perform marriages was restored on his giving proper bond with Colonel George Mason and Mr. Robert Townshend, his securities.

It appears Parson Waugh zealously celebrated marriages. In 1688 he joined in matrimony Mary Hathaway, aged about nine years, to Mr. William Williams of Stafford County. The suit instigated in 1691 to declare this marriage null and void, couple with the bitter burgesses election of the same year in which the Parson's candidate Captain Martin Scarlett, was elected over Colonel William Fitzhugh, caused feeling to run high in Stafford County. Counsel for the complainant, Mary Hathaway, was Captain George Brent of Woodstock and Colonel William Fitzhugh of Bedford; counsel for the defendant, William Williams, was Mr. Sampson Darrell and Mr. Robert Collis. Much testimony was heard by the gentlemen justices and they ruled that the marriage de facto made by Mr. John Waugh, Clerk, between Mary Hathaway and Mr. William Williams is not good de jure unless at the time Mary Hathaway arrives at the age of twelve years she ratifies the marriage de facto "but if she then publickly disclaim the said marriage and protest against it, then it is the Judgment of this Court tha the aforesaid marriage de facto is utterly null and void as if the same had never been had or made." However, Mr. John Withers [the maternal grandfather of Mary Hathaway] and Mr. Mathew Thompson, two of the gentlemen justices of Stafford County court then sitting, dissented from the majority opinion and stated they were "of opinion that the said Mary Hathaway is the wife of the said William Williams not only [now] but alsoe when she shall arrive at the age of twelve years and that not only de facto but de jure it appearing to them that she was married by the said Mr. John Waugh, Clerk, as aforesaid, and that by consent of her guardian and did there-fore order the clerk to enter their dissent upon the records accordingly." However on the 28th of December 1691, "the very day by the mercy of God that I am twelve years old," Mary Hathaway appeared before "Mr. John Waugh, an orthodox minister of God's word, Captain Malachy Peale, Judge of the Court of Stafford County, Mr. Edwar Thomason of their Majesties Justices of the Peace in Quorum for the said county, Captain George Mason, their Majesties High Sheriff of the same county and the rest of the worthy Gentlemen here present" in the hall of the house of Captain George Mason and did there declare her marriage to Mr. William Williams to be null and voi by reason of "infancy and impuberty as well as force and fraud at the time of the contract and that by no means I can entertain a thought of ever receiving him for a spouse or husband" ... "and soe I bid the said Mr. Williams heartilie farewell and wish him a very good fortune."

Mary Hathaway was the only child and heir of Thomas Hathaway of Aquia and Mary Withers, his wife, who was the daughter of Captain John Withers (16 -1698). About 1702 she married Captain Thomas Lund of Saint Paul's Parish and their only child to leave issue was Elizabeth Lund (circa 1707-circa 1775) who married on December 22, 1726 Townshend Washington (1705-1743) of Green Hill, Saint Paul's Parish. This couple had several children among whom was Lund Washington (1737-1796) who was for more than twenty five years the trusted manager of the Mount Vernon estate.

The Reverend Mr. John Waugh was constantly meddling in politics. On September 9, 1680 John Pinnet, aged 35 years, deposed in Stafford County court "that sometime after the Burgesses came from Towne" [Jamestown] ... he was at "Choppawomsicke Churc which is kept at Thomas Barton's" ... and "several of ye company being together be-fore the sermon, some of ye company did aske Mr. Waugh what news from Towne" and he

replied that "we had chosen Mr. Fitzhugh a Burgess for George Brent to get him a
Commission to Peace and that he was for his own self-interest." Parson Waugh
never lost an opportunity to voice his disapproval of Colonel William Fitzhugh, a
Tory, and Colonel George Brent, a Roman Catholic.

From this record we learn that there was a church or chappel as early as 1680
on Chopawamsic Creek and Parson Waugh had doubtless come up by boat from his home
on the south side of Potomac Creek to officiate.

Although never a resident of Overwharton Parish the influence of Colonel William Fitzhugh of Saint Paul's Parish was strongly felt there during the last quarter
of the Seventeenth Century. From 1677 to 1682 he represented Stafford County in
the House of Burgesses with Colonel George Mason, but in the second session of 1682
Colonel Mason was replaced by Captain Martin Scarlett. In the session of 1684, Colonel George Mason and Colonel William Fitzhugh were members of the House of Burgesses but in the sessions of 1685-1686 Samuel Hayward and Martin Scarlett represented
Stafford County.

At this time Captain George Brent of Woodstock was Attorney General of Virginia. In 1684 he had been rewarded from the public funds 1,000 pounds of tobacco "as
a Gratuity and his Corporall paid 400 pounds of tobacco and to each of his nineteen
men 250 pounds of tobacco as a free and voluntary Benevolence" by the House of Burgesses for their good services against the Indians particularly when they marched
to the assistance of Captain Cadwallader Jones and the inhabitants of Rappahannock
when the Seneca Indians infested those parts. However, in 1686 Captain Brent was
relieved of his office by his Excellency Francis, Lord Howard, Baron of Effingham,
his Majesties Lieutenant and Governor General of Virginia, and Edmund Jennings,
Esq., appointed in his stead. His removal was probably due to his failure to promptly prosecute his friend Colonel William Fitzhugh who was accused of having misre-
presented the amount of the claim that the Assembly in 1682 had ordered paid to him
and also had collected from Stafford County 4,000 pounds of tobacco as payment for
his services as a member of the House of Burgesses in 1685 whereas he had not been
present at that session. Before the charges were heard, Colonel Fitzhugh filed
charges against Captain Martin Scarlett, his political enemy and the recently elected member of the House of Burgesses from Stafford County, whereupon the House dropped their intentions of prosecuting the impeachment but ordered all the papers in
the case to be delivered to George Brent, the King's Attorney General, with the intent that the cause should be prosecuted by him before the General Court of Virginia. Captain Brent was relieved of his office soon after the dissolution of the
Assembly of 1686 by Lord Effingham and with Colonel George Mason was elected a member of the House of Burgesses for 1688. At this session, when the Fitzhugh matter
again came up, he informed the House when the report of the Committee of Proposition
and Grievances was under consideration - in which the conduct of Colonel Fitzhugh
was characterized as "the abuse put upon Stafford County and the whole country by
Lieutenant Colonel William Fitzhugh" - that he would deliver the papers in the case
to Edmund Jennings, Esq., the newly appointed Attorney General of Virginia, as soon
as that gentleman came to Jamestown and the House sent an address to the governor
requesting him to prosecute the case without fail at the next meeting of the General
Court. It appears that Colonel Fitzhugh's counter-charges quelched the matter as
no further official record is to be found. Colonel Fitzhugh, Stafford's wealthiest
Seventeenth Century citizen, continued to be highly respected by his contemporaries.

The 1690's witnessed considerable political change in Stafford County. Due to the influence of the Reverend Mr. John Waugh, Captain Martin Scarlett was again elected to the House of Burgesses in 1691, and with Colonel George Mason (16 - 1716) was seated in that honorable body. However, in the March session of 1693 Captain Scarlett was forced to return to his home on Occoquan Bay in upper Stafford [now Prince William] County due to illness and it must have been very displeasing to him when he learned that Colonel William Fitzhugh was returned as a Burgess from Stafford County.for the October 1693 session. In 1695 Colonel George Mason and Captain Thomas Owsley were elected Burgesses from Stafford County, but shortly Captain Owsley was elected sheriff of Stafford County. Martin Scarlett, although he lay on a sick bed, was elected to replace Captain Owsley, but he died in 1695 and his tombstone may be seen upon his plantation, Deep Hole, in Prince William County.

In unseating Colonel Fitzhugh in the 1691 election, Captain Scarlett grievously hurt his opponent's feelings and Fitzhugh complained to the gentlemen justices of Stafford County court with hot indignation that Scarlett had asserted publicly during the canvass "that neither Law nor Justice had been administered in this County since I sat upon the Bench for nothing was Law or Justice but what I [Fitzhugh] said was soe." Resenting this imputation, Fitzhugh reminded the Court that he had been their colleague since 1683 when he was commissioned second in rank to Colonel George Mason and after his death in 1686 had succeeded him as presiding magistrate and had always polled the Court before assuming to speak for it. In this situation, he complained, Scarlett's charge did not merely reflect upon him but was so heinous an insult to the Court itself that out of respect for that cornerstone of local government, as well as in assertion of his own dignity, he felt compelled to refuse to sit on the bench again until Scarlett had received a sufficient punishment. The Court was evidently embarrassed, for several of them were Scarlett's political allies, but Scarlett himself came to their support. From his own seat on the bench he made a vigorous and manly answer and ultimately assured Colonel Fitzhugh that he had no intention of reflecting upon his character. Much relieved the Court again summoned Fitzhugh to preside over its deliberations, whereupon in November 1691 he wrote them another letter, violently attacking Parson Waugh, his chief political enemy. Parson Waugh had called Fitzhugh a Papist in court before the gentlemen justices as they were "taxing him for his ill behaviour" in inciting "a most mischievous and dangerous Riot." Fitzhugh said that the present incident he can hardly believe emanated from a man of reason and learning "and a Clergyman too and one that not long since has been at considerable charge and Trouble for Passionate`Expressions of a far inferiour nature" than this.

It appears Colonel Fitzhugh never again took his seat on the bench of Stafford County court and Captain Malachi Peale officiated as the presiding magistrate. Fitzhugh seems, however, to have held the county standard as twice in February 1692 and again in November 1693 the court ordered that it be removed from Fitzhugh's house to that of Captain Peale at Marlborough where the court had been appointed to be held.

In 1693 Colonel William Fitzhugh and Colonel George Brent were appointed agents for the Northern Neck of Virginia by the Right Honorable Katherine, Lady Culpeper, Proprietress of that extensive domain. This was a very lucrative position and these gentlemen busied themselves with their offices and for themselves patented thousands of acres of land in the upper regions of Stafford County which was then being rapidly settled.

In the Burgess election of 1696 following Captain Martin Scarlet's death, Colonel George Mason and Captain John Withers were elected and they served until the latter's death in 1698. At the ensuing election in 1699 Parson Waugh apparently could not find another candidate worthy of his support and got himself returned as a Burgess for Stafford County. This was a daring attempt to set aside a political precedent in Virginia, and it failed. Following the practice of the English Parliament, which prohibited a clerk to sit in that body, and the Assembly's own previous determination to the same effect, Waugh was promptly unseated by the Assembly; "being a Clergyman," they said, he was "disabled from Serving as a Burgess." Colonel Rice Hooe (circa 1660-1726) of Saint Paul's Parish was "duly elected and returned Burgess" for Stafford County on May 18, 1699 in the room of the Reverend Mr. John Waugh. Colonel Hooe married in 1699, as his third wife, Frances (Townshend) Dade Withers widow successively of Francis Dade, Junior, (1659-1694) and Captain John Withers (16 -1698).

It must have been a great satisfaction to Colonel William Fitzhugh to see his eldest son, young Captain William Fitzhugh (circa 1678-1713), elected to the House of Burgesses in 1700; he served with Colonel George Mason (16 -1716). In 1712, upon the recommendation of Governor Alexander Spotswood (1676-1740), Fitzhugh was elevated to the Council, however, he died in the fall of 1713 after serving but a year. In 1714 his brother, Captain Henry Fitzhugh of Bedford (1687-1758), was elected to the House of Burgesses with John Waugh, Junior, (16 -1716) and in 1718 his brother George Fitzhugh, Gentleman, (169?-1722) served with the third Colonel George Mason (1690-1735). Later other Fitzhughs served in that distinguished body.

The largest legacy which Overwharton Parish received during the Seventeenth Century was from Doctor Edward Maddox. The last will and Testament of Doctor Edward Maddox "of Stafford Parish, Stafford County, in the Colony of Virginia" was dated June 23, 1694; it was admitted to probate on December 11, 1694. His only child, Amy Maddox, married without his approbation, Thomas Derrick, and for this reason Doctor Maddox made the following bequest:

> "I first give and bequeath this plantation whereupon I now
> live and all the lands thereto appertaining and to me belonging
> to be and forever after to continue as a glebe and manse for the
> reception and encouragement of a pious and able minister in that
> parish wherein I now live being commonly known and called by the
> name of Stafford, or the upper parish of Stafford County; and
> that after my decease it be well and truly improved and managed
> at all times for the intent above said excepting that while there
> is no minister to serve ye cure in the said parish then I will
> and desire that the said plantation and land together with all its
> profits and advantages (before the time of vacancy above said) fully
> improved and laid out for the relief and support of such poor and
> indigent as in the said parish shall seem most in want at the dis-
> cretion of the church wardens and vestry of the above said parish
> for the time being."

Doctor Maddox's plantation consisted of between 450 and 500 acres on Passapantanzy Creek not far from the plantation of the Reverend Mr. John Waugh. It was
enjoyed as a glebe by the curate of Stafford [later Overwharton] Parish until after
the death of the Reverend Mr. Robert Buchan in 1804 when Doctor Maddox's descendants instigated suit claiming it was no longer being used as stipulated in his last
will and Testament and recovered it.

The clerical duties of the Reverend Mr. John Waugh as rector of Stafford Paris
seem to have come to an abrupt ending in 1700 when, consistent to his own self-will
ed way and his presistence in making his Virginia parish a Gretna Green for runaway
couples from Maryland for whom he performed the ceremony of marriage without benefi
of banns or license, he was for the last time suspended and fined. He did not agai
resume pastoral work and seems to have retired to his plantation, Overwharton, and
was succeeded by the Reverend Mr. John Fraser.

As I have been unable to discover a list of vestrymen in Stafford Parish during the period the Reverend Mr. John Waugh was at his height politically, I will
list some of the prominent men of the county some of whom were certainly on the
vestry of their parishes. This list is taken from a recording of those Justices
and Militia officers present at Stafford County courthouse on March 9, 1692 "in a
Tryal of the Indians which were taken and Brought into the Custody of Capt. George
Mason, high sheriff of this County, by Lieut. David Straham, lieutenant of the Ran-
gers." Those whose names are marked thus [#] were residents of Stafford Parish
and those whose names are marked thus [*] were residents of Chotank Parish.

	# Capt. Malachy Peale	
# Capt. George Mason	# Ensign Joseph Sumner	# Capt. John Withers
# Capt. Martin Scarlet	# Lieut. David Straham	* Ensign Thos.Gilson
* Mr. Richard Fossaker	of the Rangers	* Ensign John West
* Mr. Philip Buckner	# Lieut. Sampson Darrell	# Capt. Wm. Downing
# Mr. Matthew Thompson	* Mr. Robert Alexander	

In 1698 the militia officers in Stafford County were as follows: # Major
George Mason (16 -1716); # Captain Thomas Owsley (1663-1700); # Captain Joseph
Sumner (16 -1723) and * Captain Robert Alexander (16 -1704). Of these there is
a record dated October 19, 1699 indicating that George Mason was a church warden
in Stafford Parish.

It appears from various records that the upper parish of Stafford County,
called Stafford Parish and the lower parish of Stafford County, called Chotank Parish, did not officially come to be known as Overwharton Parish and Saint Paul's
Parish, respectively, until about 1700. The earliest use of the names Overwharton
Parish and Saint Paul's Parish appears in an official list of the Virginia parishes
in 1702 and these names have survived to the present day.

As no list has been located of the church wardens and vestrymen of Overwharton
Parish when it first came into existence as such, I wish to cite the following records which show the prominent men of Stafford County, some of whom were certainly
on the vestry of their parishes. Those names are marked thus [#] were residents
of Overwharton Parish and those whose names are marked thus [*] were residents of
Saint Paul's Parish.

By a writing dated the 30th of September 1701 at Williamsburg, Colonel Francis Nicholson, Governor of Virginia, appointed the following gentlemen as a Commission of the Peace for Stafford County:

# George Mason	* Rice Hooe	# Joseph Sumner	* William Bunbury
* Robert Alexander	* Richard Fossaker	# John Waugh, Jr.	# John West
# Mathew Thompson	* John Washington	* Edward Hart	* Charles Ellis

The following gentlemen served at various times in 1702-1703 as Justices of
Stafford County:

# Colonel George Mason	# Captain Joseph Sumner	# Mr. Mathew Thompson
* Lt. Col. Rice Hooe	* Captain Philip Alexander	* Mr. Robert Alexander
* Captain Charles Ellis	* Captain Thomas Clifton	* Mr. Richard Foote
* Captain Richard Fossaker	# Captain John West	* Mr. William Bunbury
* Mr. Edward Hart	* Mr. Thomas Gilson	# Mr. Thomas Gregg
# Mr. John Waugh, Jr.	* Mr. John Washington	# Major W.ᵐ Fitzhugh
		[Clerk of the Court]

On the 13th of March 1703 the following gentlemen signed a Memorial to Her
Majesty, Queen Anne, in regard to the death of her late brother-in-law King William:

* Robert Alexander	* William Bunbury	# John West	* William Fitzhugh
* John Washington	# Thomas Harrison	# John West, Jr.	* Benjamin Colclough
# Mathew Thompson	# George Mason	# John Peake	# George Anderson
# Giles Travers	# Moses Lynton	# G. Mason	* Thomas Lund
* Richard Fossaker	# Alexander Waugh	* Thomas Gilson	* Philip Alexander
	* Charles Ellis	* Edward Hart	

In a list of the militia for the various counties of Virginia dated the 17th
of June 1703, which was certified to Her Majestry, Queen Anne, the following field
officers are named for Stafford County:

			* Charles Ellis
			# George Anderson
COLONEL:	# George Mason		# John West
LT. COL:	* Rice Hooe	CAPTAINS:	# Edward Mountjoy
MAJOR :	* William Fitzhugh		# Thomas Harrison
			* Richard Fossaker

In 1702 the clerk of Stafford County was Major William Fitzhugh of Saint
Paul's Parish; the sheriff was Captain Charles Ellis of Saint Paul's Parish and
the sub-sheriff was Captain George Anderson of Overwharton Parish.

After 1702 there are frequent references in the court records to both Overwharton Parish and Saint Paul's Parish, but perhaps the earliest two such references are to be found in two deeds now of record at Stafford Court, viz: by deed
dated the 22nd of March 1704 Edward Hinson is described as of Overwharton Parish
and by deed dated the 11th of October 1704 Thomas Kitching is described as of
Saint Paul's Parish.

The Reverend Mr. John Fraser was ordained by the Bishop of London on August
29, 1700; he received the King's Bounty for Virginia on September 18, 1700 and
shortly was received as curate of Overwharton Parish. In 1701 he was paid a fee

for preaching the funeral of William Perkins. On April 20, 1702 "John Fraser, Minister of Overwharton Parish," witnessed the last will and Testament of Peter Beach and on August 10, 1702 "J̇ọ Fraser, Minister of Overworton," witnessed a legal document for George Mason as attorney for Brice Cockram, Merchant, of the Kingdom of Ireland. The Reverend Mr. John Fraser held the charge as minister of Overwharton Parish but a short time and removed to Maryland.

After the departure of the Reverend Mr. John Fraser it appears from an entry in the Journals of the House of Burgesses dated March 27, 1703, that there was some thought of consolidating the parishes of Overwharton and Saint Paul's as we find that Colonel Rice Hooe and Mr. Richard Fossaker, the Burgesses representing Stafford County, presented a proposition "for consolidateing yᵉ parishes of Overworton and Saint Paul's in yᵉ said county" and same "was referred to yᵉ Committee of Propositions and Grievances." Nothing else appears in regard to the proposal, however, it appears Overwharton Parish was without a minister the following year.

In the year 1703, at the request of Commissary Blair, Sir Edward Northey, Attorney-General of England, rendered a formal opinion in which he stated vestries of the several parishes in Virginia had the right to select the ministers whom they desired to serve as rectors of their parishes - this right having been acknowledged and confirmed by the laws enacted by the General Assembly of the colony. But, inasmuch as no law of Virginia dealt with the case of a vestry who employed a minister as incumbent and failed to present him to the governor for induction into the rectorship of the parish, he declared that, in such cases, the laws of the Church of England as adopted by Parliament were in force, and that whenever a vestry had failed to present a minister to the governor for induction into the rectorship within six months from the beginning of a vacancy, the governor had the right to appoint a minister of his own choosing and induct him into the rectorship of the parish, regardless of the desires or wishes of the vestry or parishioners.

This opinion was reported to the Council by the governor and recorded in its minutes of March 3, 1704. By order of that body, Governor Nicholson sent a copy of the opinion to the churchwardens of every parish in the colony, with the instruction that it should be copied into the vestry records and read and discussed at a meeting of the vestry called for that purpose, with the further instruction that each vestry report to the governor its opinion as to the enforcement of the law as interpreted by the Attorney-General.

In response to the governor's inquiry, the Church Wardens of Overwharton Parish replied as follows:

"October ye 21st, 1704
"Wee the Church wardens of Overworton Parish in Virginia by order of the said Vestry do humble Acquaint your Excellency that they are and shall be ready to yield all due Obedience to the 3d Act of Assembly Intituled Gleabe to be laid out, as Soone as it shall Please God to Supply us with a Minister and shall take Care for to provide for a Minister According to Law."

The activities of the vestries of the colonial Virginia parishes were closely knit to the county court and in the latter records we find many indentures by which orphans and indigent children were put apprentice for a term of years. On March 13,

1707 Captain Edward Mountjoy, church warden of Overwharton Parish in the county of Stafford, and Mr. George Mason, jun! (son of Colonel George Mason), agreed that the said George Mason, Junior, should take as an apprentice a bastard mulatto girl, the newly born daughter of Mary Allen named Mary Allenson, and the said child to serve him after the manner of an apprentice until she is thirty one years of age.

In 1711 the Reverend Mr. Alexander Scott (1686-1738) began a notable ministry in the parish. He was born in Dipple Parish, Elgin [now Moray], Scotland, the son of the Reverend Mr. John Scott, M.A., (circa 1650-1726). He received the King's Bounty for Virginia on October 10, 1710 and settled on Potomac River in Stafford County just below Chopawamsic Creek; he called his plantation Dipple. He married on May 20, 1717, Madam Sarah (Gibbons) Brent (1693-1733), daughter of William Gibbons, Esquire, of Wiltshire and widow of William Brent, Esquire, (circa 1677-1709) of Richland, Overwharton Parish, which estate lies about two miles down the Potomac River from Dipple. William Brent, son of Colonel Giles and Mary (Brent) Brent and grandson and heir entail of Colonel Giles Brent (circa 1600-1672), went to England in 1708 to claim the estates of Stoke and Admington in Gloucestershire and married there on May 12, 1709 the aforementioned Sarah Gibbons; he died on November 26, 1709 in Middlesex, England, leaving his wife enceinte and their son William Brent (1710-1742) was born the 6th of March following his father's death. When he was seven, his widowed mother brought him to Stafford County to claim the vaste estates to which he was entitled as the only surviving male heir of his distinguished great-grandfather, Colonel Giles Brent, "first citizen" of Stafford County. Because of his great wealth he was called "Squire Brent;" he resided at Richland which handsome manor house was burned by the British during the Revolutionary War while occupied by Colonel William Brent (1733-1782) only child of "Squire" Brent to survive infancy.

The Reverend Mr. Alexander Scott's official report of his church work, made in 1724 to the Lord Bishop of London, who had direct supervision of the Church in America, is interesting and enlightens us considerably as to his charge.

"Overwharton Parish, 1724. I went from England in the year 1710 in the latter end thereof and arrived here in 1711. I have no other Church or Parish but this. I was Licensed by the Rt. Rev. Henry, Lord Bishop of London, to officiate in this Colony of Virginia. I was sent to this Parish with a Letter from the Governor and another from the Commissary to the Vestry who received me without induction, that being not common. I do ordinarily reside in the parish wherein I do now exercise my function. The bounds of my Parish is not known it being a frontier parish but is inhabited near 80 miles in length and in some places near 3 miles, in others near 20 miles in breadth and about 650 families. There are no Indians nor other Infidels among us but Negro Slaves the Children of whom and those of them who can speak and understand the English Language we instruct and baptise if permitted by their Masters. Divine Service is performed but once every Sunday either in Church or Chappels by reason of the Great distance the inhabitants have to Church or Chapel, Some living about 15 miles distant from either & the plantations being but thin seated. Notwithstanding I have then generally as full a congregation as

either Church or Chappels can contain and can well be expected
in such a thin seated place. I administer the Sacrament of the
Lord's Supper 6 times a year, and generally have betwixt 80 &
100 Communicants each time. I catechise the youth of my parish
in Lent and a great part of the Summer.

"Our Church is tolerably well provided; our two Chappels
want a pulpit Cloth, reading Desk Cloth, Communion table cloth,
and vessels for the Communion. The value of my living is very
uncertain being paid in Tobacco the quantity 16, 000 lb. Tobacco
yearly & being in a frontier place may be worth communibus annis
5 shillings for each hundred pounds and very often not so much
worth. The glebe lies so inconvenient at the lower end of the
parish that I was obliged to lease it out and purchase a convenient plantation near the middle of the parish for myself.
There is no house upon it for its being so inconvenient that it
must be leased out it did not seem needful to build one. I preached at the Church and one of the Chappels near to which the inhabitants are thickest seated every Sunday by turns and at the other
Chappel 6 times a year. There is no public school for the instruction of youth, and there is no Parochial Library.

                                        Alexander Scott"

     In the absence of the vestry books of Overwharton Parish during the Eighteen-
th Century, a report made in 1726 by Governor Hugh Drysdale covering the "present
state of Virginia" is most valuable. Here are listed the prominent men of Stafford County, some of whom were vestrymen.

                          STAFFORD COUNTY
          Acres of Land: [blank]
          Tithables   : 1, 800
          Sheriff   : William Storke[1]
          Coroner   : Henry Fitzhugh
          Justices of the Peace: Rice Hooe, Dade Massey, Henry Fitzhugh,
                       William Storke, Thomas Hopper, Thomas Harrison,
                       Townsend Dade, John Fitzhugh (Quorum), French
                       Mason, Abraham Farrow, Charles Broadwater, John
                       Linton, Anthony Thornton, Rice Hooe, jun., and
                       Robert Alexander
          Burgesses   : George Mason and William Robinson
          Clerk of the County Court: Catesby Cocke
          Land Surveyor: Henry Conyers
          Parishes   : Saint Paul's and Overworton
          Ministers   : Mr. Steward [Stuart] and Alexander Scott
          No. Militia : Horse, 202 - Foot, 370
          County Lieutenant: Robert Carter
          Sort of Tobacco : Arronoco

---

1 - William Storke, Gentleman, was appointed sheriff on April 25, 1726 by Lieuten-
    ant-Governor Hugh Drysdale; he died in office and on September 20, 1726 Robert
    Carter, Esq., appointed Anthony Thornton sheriff "in the room of William
    Storke, Gentleman, deceased."

In July 1726 Governor Hugh Drysdale also sent to England "An Account of all Births and Deaths of Free people and Slaves within the Colony of Virginia from the 15th day of April 1725 to the 15th of April 1726" as reported to him by the ministers of the various parishes. For Overwharton Parish his report was as follows:

BIRTHS: Free Persons: Males 19; Females 26
        Slaves   : Males 12; Females 18
BURIALS: Free Persons: Males 13; Females 17
        Slaves   : Males 6; Females 3

These figures furnish ample evidence that the recordings during the early [1723-1738] years of The Register of Overwharton Parish 1723-1758 are far from complete.

In 1729 Governor William Gooch sent a report to England covering the "present state of Virginia" and the portion of it as concerns Stafford County is given below.

STAFFORD COUNTY

Acres of land : [blank]
Tithables   : 2,060
Sheriff   : Abraham Farrow
Coroner   : Dade Massey
Burgesses   : Anthony Thornton and John Fitzhugh
Justices of the Peace: Dade Massey, Thomas Harrison, Townsend
                Dade, John Fitzhugh, French Mason, Abraham
                Farrow, Charles Broadwater, Anthony Thornton,
                Henry Fitzhugh (Quorum); Dennis McCarty, Elias
                Hore, Thomas Grigsby, John Washington, William
                Triplett, William Lynton, Peter Hedgman and
                Francis Awbrey
County Clerk : Catesby Cocke
Parishes   : Saint Paul's and Overwarton
Ministers   : Mr. Steward [Stuart] and Mr. Scott
Surveyor   : James Thomas
County Lieut. : Robert Carter, Esq.[r]

By Act of Assembly in 1730, Prince William County was formed "on the heads of Stafford and King George counties" to be effective March 25, 1731: "all the lands on the heads of the said counties above Chopawamsick Creek on Potomac River, Deep Run on the Rappahannock River and a south west line to be made from the head of the North branch of the said creek to the head of said Deep Run" shall be called and known by the name of Prince William County. Thus Overwharton Parish lost that extensive domain which it formerly had now embracing the counties of Prince William, Fairfax, Loudoun, Arlington, the Potomac watershed of Fauquier County, and the City of Alexandria.

The birth of Prince William County must have delighted the aging Reverend Mr. Alexander Scott; new parishes would be formed and he would not be called upon to travel far from Dipple. Doubtless, he seldom officiated in the remote parts of his parish anyway, confining his ministry to services at Aquia and Potomac churches. In the more remote parts of his parish there were probably several chapels where lay readers performed services at irregular intervals.

The Reverend Mr. Alexander Scott had no child and after the death of his wife he invited his much younger half-brother, the Reverend Mr. James Scott, M.A., (17 -1782) to come to Virginia and reside at Dipple. This he did and he inherited that well known seat. He married _circa_ 1738 Sarah Brown (1715-1784), daughter of Doctor Gustavus Brown (1689-1762) of Rich Hill, Charles County, Maryland, and his wife nee Frances Fowke (1691-1744), daughter of Colonel Gerard Fowke (1662-1734) and his wife nee Sarah Burdett of Charles County, Maryland. For an account of the distinguished lineages of the last named couple see Jester and Hiden: Adventurers of Purse and Person, Virginia, 1607-1625, pages 192 and 331 and Hayden: Virginia Genealogies, page 156 et seq. Frances (Fowke) Brown (1691-1744) died while on a visit to her daughter and was buried at Dipple.

In 1745 the Reverend Mr. James Scott became rector of Dettingen Parish, Prince William County, and continued that charge until his death, a period of thirty seven years. Although two wills directed that tombstones should be placed over the graves at Dipple of the Reverend and Mrs. James Scott this was never accomplished. In 194? this ancient cemetery and adjoining property was taken into the Quantico Marine Base and the remains of those interred at Dipple and the tombstones removed to Aquia Churchyard. The handsome tombs of the Reverend and Mrs. Alexander Scott were among those moved. They are inscribed:

[In relief, an hour-glass, beneath which is a skull and cross bones, and under that an angel, head and shoulders, winged.]

Here Lyeth the body of the Rev'd Alex: Scott, A.M., & Presbyter of the Church of England; who lived near twenty eight years minister of Over - wharton Parish, and died in the fifty third year of his age. He being born the twentieth of July A.D. 1686 and departed this life the first day of April 1738.

[Beneath this inscription is the coat of arms of the Reverend Mr. Scott, surrounded by the motto, Gaudia Nancio Magna. The Arms: "on a bend a star between two crescents, in a bordure eight stars." The Crest: "a dove." Beneath the crest an Esquire's helmet with visor closed.]

[In relief, two winged angels, each holding a globe in the one hand, and a palm branch in the other. Under these are the words, memento mori, with the usual skull and cross bones.

Here Lyeth the body of Sarah, the wife of the Rev'd. Alex'r: Scott, A.M., Minister of Overwharton Parish, & Formerly wife and widow of William Brent of Richland, Gentleman. She exchanged this life for a Better About the 41st year of her age on Monday at one o'clock of October 29th, 1733.

[There is some reference on the stone to the issue of the deceased by Mr. Brent and also an inscription in Latin but not enough can be brought together to reproduce here.]

The following tombs were also removed from the Scott family cemetery at Dipple to Aquia Churchyard:

Here lyeth the body of
Frances the wife of Dr.
Gustavus Brown of Charles
County in Maryland. By her
he had twelve Children, of
whom one son and seven daughters survive her. She was
a daughter of Mr.Gerard Fowke,
late of Maryland, and descended from the Fowkes of Gunston
Hall in Staffordshire. She
was born February the 2d,
1691, and died much lamented
on the 8th of November 1744
in the 54th year of her age.

[At the head and perpendicular to this
ancient horizontal tombstone, a descendant has erected a granite memorial
stone duplicating the original inscription, above given. Then follows:

The above Epitaph copied from the
old gravestone now mouldering at its
feet was the tribute of a mourning
husband to a beloved wife 138 years
ago. Among the descendants of the
seven daughters mentioned on it are
many widely scattered between the
Lakes of Canada and the Gulf of Mex-
ico and the Atlantic Ocean and the
Mississippi being honoured names
but whose names give them no clue
to their descent from their remarkable ancestress
                FRANCES FOWKE
To enable those who are aware of it
to visit her last resting place and
to identify and preserve it a great-
grandson of her eldest daughter
Frances, wife of the Rev. John Moncure,
Rector at that time of Aquia and Potomac Churches and whose remains with
those of his wife rest in the Church
first named near the alter has caused
this tablet of granite bearing on its
surface a more durable copy of the
original inscription to be erected to
            her memory.]

[Skull and Cross Bones]

Here lies the Body of
            CHRISTIAN
the wife of John Graham Merch.^{t}
and daughter of Doctor Gustavus
Brown. She departed this life the
17th of September 1742 in the 23^{d}
year of her Age when she had been
married not quite two months.
There was no person more universally esteemed nor more sincerely
lamented by her acquaintances.

In Memory of
ROBERT HORNER
Born Jan. 21, 1718
in Ripon, England.
Died Sept. 8, 1773
Married Ann, daughter
of Gustavus Brown,M.D.

Sacred to the Memory
of my son
Richard Marshall Scott
eldest son of
Gustavus Hall Scott
Born May 11, 1807
Died Sept. 21, 1847

By his last will and Testament dated January 19, 1737 which was admitted to probate April 11, 1738, the Reverend Mr. Alexander Scott made the following bequest:

> "Item: I give and bequeath to the church near the head of Acquia in this Parish thirty pounds sterling money of Great Britain to be paid within a year and a half after the proof of this will by my executors hereinafter named to the Church Wardens and vestry of the said parish for the time being to buy a silver pottle flaggon, a silver pattin and good substantial silver pint chalice and cover for the communion service in the said church and each of them to have engraved these words, Given by the Rev. Alexander Scott, A:M. late Minister of this Parish and the date when given else that my executors herein after named shall within the time before mentioned send for the above mentioned flaggon, Pattin, challice and cover and have them wrought of good sufficient and substantial workmanship."

The directions of the Reverend Mr. Scott were carefully followed and the handsome communion service has been carefully guarded for more than two hundred years. To insure its survival, it was buried during the Revolutionary War, the War of 1812 and the Civil War. Each piece is inscribed: "The Gift of the Rev. Mr. Alex: Scott, A.M., late Minister of this Parish. Anno. 1739."

AQUIA CHURCH COMMUNION SERVICE
1739

The Reverend Alexander Scott also bequeathed three thousand pounds of Tobacco for cloathing and schooling three of the most needy and poor children in Overwharton Parish. He was succeeded as rector of Overwharton Parish by the Reverend John Moncure (circa 1714-1764) and he served the parish twenty six years exerting a marked influence over his parishoners; during his term as curate Aquia Church was built.

The appointment of the Reverend Mr. John Moncure as minister of Overwharton Parish may not have been accomplished without some opposition. So soon as Governor William Gooch heard of the death of the Reverend Mr. Alexander Scott, he immediately dispatched a letter to the Lord Bishop of London under date of April 20, 1738:

> "As I was always cautious in recommending any person
> from hence to Your Lordship for Ordination, so from the same
> care I can assure Your Lordship, upon the Testimony of sev-
> eral worthy Gentlemen who have known the Bearer, Mr. George
> Fraser, many years, that he is an unexceptionable man in his
> Life and Conversation, a constant Churchman and Communicant,
> And that, Mr. Scott, Minister of the Parish where Mr. Fraser
> lived, being lately Dead, they one and all desire this Gentle-
> man may succeed him and therefore I hope Your Lordship will
> find him in all other Respects qualified. He has been a
> schoolmaster in a private Family."

The Reverend Mr. George Fraser received the King's Bounty for Virginia from the Bishop of London on August 20, 1738 and took up a charge in Dale Parish, Chesterfield County, which he appears to have held for more than twenty years. The inventory of the estate of "the Reverend Mr. George Fraser, deceased," was recorded in Chesterfield County in 1762. He was probably the son of the Reverend Mr. John Fraser, rector of Overwharton Parish 1701-1702, but he was never rector of Overwharton Parish.

While the precise details are unknown, by some means the Reverend Mr. John Moncure was assigned to Overwharton Parish prior to the arrival of the Reverend Mr. George Fraser in Virginia. On January 26, 1738 John Moncure witnessed a deed from Thomas Grayson of Deal in Kent, England, conveying to Thomas Turner, Gentleman, of King George County, 500 acres of land on the Rappahannock River in Spotsylvania County about four miles below Fredericksburg. He must have been bound for Virginia at this time as with other witnesses he proved the deed at Spotsylvania County court on July 4, 1738. This record proves that the Reverend Mr. John Moncure came to Virginia in 1738.

The Reverend Mr. John Moncure was born in the parish of Kinoff, County Mearns (now County Kincardine), Scotland, about the year 1714. The year of his birth was approximated by the Reverend Mr. Horace Hayden in his Virginia Genealogies, page 424, to be circa 1709-1710 and others have followed him in so stating; I do not know upon what record, if any, this approximation was made by the Reverend Mr. Hayden. However, in a deposition at Stafford County court on June 13, 1759 in connection with the proving of the will of Travers Cooke, Gentleman, the Reverend Mr. John Moncure stated he was then forty five years of age. It thus appears he was born in or about the year 1714.

Although born in Scotland, the Reverend Mr. John Moncure was of French ex-
traction, being descended from a French Protestant ancestor who fled France in
consequence of the persecution that took place there after the Reformation in the
early part of the Sixteenth Century. Mrs. Jean (Moncure) Wood (1753-1823), the
youngest child of the Reverend Mr. Moncure, stated in a genealogical letter in
1820 that her father had an excellent education and had made considerable progress
in the study of medicine, when he received an invitation to seek an establishment
in Virginia. He came to Virginia about 1733 and lived two years in a gentleman's
family as a private tutor in Northumberland County. During that time, although
teaching others, he was closely engaged in the study of divinity and at the commencement of the third year from his arrival returned to Great Britain and was
ordained a minister by Bishop Edmund Gibson, Lord Bishop of London. He returned
to Virginia in 1738 and upon the death of the Reverend Mr. Alexander Scott (1686-
1738) succeeded him as curate of Overwharton Parish.

The Reverend Mr. John Moncure was married on July 9, 1741 to Frances Brown
(1713-1770), eldest daughter of Doctor Gustavus Brown of Rich Hill, Charles County, Maryland, and Frances Fowke, his wife, who have been mentioned in detail on
page 186. They had four children to survive infancy, viz:
>   (1) Frances Moncure (1745-1800) married on October 7, 1762
>   Travers Daniel, Senior, (1741-1824) of Tranquility and
>   Crow's Nest. He served as surveyor of Stafford County
>   1763-1792 and also as a justice of the county court.
>   Mr. and Mrs. Daniel are buried, with other members of
>   their family, in the family cemetery at Crow's Nest on
>   Accakeek Creek near its conflux with Potomac Creek.
>   They had eleven children.
>   (2) John Moncure (1747-1784) of Clermont, Stafford County;
>   he married Anne Conway, daughter of George and Ann
>   (Heath) Conway of Lancaster County, Virginia; they had
>   five children.
>   (3) Anne Moncure (1748-   ) married Walker Conway and had
>   three children. He was a brother of Anne (Conway) Mon-
>   cure, above mentioned.
>   (4) Jean Moncure (1753-1823) married in 1775 Governor James
>   Wood (1741-1813) of Virginia; they had no issue. He is
>   buried in Saint John's Churchyard, Richmond, Virginia,
>   and she is buried in the Robinson family cemetery, Pop-
>   lar Vale, Byrd Park, Richmond, Virginia.

The Reverend Mr. Horace Hayden in his Virginia Genealogies [1891] gives an excellent account of the Moncure family as well as those with whom they were connected.

The Reverend Mr. John Moncure regularly officiated at Aquia and Potomac churches. He may have had an assistant curate as John Mercer, Esq., of Marlborough records the Reverend Mr. John Phipps came to Virginia in 1746 and on March 3, 1747
he baptized John Moncure [Jr.] (1747-1784). The Reverend Mr. Phipps was a tutor
for some years in the family of John Mercer, but I have no further information
concerning him.

During the ministry of the Reverend Mr. John Moncure Aquia Church was built.
He died on March 10, 1764 and his last will and Testament remains of record. He

and his wife are buried under the chancel at Aquia Church. Upon one of the large marble stones covering the chancel is engraved:

IN MEMORY
OF THE RACE OF THE HOUSE
OF
MONCURE

The following letter written to Mrs. Frances (Brown) Moncure (1713-1770) by her cousin the Honorable George Mason (1725-1792) of Gunston Hall, a couple of days after the death of the Reverend Mr. John Moncure, is of considerable interest.

" Gunston, 12th March, 1764

"Dear Madam-
            "I have your letter by Peter yesterday, and the day before I had one from Mr. Scott, who sent up Gustin Brown on purpose with it. I entirely agree with Mr. Scott in preferring a funeral sermon at Aquia Church, without any invitation to the house. Mr. Moncure's character and general acquaintance will draw together much company, besides a great part of his parishoners, and I am sure you are not in a condition to bear such a scene; and it would be very inconvenient for a number of people to come so far from church in the afternoon after the sermon. As Mr. Moncure did not desire to be buried in any particular place, and as it is usual to bury clergymen in their own churches, I think the corpse being deposited in the church where he had so long preached is both decent and proper, and it is probable, could he have chosen himself, he would have preferred it. Mr. Scott writes to me that it is intended Mr. Green shall preach the funeral sermon on the 20th of this month, if fair; if not, the next fair day; and I shall write to Mr. Green tomorrow to that purpose, and inform him that you expect Mrs. Green and him at your house on the day before; and, if God grants me strength sufficient either to ride on horseback or in a chair, I will certainly attend to pay the last duty to the memory of my friend; but I am really so weak at present that I can't walk without crutches and very little with them, and have never been out of the house but once or twice, and then, though I stayed but two or three minutes at a time, it gave me such a cold as greatly to increase my disorder. Mr. Green has lately been very sick, and was not able to attend his church yesterday, (which I did not know when I wrote to Mr. Scott:) if he should not recover soon, so as to be able to come down, I will inform you or Mr. Scott in time, that some other clergyman may be applied to.
            "I beseech you, dear madam, not to give way to melancholy reflections, or to think that you are without friends. I know nobody that has reason to expect more, and those that will not be friends to you and your children now Mr. Moncure is gone were not friends to him when he was living, let their professions be what they would. If, therefore, you should find any such, you have no cause to lament the loss, for such friendship is not worth anybody's concern.

"I am very glad to hear that Mr. Scott purposes to apply for Overwharton parish. It will be a great comfort to you and your sister to be so near one another, and I know the goodness of Mr. Scott's heart so well, that I am sure he will take a pleasure in doing you every good office in his power, and I had much rather he should succeed Mr. Moncure than any other person. I hope you will not impute my not visiting you to any coldness or disrespect. It gives me great concern that I am not able to see you. You may depend upon my coming down as soon as my disorder will permit, and I hope you know me too well to need any assurance that I shall gladly embrace all opportunities of testifying regard to my deceased friend by doing every office in my power to his family.

"I am, with my wife's kindest respects and my own, dear madam, your most affectionate kinsman,

George Mason"

The first brick church built in Overwharton Parish stood upon the narrows of Potomac Creek - it was called Potomac Church; it is not now standing and historical facts concerning it are meager. The second substantial church built in Overwharton Parish is standing and called Aquia Church. I will discuss these two edifaces separately.

AQUIA CHURCH

How many frame buildings preceeded the present brick Aquia Church is not known. We do know that near or upon this site since shortly after the county of Stafford was created, divine services have been held - a period of almost three hundred years.

There is a reference in the court records in 1738 that the key to Aquia Church was stolen by Richard Watson, an absconding indented servant of the Reverend Mr. Alexander Scott. With considerable difficulty, both Watson and the key were recovered.

The following advertisement appeared in the Virginia Gazette of June 6, 1751:

"The Vestry of Overwharton Parish, in the County of Stafford, have come to a Resolution to build a large Brick Church, of about 3,000 Square Feet in the Clear, near the Head of Aquia Creek, where the old Church now stands. Notice is hereby given, That the Vestry will meet at the said Place, to let the same, on Thursday, the 5th Day of September next, if fair, if not, the next fair Day. All Persons inclinable to undertake it are desired to come then, and give in their Plans and Proposals.

Benjamin Strother
Peter Daniel
Churchwardens"

The contract to build Aquia Church was awarded to Mourning Richards of Drysdale Parish, King and Queen County, master builder and architect. The unfortunate

accident which befell the new church as it neared completition is recorded in the
Virginia Gazette of March 21, 1755:

> "We hear from Stafford County, that the new Church at
> Acquia, one of the best Buildings in the Colony (and the old
> wooden one near it) were burnt down on the 17th Instant, by
> the Carelessness of some of the Carpenters leaving Fire too
> near the Shavings, at Night, when they left off work. This
> fine Building was within two or three Days Work of being com-
> pletely finished and delivered up by the Undertaker, and this
> Accident, it is said, has ruined him and his Securities."

During the time Aquia Church was being constructed, Mourning Richards became
indebted to Colonel Nathaniel Harrison (1713-1791) of Eagle's Nest in Saint Paul's
Parish. Colonel Harrison had removed there a few years before from Brandon on the
James River, upon his marriage to Lucy (Carter) Fitzhugh (171?-1773), widow of Colonel Henry Fitzhugh (circa 1706-1742) and mother of William Fitzhugh, Esq., (1741-
1809) of Chatham. Colonel Harrison obtained a judgment against Mourning Richards
at King and Queen County court on October 28, 1753 for this debt of £238:3:0 and
in order to secure it, Richards gave Colonel Harrison a mortgage on eleven Negro
slaves. Already thus encumbered, the burning of the nearly completed Aquia Church
placed Mourning Richards in extremely embrassing financial circumstances as we see
from the following announcement in the _Virginia Gazette_ of May 16, 1755:

> "TO ALL CHARITABLE AND WELL-DISPOSED CHRISTIANS
>
> "Mourning Richards, most humbly represents, That, in
> the year 1751, he contracted with the Vestry of Overwharton
> Parish, in the County of Stafford, to build a very large and
> beautiful Church, near Aquia Creek, for 111,000 pounds of Tob-
> acco, which Building he carried on with all possible Diligence
> and made Sundry Alterations and Additions, at the Request of
> the Vestry, who proposed paying him for so doing 20,000 pounds
> of Tobacco more than the first Contract: That he had got the
> Church in such Forwardness, that he should have been able to
> have delivered the same to the Vestry in a short Time, and then
> was to receive the Ballance of his Tobacco, having received only
> 75,000 pounds; but, on the 17th Day of February last, while he
> was absent on his necessary Business, the whole Building was ac-
> cidently consumed by Fire, which has reduced him and his Family
> to very great Distress, he being utterly unable to rebuild the
> said Church. And, therefore, he most humbly prays your Aid and
> Assistance.
> "I know the above Facts to be true.
>   Peter Hedgman"

Major Peter Hedgman (circa 1700-1765) was a gentleman justice of Stafford
County for many years and served as a member of the House of Burgesses 1742-1758.
This advertisement seems in some measure to have resolved the financial difficulties of Mourning Richards and he erected the building now standing over the south
door of which, in a contemporary cutting, is inscribed:

"Built
A.D. 1751.   Destroyed by Fire
1754.   Rebuilt A.D. 1757 By
Mourning Richards Undertaker
William Copein   Mason"   1

William Copein, stonemason, also built Pohick Church 1769-1774, the undertaker of which was Daniel French (1723-1771) who died before the edifice was completed. The baptismal font now in Pohick Church bears the date A.D. 1773; it was
made by William Copein after "a Plate in Langley's Designs ... for the price of
six pounds, he finding for himself everything." The similarity of the doorways
of Pohick Church and Aquia Church may be seen in the detail drawingsmade by George
Carrington Mason, Historiographer, Diocese of Southern Virginia, and reproduced in
his Colonial Churches of Tidewater Virginia [1945], Plates 86 and 87.

Thomas Green, Esq., (1798-1882), attorney at law, left a genealogical account
of his family. His mother, nee Fanny Richards, wife of General Moses Green (1770-
1857) of Fauquier County, was the daughter of Captain John Richards (1734-1785) of
King and Queen, Essex, King George and Stafford counties whose family is detailed
by Colonel Brooke Payne in The Paynes of Virginia, pages 83-84. Mr. Green indicates his great-grandfather, William Bird Richards of Drysdale Parish, King and Queen
County, had a sister and a brother, viz: Catherine ("Kitty") Richards, wife of the
Reverend Mr. Robert Innis, and Mourning Richards "a bricklayer who built Aquia
Church;" he married and left an only child, Mrs. Trent of King William County.

Aquia Church is built in the form of a Greek cross, with two tiers of windows
set in very thick walls. There are three double door entrances; one in each arm
of the cross with the alter in its east end. Against the reredoes of white wood-
work are four arched panels in black, inscribed in English script by William Copein with the Ten Commandments, the Apostles' Creed and the Lord's Prayer. At the
southeastern re-entrant angle stands the original "three decker" pulpit, with its
great sounding board. The pews are square. Over the west entrance is the gallery,
supported by large pillars and reached by winding stairs. This was the slave gallery in former days. On the front of the gallery a panel bears the names of the minister, church wardens and vestrymen, when the present edifice was completed. This
unusual plaque is also the work of William Copein; it is inscribed:

JOHN MONCURE.	Minister	
Peter Hedgman.	Benjamin Strother.	
John Mercer.	Thomas Fitzhugh.	
John Lee.	Peter Daniel.)	Church
Mott Doniphan.	Travers Cooke.)	Wardens.
Henry Tyler.	John Fitzhugh.	
William Mountjoy.	John Peyton.	

Vestrymen
1757   Wm Copein Pixnit

Some account of these church wardens and vestrymen and their families will be
found in Section VII.

---

1 - The notices from the Virginia Gazette of 1755, quoted on page 193, make it
   certain that the church was destroyed by fire in 1755 and not in 1754.

While the evidence is scant, it is conclusive that all of the Reverend Mr. Moncure's parishoners were not in complete harmony with the decision of the vestry and church wardens to erect the handsome edifice at Aquia in 1751; the thought of being taxes for the destruction of the first church built by Mourning Richards in order to relieve his distressed financial situation caused much dissatisfaction in Overwharton Parish a few years later.

The third quarter of the Eighteenth Century witnessed a steady increase in the number of dissenters from the Established Church. Particularly active were the Baptists and the general decline of Episcopalism throughout Virginia, which was to be so well defined a few years later, had already clearly shown itself in Overwharton Parish, indeed, I believe more so than in any other parish in eastern Virginia.

In 1757 Stafford County was represented in the House of Burgesses by Major Peter Hedgman (circa 1700-1765) of Overwharton Parish and William Fitzhugh, Esq., (1725-1791) of Marmion in Saint Paul's Parish, both staunch supporters of the Episcopal Church. However, these gentlemen seem to have been caught off guard on April 18, 1757 when a petition was presented to the House of Burgesses in Williamsburg signed by "sundry inhabitants of Overwharton Parish complaining of the illegal, arbitrary and oppressive proceedings of the present vestry of the said Parish and praying that the same may be dissolved." Of course Hedgman and Fitzhugh were influencial enough to have this petition rejected and the House accommodated them immediately on May 2, 1757.

On June 2, 1757 the House of Burgesses granted leave to its members from the county of Stafford "to bring in a Bill to impower the Vestry of Overwharton Parish to levy for Mourning Richards a reasonable satisfaction for rebuilding a church at Aquia and same was referred to Mr. Charles Carter to prepare and bring in the same." This was promptly done and the bill was passed on June 8, 1757.

But the dissenters in Overwharton Parish refused to be silenced by the Episcopalian gentry and for the next ten years filed frequent petitions in the House of Burgesses clearly declaring their disapproval of the manner ecclesiastical affairs were administered there. Finally, at the fall session of 1769, the House of Burgesses passed an act which recited that there are "divisions among the vestry of the parish of Overwharton, in the county of Stafford, that the affairs of the said parish have for sometime been neglected and mismanaged" and by this act dissolved the vestry. A new vestry was ordered to be elected on September 20, 1770 and to consist of "twelve of the most able and discreet persons, being freeholders and resident in" the said parish. It appears from the proceedings that the levies in Overwharton Parish for the last two years had not been laid by the vestry and creditors of the parish remained unpaid - the new vestry were directed to lay the levy "and assess upon the tithable persons of the said parish all such sums of money and quantities of tobacco as ought to have been levied and assessed by the said present vestry."

This action did little to squelch the dissenters and dissatisfaction continued both in their ranks and among the vestry. It appears the number of persons were increasing who would no longer pay tribute to support a church they had no intentions of attending.

Before the election of the new vestry as ordered by the House of Burgesses was accomplished, a delegation from Overwharton Parish appeared before the Committee of Propositions and Grievances of the House of Burgesses in regard to the continued dissatisfaction there. These men, William Garrett, John Mauzy, Bailey Washington, Thomas Mountjoy, Yelverton Peyton, Humphrey Gaines, William Adie, Andrew Edwards and Joseph Thacker protested against the irregular actions of the Vestry of Overwharton Parish and on June 18, 1770 the House found their grievances "reasonable." We note that several of these men were members of aristocratic families of Stafford County and it must be conceeded that from this time forward the decline of the Established Church in Virginia was rapid.

In advertising his plantation in Overwharton Parish for sale in the Virginia Gazette on August 1, 1771, John Ralls, Senior, not only informs the people of the convenient location of the place for trade but is quite informative as to its proximity to the various houses of worship in its environs. In offering to sell his plantation Beulah of 780 or 785 acres where he formerly lived for the benefit of "my younger Grandsons," he says: "The Situation of the Place is convenient to Trade, lies fourteen Miles from the Falls of Rappahannock, twelve from Dumfries, on Potomack, seven from Aquia Warehouse, the same Distance from Aquia Church, six from the Quaker Meeting House, five from the Baptist Meeting House, in Fauquier County, four from Chapwasmick Meeting House, in Stafford County, and not quite three miles from Two Grist Mills." He continues giving a full description of the plantation and says since 1756 the "very fine Apple Orchard" has averaged yielding seven or eight Thousand Gallons of Cider a year which is as good as any on the Continent."

Thus we see that the Baptist meeting house at Chapwasmick in Stafford County had been erected - in fact the record book of this church, beginning in 1766, indicates a large membership consisting of many former Episcopalians whose names are found upon The Register of Overwharton Parish.

On March 5, 1772 the House of Burgesses again fanned the flames of insurrection by ordering that the "tithables of Overwharton Parish be levied for 4,686 pounds of tobacco and £ 1:11:3 current money" for expenses incurred in the prosecution of certain petitions presented to the last General Assembly for dissolving the vestry of the said parish.

Dissatisfaction mounted over the election of a new vestry as ordered by the General Assembly as well as their actions and non-actions. A petition "of sundry inhabitants of Overwharton Parish" received by the House of Burgesses on May 9, 1774 set forth "that the Election of Vestrymen in the said Parish, by virtue of a late Act of the General Assembly, was made in an unfair and illegal manner." While the situation was perhaps not as tense as in the time of Parson Waugh a hundred years before, it was evident that the doctrine of separation of church and state was firmly fixed in the minds of many. These dissenters kept their views constantly before the public and as the outbreak of the Revolutionary War approached it was certain that they had won their fight.

By an act passed at the Capitol at Williamsburg on October 7, 1776, in the First Year of the Commonwealth, "the different societies of Dissenters" were exempt "from contributing to the support and maintenance of the church as by law established." This act states that the purpose is to extend "equal liberty, as well religious

as civil, may be universally extended to all the good people of this Commonwealth."
By this act all dissenters were decreed "totally free and exempt from all levies,
taxes, and impositions" ... "towards supporting and maintaining" the Established
Church. However the glebe lands, churches and chapels were reserved to the use of
the parishes as previously established as well as all books, plate, and ornaments
belonging to them.

The passage of this and other acts greatly spurred the Revolutionary cause,
and united the people of Overwharton Parish who were great suffers in that struggle
fought for freedom from the English crown. After the termination of the war many
families moved to Kentucky and elsewhere. Significant is the fact that most of the
family and immediate connections of the Reverend Mr. Moncure remained in Stafford
County and its environs and with a few other loyal Episcopalian families by some
means preserved Aquia Church though Potomac Church was allowed to crumble.

The Honorable George Mason of Gunston Hall in his letter to his cousin, Mrs.
Frances (Brown) Moncure, widow of the Reverend Mr. John Moncure (circa 1714-1764),
[which has been quoted verbatim on pages 191 and 192] states he is "very glad to
hear that Mr. Scott purposes to apply for Overwharton Parish." He refers to the
Reverend Mr. James Scott (17 -1782), then rector of Dittengen Parish in adjoining
Prince William County, who was Mrs. Moncure's brother-in-law. We have no particu-
lars, but the Reverend Mr. Scott continued his charge in Dettingen Parish until his
death. Bishop William Meade in his Old Churches and Families of Virginia intimates
the Reverend Mr. Moncure was succeeded by the Reverend Mr. Charles Green (1711-1765),
rector of Truro Parish in Fairfax County, but this is without foundation as he died
the following year yet rector of Truro Parish and his last will and Testament remains of record in Fairfax County, Virginia.

The Fitzhugh family register furnishes evidence that the Reverend Mr. Moncure
was succeeded by the Reverend Mr. Clement Brooke (1730-1808); this is quoted in detail on page 232, and shows he was rector of Overwharton Parish early in 1765. Of
distinguished ancestry, he was born at Brookfield, Prince George's County, Maryland, the son of Thomas and Lucy (Smith) Brooke. He held several charges in Maryland before coming to Virginia where he was minister of Overwharton Parish for about
eleven years. He was loyal to the American cause and was a member of the Committee
of Safety of Stafford County in 1774. He married his cousin Anne Murdock and had
five children, viz: (1) Kitty Murdock Brooke, born March 11, 1775, married Isaac
Lansdale; (2) Thomas Brooke, born August 27, 1776, married Elizabeth Bowie; (3)
Anne Addison Brooke, born July 28, 1778; (4) William Murdock Brooke, born November
17, 1779 and (5) Clement Brooke, Junior, born April 2, 1781, married Ann Eleanor
Whitaker. About the beginning of the Revolutionary War the Reverend Mr. Clement
Brooke returned to Maryland and died there.

Various petitions were received by the House of Burgesses beginning in 1769
"for a new modelling of the counties of Richmond, Westmoreland, King George and
Stafford." Finally on the 3rd of June 1775 the House of Burgesses ordered "that
leave be given to bring in a bill for altering and establishing the boundries of
the counties of King George and Stafford and Mr. Jones, Mr. Fitzhugh, and Mr. Charles
Carter of Stafford, do prepare and bring in the same." The Honorable Joseph Jones
(1727-1805) of Spring Hill and the Honorable William Fitzhugh (1741-1809) of Chatham
represented King George County, while Colonel Charles Carter (1733-1796) of Ludlow

represented Stafford County. Judge Joseph Jones presented the bill to the House
and the Council shortly concurred but before the bill was signed, the Honorable
John Murray, Earl of Dunmore, lieutenant governor of Virginia, fled from Williamsburg and took refuge on a British man-of-war and the Royal Government in Virginia
was dissolved; the Revolution had begun. However, on the 15th of October 1776 the
bill was again presented to the legislators assembled at Williamsburg and that
assembly ordered extensive alterations in the boundries of King George and Stafford
counties to be effective the 1st of January 1777.

Since the formation of Stafford and King George counties the upper or western
section of the Northern Neck penisula had been about equally divided between the
westward extensions of Westmoreland County on the Potomac River and Richmond County
on the Rappahannock River. Thus the counties of Stafford [formed from Westmoreland
County in 1664] and King George [formed from Richmond County in 1721] were long and
narrow and were divided by the natural ridge of the Northern Neck, that is to say,
that territory which was drained by the Rappahannock River was King George County
and that territory which was drained by the Potomac River was Stafford County. A
more convenient division of Stafford and King George counties was effected by the
Act of 1776. This directed that the two counties be divided about the middle across
the Northern Neck penisula, beginning at the mouth of Muddy Creek on the Rappahannock River and following it upstream to its headwaters near where present Route 218
crosses it and thence in a straight line [which presently divides the farms of Mrs.
Thomas Benton Gayle, Senior, and her son Robert Lee Gayle] to the head spring of
Whipsewasin [Whipewaughson] Creek, and thence down the meanders of the said creek
to its junction with Potomac Creek and thence down this creek to Potomac River.

By this approximately North-South division of the two counties, the lower
portion of Stafford County along the Potomac River was given to King George County
and the upper portion of King George County along the Rappahannock River was given
to Stafford County. The entire bounds of colonial Saint Paul's Parish fell into
King George County, but the major portion of Overwharton Parish remained in Stafford
County. However, Overwharton Parish lost to King George County that land drained by
the Potomac River on the south side of Potomac Creek between Whipsowason Creek and
Passapatanzy Creek which had been the domain of Prince Japasaw and later of Colonel
Henry Meese, Parson John Waugh, the Sumners and Doctor Edward Maddox who bequeathed
his plantation as a glebe for Overwharton Parish in 1694.

In this extensive alteration of boundry lines most of Brunswick Parish, King
George County, was thrown into Stafford County: to be exact, the portion acquired
by Stafford County included that territory in the Rappahannock watershed between
Muddy Creek and Deep Run, but this territory was not added to Overwharton Parish
but remained a part of Brunswick Parish. Brunswick Parish had three colonial churches. The earliest was on the present Stafford County side of Muddy Creek immediately
on the left hand side of Route 3 before one crosses the creek; the site is fortunate-
ly marked by a lone tombstone to Mr. George Mayers (1713-1755) although the Reverend
Mr. Daniel McDonald (17 -1762) is also buried there. Before the Revolutionary War
Muddy Creek Church was abandoned and Lamb's Creek Church, now standing, replaced it
as the lower parish church of Brunswick Parish. The upper parish church of Brunswick Parish was at Falmouth on the hill where now stands the remains of the old brick
church surrounded by the cemetery. The glebe of Brunswick Parish was the present
farm of Mr. Robert Lee Gayle on Muddy Creek; it is yet called The Glebe Farm.

The Reverend Mr. Clement Brooke was succeeded as rector of Overwharton Parish by the Reverend Mr. Robert Buchan (17 -1804), a bachelor. He was licensed by the Bishop of London for Virginia on March 16, 1772 and received the King's Bounty on March 20, 1772. Various published accounts say the Reverend Mr. Buchan was minister of Overwharton Parish 1785-1804, but I find him in the vicinity in 1773 and believe he immediately followed the Reverend Mr. Brooke in his charge. In 1773 the Reverend Mr. Buchan stood as godfather at the baptism of Sidney Wishart (1773-1841), youngest child of the Reverend Mr. John Wishart (17 -1774), then rector of Brunswick Parish. As rector of Overwharton Parish, he certified that on February 26, 1780 he married Doctor George French (1751-1824) of Fredericksburg, Virginia, to Anne Brayne Benger, daughter of John Benger, Esq., (17 -1766), late of Spotsylvania County, Virginia.

Among the Stafford County court records is an interesting recording of an "Account of Parochial Property - Overwharton Parish, 1785." The record reads:

"At a Vestry held for the Parish of Overwharton at the Glebe of same August 20, 1785:

PRESENT

Robert Buchan   Minister

Thomas Mountjoy)
John R. Peyton)   Church wardens

John Mountjoy   )
William Garrard)
Moses Phillips)   Vestrymen
Elijah Threlkeld)
George Burroughs)
James Withers   )

"Pursuant to an Act of Assembly, we the Minister and Vestry of Overwharton Parish proceeded to value the real and personal estate of the said Parish, do find:

235 acres of land worth £ 15 per annum
100 acres of land for the Poor House

Chalice and plate at Aquia Church   £ 5 1/2
       Do   at Potomac Church £ 6 1/2"

The document is signed by the above mentioned minister, church wardens and vestrymen of Overwharton Parish.

It appears that both Aquia Church and Potomac Church were in regular use in 1785 and from all inferences I can gather, they continued so during the lifetime of the Reverend Mr. Buchan, but both suffered neglect after his death. The complete lack of vestry records during this period leaves us ignorant of many details.

The Fredericksburg _Virginia Herald_ of Tuesday, January 31, 1804 carried the following obituary:

> "Died, on Wednesday the 25th inst., at his seat
> in Stafford County, the Rev. Robert Buchan, a
> Gentleman of exemplary piety, integrity and
> erudition."

By his last will and Testament the Reverend Mr. Robert Buchan bequeathed "to my successor in the Parish of Overwharton, if a minister of the Protestant Episcopal Church, my surplice, but if the parish should not obtain one of that persuasion my executors may dispose of it as they think fit." This phraseology indicates some doubt in the mind of the testator if Overwharton Parish would be served by a clergyman of the Protestant Episcopal Church. The indications are that the parish was without a minister for a number of years. The Reverend Mr. Buchan had resided on his own plantation near Potomac Church but had enjoyed the glebe on the south side of Potomac Creek which had been bequeathed to the parish in 1694 by Doctor Edward Maddox. After his death, Doctor Maddox's heirs instigated a chancery suit claiming that the glebe so devised by their ancestor had fallen into disuse by the parish and thus had reverted to them. The facts recited in this cause and other indications lead us to the conclusion that the fifteen years following the death of the Reverend Mr. Buchan witnessed the lowest period of Episcopalian interest in Overwharton Parish.

Bishop William Meade informs us that the Reverend Mr. Thomas Allen took charge of Overwharton Parish in 1819 and labored hard for its resuscitation, preaching alternatively at Dumfries and Aquia churches. At a subsequent period, the Reverend Mr. Prestman gave all his energies to the work of the revival of Aquia Church and while the labors of both were of some avail to preserve Aquia Church from utter extinction, it did not rise to anything like prosperity until the last half of the Nineteenth Century, from which period the minutes of the vestry have been preserved.

Writing in 1857, Bishop Meade reflects upon a visit to Aquia Church in 1838 while he was Assistant-Bishop of the Protestant Episcopal Church in Virginia. This account is interesting and is quoted here in full:

> ... "It stands upon a high eminence, not very far from the
> main road from Alexandria to Fredericksburg. It was a mel-
> ancholy sight to behold the vacant space around the house,
> which in other days had been filled with horses and carriages
> and footmen, now overgrown with trees and bushes, the limbs
> of the green cedars not only casting their shadows but rest-
> ing their arms on the dingy walls and thrusting them through
> the broken windows, thus giving an air of pensiveness and gloom
> to the whole scene. The very pathway up the commanding emin-
> ence on which it stood was filled with young trees, while the
> arms of the older ones so embraced each other over it that it
> was difficult to ascend. The church had a noble exterior, be-
> ing a high two-story house, of the figure of the cross. On
> its top was an observatory, which you reached by a flight of
> stairs leading from the gallery, and from which the Potomac

and Rappahannock Rivers, which are not far distant from each
other, and much of the surrounding country, might be seen.
Not a great way off, on another eminence, there might be seen
the high, tottering walls of the Old Potomac Church, one of
the largest in Virginia, and long before this time a deserted
one. The soldiers during the last war with England, when English vessels were in the Potomac, had quartered in it; and it
was said to have been sometimes used as a nursery for cater-
pillars, a manufactory of silk having been set up almost at
its doors. The worshippers in it had disappeared from the
country long before it ceased to be a fit place for prayer.
But there is hope even now for the once desolated region about
which we have been speaking. At my visit to Old Aquia Church
in the year 1837, to which I allude, I baptized five of the
children of the present Judge Moncure, in the venerable old
building in which his first ancestor had preached and so many
of his other relatives had worshipped. He had been saving them
for that house and that day. I visited once more, during the
last spring, that interesting spot. Had I been suddenly dropped
down upon it, I should not have recognised the place or building.
The trees and brushwood and rubbish had been cleared away. The
light of heaven had been let in upon the once gloomy sanctuary.
At the expense of eighteen hundred dollars, (almost all of it
contributed by the descendants of Mr. Moncure,) the house had
been repaired within, without, and above. The dingy walls were
painted white and looked new and fresh, and to me it appeared
one of the best and most imposing temples in our land. The
congregation was a good one. The descendants of Mr. Moncure,
still bearing his name, formed a large portion. I was told that
all those whom I had baptized eighteen years ago (some of whom,
of course, were not babes at the time) were there and meant to
make it their home. The country, which seemed some time since
as if it were about to be deserted of its inhabitants by reason
of sickness and worn-out fields, is putting on a new aspect.
Agriculture is improving. A better population is establishing
itself in the county, and at the end of a century there is an
encouraging prospect that a good society and an Episcopal congregation will be again seen around and within Old Aquia Church.
The Rev. Mr. [Henry] Wall is now their minister."

The Reverend Mr. Henry Wall (1818-1889) was a native of Ireland; he graduated
from Trinity College, Dublin, and was ordained Deacon in 1852 and Priest in 1853.
After some years as rector of Aquia Church, he served as rector of Saint John's
Church in Richmond and in 1870 the College of William and Mary bestowed the honorary degree of Doctor of Divinity on him. He married first, in 1856, Judith Woodford
Hansford (1828-1864), and secondly, in 1866, her sister, Julia Wallace Hansford;
they were the daughters of Addison Hansford, Esq., (1800-1850) of Green Height,
King George County, who served as clerk of the Virginia Senate 1824-1849, and his
wife nee Julia Wallace (1802-1882). Mrs. Hansford was the granddaughter of Doctor
Michael Wallace (1719-1767) of Ellerslie, King George [now Stafford] County, and
his wife Elizabeth Brown, one of the nine beautiful daughters of Doctor Gustavus

Brown (1689-1762) of Rich Hill, Charles County, Maryland, who is mentioned on page 186. Thus we see that Mrs. Henry Wall was a cousin of the Moncures and the several other families of that large connection who were then struggling to revive Aquia Church.

The vestry book covering the years 1852-1888 reveals an appalling resolution of the vestry in 1869. Because an infirm rector was having difficulty climbing the steps of the handsome three decker colonial pulpit, the vestry decided to dismantle it and erect a new pulpit on the floor level. Captain Sydney Smith Lee (1802-1869), elder brother of General Robert Edward Lee (1807-1870), who was a vestryman in Overwharton Parish, reported he had received seventy dollars "from friends in Alexandria" to carry out the project and thus he was put in charge of the demolition. The next recording is a happy one! "While making preparations to carry out the above object, he [Captain Lee] departed this life" and the project went to rest with him. Aquia Church had again been spared.

Today Aquia Church stands in all its colonial glory. The edifice is in an excellent state of repair, has a recently installed modern heating system, and the grounds and cemetery surrounding it are well kept. Under the leadership of Mrs. Robert V.H. Duncan, a descendant of the Reverend Mr. John Moncure and president of the Aquia Church Association, a handsome parish house in site of the church was dedicated on Sunday, July 9, 1961, by Suffragan Bishop Samuel B. Chilton of Virginia. May the work of the parish go forward under the rectorship of the Reverend Mr. Arthur E. Booth, and Old Aquia forever stand that future generations may reflect upon all that it represents for it alone is the sole surviving handsome colonial structure of any description in Overwharton Parish.

POTOMAC CHURCH

Recently I stood upon the site of Potomac Church; all that is evident are a few broken bricks - not even the general outline of the building remains above ground. I wished for an archeological crew to reveal the interesting details now hidden below the ground level.

The site is upon an elevation immediately upon the narrows of Potomac Creek on the right hand side of Route 608 after crossing the creek from Fredericksburg toward Brooke, Va. This now slightly travelled road was once the scene of much activity and it is indeed difficult to realize that Potomac Church, which was one of the largest colonial churches in Virginia, stood upon an eminence in this deserted region. Three wars and the complete exodus of the ancient families in the environs of Potomac Church were the cause of its destruction. Oh, that it had been so fortunate as Aquia Church and been blessed with guardian hands such as those of the Moncures which have constantly hovered over their ancestral shrine. So long has it been since the edifice was a place of worship and all of the aristocratic colonial families moved from the environs, the historians task is indeed difficult. I have discovered a few facts, but these are quite meager considering what would have been available if the Northern Army had not busied itself with the destruction of the Stafford County court records and, indeed, the church itself.

Henry Thompson, Gentleman, of Stafford County, by will dated October 23, 1691

and proved November 13, 1691, bequeathed to "the Church of Stafford ten pounds
sterling to be by the minister and Church Wardens laid out in plate for the blessed sacrament and other necessarys for the service of God and ornament of the
abovesaid Church at the head of Potomack Creek." To his last will and Testament
Henry Thompson, Gentleman, appointed as his sole executor "my Trusty Friend," the
Reverend Mr. John Waugh, and, being a bachelor, bequeathed his large estate to
various persons. Richard Waugh, Alexander Waugh and Ann Waugh, children of the
Reverend Mr. John Waugh, were bequeathed land; Joseph Waugh, the Parson's eldest
son, was bequeathed "one large seal Ring of twenty shillings price."

Probably the next bequest to Stafford Parish was that of Doctor Edward Maddox (16 -1694) which has been mentioned in detail on pages 179-180. The glebe
bequeathed by Doctor Maddox was on the south side of Potomac Creek at the lower
end of Stafford [later Overwharton] Parish and not far from Potomac Church by
water. However, the Reverend Mr. Alexander Scott found it inconvenient and pre-
ferring to be nearer the center of the parish, leased the glebe and resided upon
his own land at Dipple; this practice seems to have been followed by the several
rectors who followed him.

Until Aquia Church was erected in 1757, Potomac Church was the principal
church of Overwharton Parish, but the date of its erection is unknown. John Mercer of Marlborough records that his infant daughter Elizabeth Mason Mercer (February 16, 1730-August 31, 1732) was baptised at Potomac Church on Easter Sunday,
April 12, 1730, by the Reverend Mr. Alexander Scott.

In the _Virginia Gazette_ of April 24, 1752, Alexander Hay advertised a horse
had come to his plantation "Near Potowmack Church in Stafford County," which indicates it was a place well known in Virginia.

William Allason, Scotch merchant at Falmouth, kept meticulous account books
and in 1765-1766 these carry the accounts of James Wayton, sexton at Potomac Church.

I have previously cited on page 199 the account of the Parochial Property of
Overwharton Parish in 1785 showing that Potomac Church had a more handsome communion
service than has been preserved at Aquia Church; the whereabouts of this is unknown
to me.

Indications are that Potomac Church was a regular place of worship from the
time of its erection during the curatorship of the Reverend Mr. Alexander Scott,
until about 1804 when the Reverend Mr. Robert Buchan, who lived on his own plantation nearby, died.

The account left by Bishop William Meade quoted on pages 200-201 indicates
Potomac Church was deserted by the time of the War of 1812 and in 1838 he observes
the edifice was standing but long unfit for services. Bishop Meade seemingly did
not visit the church and the next account we have is from Benson J. Lossing who
visited Potomac Church in December 1848 and left the following account:

> ... "The plan of the interior was similiar to that of Pohick.
> The roof is supported by square columns, stuccoed and painted in
> imitation of variegated marble. The windows are in Gothic style.

The LAW, the PRAYER, and the CREED were quite well preserved
upon the walls, notwithstanding the roof is partly fallen in,
and the storms have free passage through the ruined arches.
It is surrounded by a thick hedge of thorn, dwarf cedars, and
other shrubs, festooned and garlanded with ivy and wild grape,
which almost effectually guard the venerable relic from the
intrusion of strangers."

Lossing's accompanying sketch of the ruins of Potomac Church in his Pictorial
Field-Book of the Revolution [1852], Volume II, page 422, shows a square hip-
roofed building; this is reproduced below.

RUINS OF POTOMAC CHURCH.

A traveller from Washington, D.C., writing in The Fredericksburg News of May
17, 1855, has left us some "reminiscance of our early colonial history" on Potomac
Creek and states that deserted Potomac Church was "one of the old colonial Sanctu-
aries we visited." Continuing he says:

    ... "It is said to be two hundred years old - it is made of
    English Brick and the walls still stand in defiance of the rude

neglect they have received and the painted tapestry and tables
containing the Lord's Prayer and Creed on the one hand and the
Ten Commandments on the other, are almost entirely preserved
after exposure to the storms for more than a century. As we
sat musing beneath this half roofless temple of God, encompass-
ed by its rich dark shade, we could not repel the reflection
that truly 'old things do pass away and all things become new.'
And yet there are some things which time cannot touch as he has
touched this old church! How nobly, for example, has the holy
faith to which it was dedicated withstood his ruthless savages
and how it has grown and expanded into a mighty church of mill-
ions since the primitive visitation in those days to the House
of God, in simple barges. It is a pleasant thought to know too
that great and good names are also immortal, and may never be
effaced by time, but will linger around the generations who are
to come after them, as beacons to the same bright goal they have
attained."

The next account I have of Potomac Church and its environs is from the pen
of the Honorable Peter Vivian Daniel (1784-1860); it is quoted here verbatim from
Bishop William Meade's Old Churches, Ministers, and Families of Virginia, Volume
II, pages 204-205. It would have been extremely difficult for Bishop Meade to
have found a more competent person than Judge Daniel to relate his recollections
of the Potomac Church area.

                              "Washington, November 12, 1855
      "Dear Sir:
              "In reply to your inquiries concerning the Old Potomac
      Church and its neighbourhood, I give you the following statement,
      founded in part upon tradition and partly upon my own recollect-
      ion. My maternal grandfather, John Moncure, a native of Scotland,
      was the regular minister of both Aquia and Potomac Churches. He
      was succeeded in the ministry in these churches by a clergyman
      named Brooke, who removed to the State of Maryland. The Rev. Mr.
      Buchan succeeded him: he was tutor in my father's family, and ed-
      ucated John Thompson Mason, General Mason, of Georgetown, Judge
      Nicholas Fitzhugh, and many others. Going back to a period some-
      what remote in enumerating those who lived in the vicinity of
      Potomac Church, I will mention my great-grandfather, Rawleigh
      Travers, one of the most extensive landed proprietors in that
      section of the country, and who married Hannah Ball, half-sister
      of Mary Ball, the mother of General George Washington. From Raw-
      leigh Travers and Hannah Ball descended two daughters, Elizabeth
      and Sarah Travers: the former married a man named Cooke, and the
      latter my grandfather, Peter Daniel. To Peter and Sarah Daniel
      was born an only son, - Travers Daniel, my father, - who married
      Frances Moncure, my mother, the daughter of the Rev. John Moncure
      and Frances Brown, daughter of Dr. Gustavus Brown, of Maryland.
      The nearest and the coterminous neighbour of my father was John
      Mercer of Marlborough, a native of Ireland, a distinguished law-
      yer; the compiler of 'Mercer's Abridgment of the Virginia Laws;'

the father of Colonel George Mercer, an officer in the British
service, who died in England about the commencement of the Revolution; the father also of Judge James Mercer, father of Charles F. Mercer, of John Francis Mercer, who in my boyhood resided
at Marlborough, in Stafford, and was afterwards Governor of Maryland; of Robert Mercer, who lived and died in Fredericksburg; of
Ann Mercer, who married Samuel Selden of Salvington, Stafford; of
Maria Mercer, who married Richard Brooke of King William, father
of General George M. Brooke; and of another daughter, whose name
is not recollected, - the wife of Muscoe Garnett and mother of
the late James M. Garnett.

      "Proceeding according to contiguity were Elijah Threl-
keld [1], John Hedgman, who married a daughter of Parson Spence
Grayson, of Prince William; Thomas Mountjoy, William Mountjoy,
and John Mountjoy, the last-mentioned of whom emigrated to Kentucky, having sold his farm [Millvale] to Mr. John T. Brooke, the
brother of the late Judge Francis T. Brooke, and who married Ann
Cary Selden, daughter of Ann Mercer and grand-daughter of John
Mercer. Next in the progression was the residence of John Brown,
who married Hannah Cooke, daughter of Elizabeth Travers, and granddaughter of Hannah Ball, wife of Rawleigh Travers. Next was the
glebe, the residence of the Rev. Robert Buchan. Adjoining this
was the residence, (in the immediate vicinity of the church,)
called Berry Hill, of Colonel Thomas Ludwell Lee, who possessed
another plantation, on the opposite side of Potomac Creek, called
Bellevue. The son of the gentleman last named, and bearing the
same name, removed to Loudoun [County]. Of his daughters, one
married Daniel Carroll Brent, of Richland, Stafford, and the other
Dr. John Dalrymple Orr[1], of Prince William. Next to Berry Hill was

---

1 - Colonel Thomas Ludwell Lee (1730-1778) of Bellvue and his family attended
Potomac Church; the journal of his daughter, Lucinda Lee [who married Dr.
John Dalrymple Orr (17 -1820)], throws some interesting sidelights on the
Potomac Church area. September 28, 1787: "To-day is Sunday, and I am going
to church. Brother Aylett is going in the Chariot with me. I am this moment
going to crape and dress. I shall wear my Great-Coat and dress Hat. Adieu,
till my return. ... I am returned. Mrs. Brooke, Mrs. Selden and Nancy were
all at church in deep mourning. They were very civil to me and prest me to
dine at Salvington. Mr. James Gordon is come to dinner from Chatham. Mrs.
Fitzhugh has sent me a very pressing invitation to go there this evening, and
tomorrow to the races; but I have not the smallest inclination, and shall not
go. This Mr. Gordon is a mighty clever man - I wish you could see him. I saw
a beauty at church, a Miss Threlkeld. She has hazel eyes, fine complexion and
beautiful auburn hair which hung in ringlets upon her neck." These observations were made for the writer's friend, Miss Polly Brent. She probably refers to Ann Threlkeld (1772-1828), only child of Colonel Elijah Threlkeld;
she married in 1792 Captain John Fox (circa 1770-1843), then deputy clerk of
Stafford County court who later represented that county in the Virginia House
of Delegates. For further information on the Fox, Threlkeld, &c: families,
see Tyler's Quarterly Historical and Genealogical Magazine, Volume 21, page
265 et seq.

the plantation of John Withers, on the stream forming the head
of Potomac Creek. Crossing this stream were those of John James,
Thomas Fitzhugh of Boscobel, Major Henry Fitzhugh of Belle Air,
Samuel Selden of Salvington, the husband of Ann Mercer, and lastly,
Belle Plaine, the estate of Goury Waugh, and, after his death, of
his sons, George Lee Waugh and Robert Waugh. I have thus, sir,
without much attention to system or style, attempted a compliance
with your request, and shall be gratified if the attempt should prove
either serviceable or gratifying. I would remark that the enumera-
tion given you, limited to a space of some eight or ten miles square,
comprises none but substantial people, some of them deemed wealthy in
their day, several of them persons of education, polish, and refine-
ment.

"With great respect, yours,

P.V. Daniel"

In the summer of 1861 a Civil War correspondent observed that the walls of
Potomac Church still stood on a hill between the Potomac and Rappahannock rivers;
this is the last account I have of it.

Like all the handsome homes in the vicinity, Potomac Church fell pray to the
Federal Army who occupied the Potomac Creek area at the beginning of the Civil War.
They played havoc with the entire region, destroying, by one means or another,
everything with which they came in contact. They tore down the walls of Potomac
Church and used the bricks for other purposes and at the termination of the Civil
War the entire area was one of the most desolate imaginable.

As I drive through Overwharton Parish and by boat ply the several estuaries
which lead far into it, I reflect upon the early history of the region and the many
changes time has wrought. Around the beautiful shores of Potomac and Aquia creeks
and along the Potomac River are many summer cottages and a few handsome homes. Upon
Bellevue, a high eminance overlooking the entire Potomac Creek area, which for years
was the seat of Colonel Thomas Ludwell Lee (1730-1778) and his family, is an odd
looking implacement which by its ceaseless rays directs the course of air lines.
While the government confinscated thousands of acres of land in the upper portion
of Overwharton Parish for military uses, the area in general is fastly developing
and Overwharton Parish has indeed a "new look". May old Aquia Church remain un-
altered and stand as a monument to the memory of those of the past who made our way
of life possible.

George H.S. King

Fredericksburg, Virginia
November 11, 1961

SECTION VI

MEMORIAL TABLETS

IN

AQUIA CHURCH

[SCOTT ARMS]

TO THE GLORY OF GOD
AND IN MEMORY OF
The Reverend
ALEXANDER SCOTT, A.M.
Presbyter of the Church of
England. Ordained and Licensed
for Virginia by the Lord Bishop
of London in 1710.
Minister of Overwharton Parish
from 1711 to 1738.
Born Dipple Parish, Moray
Scotland, July 20, 1686
Died April 1, 1738.
His gift, a massive silver communion
Service, still in use in Old Aquia
was buried during the Revolutionary
War - War of 1812 - and
War Between the States.

[MONCURE ARMS]

TO THE GLORY OF GOD
AND IN MEMORY OF
The Reverend
JOHN MONCURE
Born cir.1709 in Mearns Co. Scotland, came
to Virginia in 1733, Returned to England
in 1737 to be Ordained by the Lord Bishop
of London
He was minister of Overwharton
Parish from 1738 until his death. He
married Frances, Daughter of Dr.
Gustavus Brown, born in Dalkeith, Scotland.
After years of devoted service to his
Church and Community, he died
March 10, 1764, and lies
Beneath the Chancel of this Church.

TO THE GLORY OF GOD
AND IN MEMORY OF
MONCURE ROBINSON
Born in Richmond, Virginia
Feb. 2, 1802
Died Nov. 10, 1891
He so loved this church of
his forefathers that in his
will of September 11, 1873
he left an Endownment for
its Preservation.
This tablet is erected in
Gratitude by the Members
of the Congregation - 1938.

[CROSS]

TO THE GLORY OF GOD
AND IN MEMORY OF
ROBERT SOUTH BARRETT D.D.
1851 - 1896
Rector of this Church
1876
and
KATE WALLER BARRETT M.D.
1858 - 1925
Co-Founder of the
National Florence
Crittenton Mission
1898

THE
ENTRANCE DOORS
Given in 1958
Are a Memorial to
JAMES ASHBY
MONCURE
1861 - 1938
A Devoted Member
of this Church
in his youth and
always vitally
interested in
its welfare.

SECTION VII

GENEALOGICAL NOTES

CONCERNING

CHURCH WARDENS

AND

VESTRYMEN

OF

OVERWHARTON PARISH

1757

PLAQUE ON GALLERY OF AQUIA CHURCH
1757

SECTION VII

GENEALOGICAL NOTES

THE PLAQUE upon which William Copein inscribed the names of the minister, church wardens and vestrymen in Overwharton Parish in 1757 when Aquia Church was completed is attached to the front of the gallery; the inscription has been noted on page 194. Some account of these church wardens and vestrymen and their families may be of interest and I will take them up in the order in which they are named on the plaque.

MAJOR PETER HEDGMAN

Major Peter Hedgman (circa 1700-1765) was the son of Nathaniel Hedgman formerly of Lancaster County, who came to Stafford County as the overseer of the vast holdings of Colonel Robert ["King"] Carter (1663-1732). Nathaniel Hedgman acquired Rose Hill on Accakeek Creek, formerly the property and burial place of Colonel George Mason (1628-1686) and this plantation descended to his son Major Peter Hedgman. The published Letters of Robert Carter reveal that Nathaniel Hedgman met a violent death in 1721 while not attending to Colonel Carter's business as he wrote: "I have heard of late he hath been a very great deliquent from my business and lived a loose, rebelling life, which hath brought him to his untimely catastrophe. As for entertaining his son, a wild young lad that hath had no experience in the world, I can by no means think proper." On June 22, 1721 Colonel Carter wrote young Peter Hedgman that he would not consider "Your proposal of succeeding your father in my business," but rather was sending John Johnson who "hath been my overseer for some years to succeed your father as my general overseer." Despite Colonel Carter's remarks, Peter Hedgman rose to a place of political and social prominence in Overwharton Parish and died testate in 1765 after serving as vestryman, justice, militia officer and representing Stafford County in the House of Burgesses 1742-1758.

In 1943 the tomb of Margaret (Mauzy) Hedgman (1702-1754), wife of Major Peter Hedgman, was moved from Rose Hill to Aquia Churchyard. It is inscribed:

> Here lies interred the Body of
> MARGARET, the wife of
> PETER HEDGMAN
> of Stafford County, Gentleman,
> and Daughter of
> John Mauzy, Gentleman, Deceased.
> She was married
> the 21 Day of September A.D. 1721
> and had by him nine Children
> of which three Sons only survived Her.
> As she was a Woman
> of great Virtue and Goodness
> She liv'd beloved

and dy'd much lamented
by all who had the Happiness
of Her acquaintance
the 6th Day of January A.D.1754
in the 52^d Year of her Age.

Conjux Dolens

H.M.P.

John Mauzy served as a gentleman justice of Stafford County court in 1714 and probably until his death circa 1718.

Major Peter Hedgman (circa 1700-1765) and Margaret Mauzy (1702-1754), his wife, had three sons to live to maturity, viz:
  (1) William Hedgman (1732-1765) died without issue. By their last wills and Testaments both he and his father disinherited their only heir, John Hedgman (1758-1796),and bequeathed their handsome estates to others.
  (2) George Hedgman (1734-1760) married on November 27, 1756 Hannah Ball Daniel (1737-1829), daughter of Peter Daniel, Gentleman, (1706-1777), also a vestryman in Overwharton Parish. Their only child was John Hedgman (1758-1796); he married Catherine Grayson, daughter of the Reverend Mr. Spence Grayson (1734-1798), rector of Dettingen Parish, Prince William County, and left issue. Hannah Ball (Daniel) Hedgman married secondly on March 12, 1765 Gilson Foote, Gentleman, (1736-1770) of Fauquier County and thirdly, John Hardy (17 -1794) of Stafford County. The above account will correct several errors in Virginia Genealogies, page 303, by the Reverend Mr. Horace E. Hayden.
          Writing from Ferry Farm, her home in the present county of Stafford, Mrs. Mary (Ball) Washington (1708-1789), then the widow of Captain Augustine Washington (1694-1743), informed her half-brother, Joseph Ball, Esq., (1689-1760) then residing at Stratford, England, of the situation of some of their relatives. She concludes her letter thus: "Mr. Daniel and his wife and family is well. Cozen Hannah has been married and lost her husband. She had one child, a boy. Pray give my Love to Sister Ball and Mr. Downman and his Lady and I am Dear Brother, Your Loving Sister, Mary Washington." The letter was docketed as received on July 2, 1760.
  (3) John Hedgman (1741-circa 1764) married circa 1763 Frances Morton (1746-ante 1795), daughter of George Morton, Gentleman, (1717-1765) of King George County, and Lucy Baylor, his wife, who was the daughter of Colonel Robert Baylor of King and Queen County. John Hedgman died childless and his widow married secondly circa 1767 Jesse Payne (17 -1770) of Goochland County and left issue. She married thirdly on March 1, 1773 in Goochland County, Doctor John K. Read (1746-1805) and had issue. Doctor Read married secondly in 1796 Helen (Calvert) Maxwell (1750-1833) and resided in Norfol Virginia.

JOHN MERCER

John Mercer, Gentleman, (February 6, 1704/5-October 14, 1768), prominent attorney-at-law, lived at Marlborough which had been the county seat of Stafford County

1691-1718. The planned port of entry at the Town of Marlborough was not a success and Mercer, after gaining title to all the town lots and a considerable acreage adjoining in Potomac Neck, established himself there. He married first on June 10, 1725 Catherine Mason (June 21, 1707-June 15, 1750), only child of Colonel George Mason (16 -1716) and his second wife Elizabeth Waugh, daughter of the Reverend Mr. John Waugh. About 1744 Mercer began construction of a handsome brick residence at Marlborough and here, his journal and account books indicate, he lived in the height of style. Mercer married secondly on November 10, 1750 Ann Roy (17 -1770), daughter of Doctor Mungo Roy of Essex County. John Mercer had a large family concerning whom considerable has been written. There is a detailed account of his family in The Virginia Genealogist, Volume 3, page 99 et seq.

CAPTAIN JOHN LEE

Captain John Lee (1707-1789) was the son of Hancock Lee, Esq., (1653-1709) of Ditchley, Northumberland County, who was the son of Colonel Richard Lee the immigrant to Virginia. His mother, nee Sarah Allerton (1671-1731), was of distinguished and unique ancestry, being the granddaughter of Isaac Allerton, a passenger on the Mayflower, 1620 and of Ensign Thomas Willoughby (1601-1658) who came to Virginia in the Prosperous, 1610, and rose to the council.

Although Captain John Lee was a resident of Overwharton Parish for over fifty years, the general index to the records of Stafford County are completely devoid of any reference to him. By inheritance, patent and purchase he was possessed of several thousand acres of land on Chapawasmic Creek in Overwharton Parish and also plantations in the adjoining counties of Prince William and Fauquier. The earliest reference I find to him is a Bill of Exchange dated August 27, 1724 and directed to George Randall, Merchant at Seren in Cork; this he signs in his characteristic manner: JN⁰ Lee. In 1724 he was granted 245 acres on Chapawasmic Creek by the Proprietors of the Northern Neck of Virginia, and he appears frequently on the records of Prince William and Fauquier counties in various land transactions as John Lee, Gentleman, of Overwharton Parish, Stafford County.

On April 24, 1731 the Council of Virginia ordered that a new commission of the Peace be prepared and that John Lee, William Brent, Henry Washington, Robert Massey, James Carter and James Markham, Gentlemen, be added to the former justices for Stafford County.

Beginning in 1741 The Register of Overwharton Parish indicates that Captain John Lee had many slaves baptized but the only other parochial record I have found of him is the recording on the plaque at Aquia Church noting that he was a vestryman in 1757.

In 1754 he was one of the several gentlemen appointed to appraise the estate in Stafford County of Thomas Lee, Esquire, of Stratford, President of Virginia. Colonel Lee died possessed of two handsome estates on Potomac Creek near Potomac Church to which his son Colonel Thomas Ludwell Lee (1730-1778) succeeded.

Philip Vickers Fithian, tutor in the family of Colonel Robert Carter of Nomini Hall in Westmoreland County, has left us an interesting bit in regard to Captain

John Lee in his journal entry of January 21, 1774:

> ... "To Day about twelve came to Mr. Carter's Captain John
> Lee, a Gentleman who seems to copy the Character of Addisons
> Will Wimble. When I was on my way to this place I saw him up in
> the country at Stafford; he was then just sallying out on his
> Winters Visit, & has got now so far as here, he stays, as I am
> told about eight or ten Weeks in the year at his own House, the
> remaining part he lives, with his waiting Man, on his Friends."

On his journey from Princeton, New Jersey, to Colonel Carter's, Fithian had
stopped on October 25, 1773 at the tavern at Stafford court house and the next day
he called at Bellevue, the seat of Colonel Thomas Ludwell Lee (1730-1778) which he
notes was "only a few Rods from Stafford Tavern;" here he first met the visiting
bachelor, Captain John Lee. On February 10, 1774 Captain John Lee was again at
Nomini Hall, this time in company with his cousin Colonel Francis Lightfoot Lee
(1734-1797) of Menokin in Richmond County and his lady, nee Rebecca Tayloe of Mount
Airy. They had dinner, read in the Virginia Gazette of the Boston Tea Party, and
drank several toasts to the King, the Queen, absent friends, the Governor of Virginia and his Lady and success to American trade and commerce. The evening was
gay and the company spent the night and continued their journey after breakfast.

Captain John Lee died August 11, 1789 in Orange County at the home of his
nephew, Major John Lee (1743-1802). By his last will and Testament dated December
8, 1787 and admitted to probate September 28, 1789 at Orange County court, he left
various legacies to friends, but the bulk of his estate to his nephew Major John
Lee with whom he spent his declining years. Major Lee's wife, nee Elizabeth Bell,
was a cousin of Captain John Lee, being a descendant of Charles Lee of Cobbs Hall.
In 1790 Major John Lee was joined by Elizabeth, his wife, in conveying the 800 acre
plantation of Captain John Lee in Stafford County to Susanna (Crump) Hewitt (1723-
1797), widow of James Hewitt of King George County, and in 1792 they disposed of
their real estate in Orange County and moved to Woodford County, Kentucky. Major
John Lee was the son of Hancock Lee, Junior, (1709-1762) and Mary Willis, his wife,
eldest child of Colonel Henry Willis (circa 1690-1740) of Fredericksburg, Virginia.

MOTT DONIPHAN

Mott Doniphan, Gentleman, (16 -circa 1776) was the second son of Captain
Alexander Doniphan (circa 1653-1717) of Richmond County and Margaret Mott, his wife.
He married Rosanna Anderson, daughter of Captain George Anderson and Mary Matthews,
his wife, of Potomac Creek, Stafford County, and in right of his wife came into
possession of a large landed estate in Overwharton Parish. His family has been detailed in Tyler's Quarterly Historical and Genealogical Magazine, Volume 26, pages
274-285 and Volume 28, pages 226-238. Mott Doniphan, Gentleman, was the great-
great-great-great-grandfather of President Harry Ship Truman.

Rosanna (Anderson) Doniphan was the only child of Captain George Anderson, who
was sheriff of Stafford county 1709-1710 and a gentleman justice in 1714, and his
wife nee Mary Matthews was the daughter of John Matthews, an early inhabitant of the
Potomac Creek neighborhood; he received a grant from the Proprietors of the Northern
Neck for 2,466 acres on Little Hunting Creek in 1694.

CAPTAIN HENRY TYLER

Captain Henry Tyler (circa 1710-1777) was descended from the prominent family of that name in York County, Virginia. In 1736 he succeeded Thomas Claiborne, Esq. (January 9, 1704-December 1, 1735) as clerk of Stafford County; he had served from 1731 until the time of his death. As the office of county clerk was then an appointive position and residence in the county not necessary, Henry Tyler probably came to Stafford County from the vicinity of Williamsburg, Virginia, bringing his commission. He served as clerk of the court until his death; for forty one years his distinctive and beautiful handwriting adorn such of the records of that period which have been preserved. He married circa 1738 Alice Strother (circa 1719-circa 1792), daughter of William Strother, Gentleman, (circa 1696-1733) and Margaret Watts, his wife. Margaret (Watts) Strother, widow, married secondly Captain John Grant, widower of Hester Foote who he married on August 17, 1727 in Saint Paul's Parish, and with him in 1738 sold Ferry Farm, the plantation of her first husband, to Captain Augustine Washington (1694-1743) who died there. Captain John Grant left issue by both wives and died testate in Prince William County about 1747/8; he must not be confused [tho he has been!] with Captain John Grant (circa 1704-1762) of King George County who is mentioned on page 135.

The will of Captain Henry Tyler was recorded in now lost Stafford County Will Book "N" [1767-1783], page 357. Henry and Alice (Strother) Tyler had issue, viz:
  (1) Betty Tyler [#]. Susanna Fitzhugh, daughter of John Fitzhugh of Bellaire, was born February 5, 1756 and was baptized "by the Rev? Mr. Moncure and had for surities Mr. and Mrs. Moncure, Mr. Henry Tyler and Miss Betty, his daughter," says the Fitzhugh family register.
  (2) Thomas Gowry Strother Tyler (circa 1740-1816) succeeded his father as clerk of Stafford County court and acted in that capacity for many years. Like his father his penmanship is distinctive and beautiful. He married Ann Fisher Adie (1756-18), daughter of William Adie (1731-1797); they were separated after having a large family of children, viz: (a) George Rodney Tyler who died without issue in 1809; (b) Thomas Tyler; (c) William Henry Tyler; (d) Elizabeth Adie Tyler; (e) John Cooke Tyler; (f) Alice P. Tyler (who was living in Stafford County in 1855); and (g) Mary Ann Tyler who married Thomas E. Baird of Alexandria, Virginia.
  (3) John Tyler, born April 17, 1743; he is said to have been insane and was taken by his sister, Mrs. Maze, to Georgia.
  (4) Henry Tyler, baptized August 18, 1746; he died testate in Prince William County in 1820. He served as a midshipman in the Navy during the Revolutionary War and also in Lee's Legion at the seige of Yorktown. He was unmarried.
  (5) Anna Tyler, baptized January 30, 1749; she married Robert Maze and moved to Georgia about 1800 taking with her an insane brother and a spinster sister [#], but if Betty or Mary Tyler the chancery papers do not say.
  (6) Mary Tyler [#], baptized March 20, 1751.
  (7) Sally Tyler married George Steptoe Blackwell of Fauquier County, Virginia.

In 1787 Alice (Strother) Tyler and her son John Tyler appear on the Personal Tax lists of Stafford County; in 1791 she last appears paying tax on seven slaves. In 1792 the Estate of Henry Tyler was taxed on six slaves, indicating his widow was deceased. The 300 acre plantation of Captain Henry Tyler was sold to Henry Fitzhugh of Bellaire in 1798.

CAPTAIN WILLIAM MOUNTJOY

Captain William Mountjoy (April 17, 1711-September 27, 1777) married Phillis Reilly (November 15, 1717-April 4, 1771) of Saint Paul's Parish; they lived at Locust Hill near Brooke. For an account of Captain Mountjoy and family see Tyler's Quarterly Historical and Genealogical Magazine, Volume 26, pages 99-104.

Elizabeth Mountjoy, daughter of Captain William and Phillis (Reilly) Mountjoy, married on December 20, 1769 in Overwharton Parish, James Garrard (1747-1822); they moved in 1783 to Bourbon County, Kentucky, and he became that state's second governor serving two terms, 1796-1804. James Garrard was the eldest son of Colonel Willian Garrard (17 -1786), a vestryman in Overwharton Parish in 1785, and Mary Naughty, his wife, who was the only daughter of John Naughty (17 -1762) of Washington Parish, Westmoreland County, Virginia.

Colonel William Garrard and William Fitzhugh, Esquire, (1741-1809) of Chatham by deed dated March 10, 1780 conveyed two acres of land, whereon the present court house of Stafford County now stands, for use of the county. The document states the reason for the joint conveyance is that "a doubt exists whether the said land is the property of Colonel William Garrard or William Fitzhugh, Esquire, of Chatham, both of whom are willing to convey same."

MAJOR BENJAMIN STROTHER

Major Benjamin Strother (circa 1700-1765), son of Captain William Strother (circa 1665-1726) and Margaret Thornton, his wife, of King George County, was a brother of William Strother, Gentleman, (circa 1696-1733) previously mentioned. Major Strother married first circa 1726 Mary (Mason) Fitzhugh, widow of George Fitzhugh, Gentleman, (169?-1722), who represented Stafford County in the House of Burgesses in 1718, and daughter of Colonel George Mason (16 -1716) and Mary Fowke, his first wife, by whom she had an only child to survive infancy, Colonel William Fitzhugh (1721-1798) who removed to Maryland. Colonel William Fitzhugh and his cousin William Fitzhugh, Esquire, of Chatham, were both intimate acquaintances of General George Washington and both often at Mount Vernon. However, in various published accounts these two William Fitzhughs have been confused and misidentified.

Major Benjamin and Mary (Mason) Strother had issue three daughters only, viz:
(1) Margaret Strother (circa 1730-May 31, 1761) who married first on October 26, 1750 John Murdock (17 -1759), son of Jeremiah Murdock, Gentleman, of King George County; he died without issue in Stafford County. She married secondly on March 10, 1760 Colonel William Bronough (1730-1800), son of Colonel Jeremiah Bronough (1702-1749) and Sympha Rose Ann Field Mason (1703-1761) of King George and Fairfax counties, by whom she had an only child, Mary Mason Bronough who married on October 2, 1792 her cousin William Fowke and died without issue. Colonel William Bronough (1730-1800) married secondly on October 13, 1762, Mary (Doniphan) Cooke (July 10, 1737-December 26, 1781), daughter of Mott Doniphan, Gentleman, previously mentioned, and widow of Travers Cooke, Gentleman, (17 -1759), subsequently mentioned, by whom he had seven children. On February 27, 1783 Colonel William Bronough married thirdly Rebecca Craine and had three children. His will, together

with many records of the family, are of record in Loudoun County, Va.
(2) Alice Strother (November 30, 1732-December , 1795) married on December
    16, 1756 Robert Washington, Gentleman, (January 25, 1730-circa 1800) of
    Woodstock, Saint Paul's Parish, Stafford County, son of Townshend and
    Elizabeth (Lund) Washington of Green Hill, Saint Paul's Parish. This
    couple had several children among whom was Lund Washington (1767-1853),
    postmaster of Washington, D.C., to whom we are indebted for a most in-
    formative family manuscript written about 1848 in which he records many
    genealogical facts of several Stafford County families which would other-
    wise have been lost. He married first on February 11, 1793 Susanna Mon-
    roe Grayson (May 29, 1768-April 20, 1822), daughter of the Reverend Mr.
    Spence Grayson (1734-1798), and secondly on April 11, 1823, Sally Johnson
    (October 9, 1797-August 15, 1871), daughter of John Johnson of Worchester
    County, Maryland. Lund Washington left issue by both wives; he and some
    other members of his family are buried in the Congressional Cemetery,
    Washington, D.C.
(3) Ann Strother was married by the Reverend Mr. William Stuart, rector of
    Saint Paul's Parish, on September 16, 1763 to John James (circa 1732-
    circa 1794). He was administrator of the estate of his father-in-law,
    Major Benjamin Strother, and seems to have succeeded to his plantation
    near Potomac Church. The inventory of his estate was recorded in now
    missing Stafford County Will Book "Y" [1793-1804], page 83. On March 6,
    1789 Lund Washington, Senior, (1737-1796) wrote General George Washington
    relating a report heard by his nephew Lund Washington [Junior] (1767-1853)
    while he was lately in Stafford County: John James of Stafford County
    said "that we should have a very pretty President at the head of our new
    government one who had paid off his debts within the time of the War with
    paper money altho it had been lent to him in specia." Lund Washington in-
    forms the General that the report was started by Colonel Mason and adds,
    "he is no friend of yours."
        John and Ann (Strother) James had a large family of whom there is
    considerable detail in the Lund Washington manuscript. John James was
    the son of George James, Gentleman, of Fredericksburg, who died in 1753
    leaving a handsome estate in Spotsylvania, Stafford and Prince William
    counties, and Mary Wheeler, his wife, only child of John Wheeler, Gentle-
    man, (1684-1746) of Overwharton Parish who bequeathed to his grandson John
    James all his land in Prince William County.

    Major Benjamin Strother married secondly on December 6, 1760 Elizabeth (Rowzee)
Waller Peyton (circa 1715-1782), widow of Charles Waller, Gentleman, (17 -1749) and
John Peyton, Gentleman, (1691-1760) both of Stafford County. There is an account of
Major Benjamin Strother and his wives in Tyler's Quarterly Historical and Genealogical
Magazine, Volume 19, pages 224-227 and the Reverend Horace E. Hayden in his Virginia
Genealogies, pages 495-498, details the family of John Peyton (1691-1760) of Stony
Hill.

CAPTAIN THOMAS FITZHUGH

    Captain Thomas Fitzhugh of Boscobell, Overwharton Parish, was born July 16, 1725
at Bedford, Saint Paul's Parish, the son of Colonel Henry Fitzhugh (1687-1758) and
Susanna Cooke (1693-1749), his wife. He married first on October 18, 1746 Catherine

Booth, his first cousin, daughter of Thomas and Mary (Cooke) Booth of Gloucester County; she died childless on February 26, 1748 and her tomb is in the family cemetery at Bedford. Thomas Fitzhugh married secondly on June 19, 1750, Sarah Stuart (February 21, 1731- November   , 1783), daughter of the Reverend Mr. David Stuart, rector of Saint Paul's Parish and had two children. He built Boscobell, renowned for generations as a place of generous hospitality. This mansion was completely destroyed by fire in 1915 and from the ashes was recovered the fire- back from the enormous parlour fire place, marked: "T.F. 1752."

   Captain Thomas Fitzhugh died on December 1, 1768 and his last will and Testa- ment was recorded in now lost Stafford County Will Book "N" [1767-1783], page 78. His only two children were:
   (1) Susanna Stuart Fitzhugh (1751-1823) who married William Knox, Esq.,(1729-
       1805), a native of Scotland, and a wealthy merchant and planter. For
       reasons unknown to me,Major Peter Hedgman and his son William Hedgman
       [see page 216] disinherited their only heir and bequeathed the major
       part of their handsome estates to William and John Knox, brothers, mer-
       chants of Falmouth. "On Monday night the 29th of May 1769 Mr. John Knox
       was most barbarously murdered in his own house in Stafford," notes William
       Allason,another Falmouth merchant, in his ledger. William and Susannah
       Knox resided many years at Windsor Lodge in Culpeper County. After his
       death their son Doctor Thomas Fitzhugh Knox (1772-1835) purchased Belmont
       near Falmouth and his widowed mother resided there 1808-1823 and is buried
       in the Falmouth cemetery. A descendant has handsome portraits of Mr. and
       Mrs. William Knox which were painted by John Hesselius at Windsor Lodge
       in 1771.
   (2) Thomas Fitzhugh (1754-1820) succeeded his father at Boscobell and married
       on January 4, 1778 Ann Rose, daughter of Colonel John Rose of Amherst
       County, Virginia. This couple had numerous children who are mentioned in
       his last will and Testament and Boscobell remained in the Fitzhugh family
       for several generations.

PETER DANIEL, GENTLEMAN

   Peter Daniel, Gentleman, (1706-1777), son of James and Margaret (Vivian) Daniel of Middlesex County, moved to Stafford County when a young man and became one of its most prominent citizens. His marriage on July 15, 1736 to Sarah Travers (171?-1788) is the first marriage recorded in The Register of Overwharton Parish and here too we find the births of their only three children. With Peter Hedgman, John Hooe, Philip Alexander, Henry Washington, Richard Bernard, Richard Foote and John Peyton, he serv- ed as a justice of Stafford County in 1745 and for many years thereafter. He was a zealous advocate for the freedom of the colonies years before the Revolutionary War and as senior presiding justice of Stafford County was the first to sign one of the many protests against the iniquitous Stamp Act. This document, dated October 5, 1765, and addressed to the Honorable Francis Fauquier, Esq., then Lieutenant Gover- nor and Commander-in-Chief of Virginia, desired him to appoint a new commission for Stafford County in which they "may be left out," was signed by Peter Daniel, John Alexander, Travers Daniel, William Bronough, William Brent, John Mercer, Thomas Lud- well Lee, Samuel Selden, Gowry Waugh, Thomas Fitzhugh, and Robert Washington, jus- tices of Stafford County court.

Peter Daniel was a member of the Committee of Safety for Stafford County in 1774. His will was recorded in now lost Stafford County Will Book "N" [1767-1783], page 344. His wife, nee Sarah Travers (171?-1788), survived him; she was one of the three children of Rawleigh Travers (16 -circa 1722), a justice of Stafford County in 1714, and Hannah Ball (circa 1683-1748), his wife, daughter of Colonel Joseph Ball (1649-1711) of Epping Forest, Lancaster County, who married secondly Captain Simon Pearson (16 -1733). Her only brother, Raleigh Travers (17 -1749), died without issue and her only sister Elizabeth Travers married John Cooke, Esq., (died 1733), late of Youghall, County Cork, Ireland, and left issue. It is an error in Hayden's Virginia Genealogies, page 295, where it is stated that Sarah Travers, at the time of her marriage to Peter Daniel, was the widow of a certain Captain Christopher Pearson. It was her mother, Hannah (Ball) Travers, widow, who became the second wife of Captain Simon Pearson (16 -1733) and was known as Madam Pearson. She had no issue by Captain Pearson but he had four children by his first wife.

Joseph Ball, Esq., (1689-1760), brother of Hannah (Ball) Travers Pearson, was solicitous of her three children when he wrote his half-niece the following letter:

"Stratford by London
2^d Novr 1749

Couz. Betty
   I have sent you by your brother Major Washington a Tea Chest, and in it Six Silver Spoons, and Strainer, and Tongs, of the same; And in one Canister 1/4 pound of Green Tea & in the other as much Bohea; and the Sugar Box is full of sugar ready broke: So that as soon as you get your Chest you may sit down, and drink a Dish of Tea.
   I rec.^d your Mother's Letter: give my Love to her, and all your brothers and sisters; and to Rawleigh Travers & Mrs. Cook, and Peter Daniel and his wife. We are all well, I thank God; and wish you all so. My wife and Daughter Join with me in Compliments. I am

Your Loving Uncle
Joseph Ball

To Miss Eliz. Washington
nigh the falls of Rappahannock
By fav.^r of Major Lawrence Washington"

Peter Daniel, Gentleman, and Sarah Travers, his wife, had three children, viz:

 (1) Hannah Ball Daniel (1737-1829) whose three marriages have been mentioned on page 216 under the sketch of Major Peter Hedgman.

 (2) Travers Daniel (May 26, 1741-June 28, 1824) married on October 7, 1762 Frances Moncure (1745-1800), daughter of the Reverend Mr. John Moncure. Their tombs, with other members of the Daniel family, are in the family cemetery at Crow's Nest. Travers Daniel was a justice of Stafford County in 1765 when his father was senior presiding justice and a member of the Committee of Safety for Stafford County in 1774. Travers and Frances (Moncure) Daniel had eleven children who are detailed in Hayden's Virginia

Genealogies, pages 304-305, but I will here mention only their youngest son, the Honorable Peter Vivian Daniel (1784-1860), who has left us the interesting account of the Potomac Creek section of Overwharton Parish which is quoted on pages 205-206.

(3) Elizabeth Travers Daniel born May 16, 1745; died in infancy.

TRAVERS COOKE, GENTLEMAN

Travers Cooke, Gentleman, (circa 1730-1759) was the only son of John Cooke, Esq., (died 1733) and Elizabeth Travers, his wife, mentioned on page 223. He lived but two years after the completion of Aquia Church, having married on February 26, 1754, Mary Doniphan (1737-1781), daughter of Mott Doniphan, Gentleman, also a vestryman in Overwharton Parish. Mary (Doniphan) Cooke married secondly on October 13, 1762 Colonel William Bronough (1730-1800) and had issue seven children. The only child to survive infancy of Travers and Mary (Doniphan) Cooke was Colonel John Cooke (1755-1819) who married on November 18, 1784 Mary Thomson Mason, daughter of the Honorable George Mason (1725-1792) of Gunston Hall. Colonel Cooke was possessed of a very handsome estate including Marlborough which he acquired from the Mercers. Colonel and Mrs. Cooke had a large family of children but I will mention only their daughter Sarah Mason Cooke (1791-1861) who, as the widow of Wilson Cary Selden (1772-1822) of Salvington, married secondly on March 15, 1825 her cousin Doctor Robert Osborne Grayson (1789-1841), grandson of Colonel William Bronough (1730-1800) and Mary Doniphan, his second wife, mentioned on page 220. Their son was Doctor John Cooke Grayson (1832-1894) of Salubria, Culpeper County and he was the father of the late Admiral Cary Travers Grayson (1876-1938), personal physician of President Woodrow Wilson and president of the American Red Cross.

JOHN FITZHUGH, GENTLEMAN

John Fitzhugh, Gentleman, of Bellaire, Overwharton Parish, was born June 30, 1727 at Bedford, Saint Paul's Parish, the son of Colonel Henry Fitzhugh (1687-1758) and Susanna Cooke (1693-1749), his wife. Like his older brother Thomas Fitzhugh of nearby Boscobell, he was baptized by the Reverend Mr. David Stuart; he had "for surities Mr. Mordecai Cooke and Mr. William Brent of Peace Neck, also Mrs. Ann and Elizabeth Buckner, his aunts." He was married on October 30, 1746 to Alice Thornton (August 21, 1729-March 5, 1790), daughter of Rowland Thornton, Gentleman, (1685-1742) of Crow's in King George County and Elizabeth Catlett (1689-1751), his wife; they had thirteen children.

The family of Colonel William Fitzhugh of Bedford is so closely associated with the history of Stafford County, I wish to give a brief outline of the male members who so often appear on the colonial records.

Colonel William Fitzhugh (January 9, 1651-October   ,1701) was married on May 1, 1674 to Sarah Tucker (August 2, 1663-post 1701), daughter of John Tucker of Westmoreland County. Colonel Fitzhugh entered into a marriage agreement on August 26, 1674 with Mrs. Rose Garrard, widow of Mr. John Tucker, for his marriage with her daughter Sarah Tucker and same remains of record in Westmoreland County Deeds, Patents &c: 1665-1677, pages 200-201. They had one daughter who died without issue and five sons, viz:

(1) William Fitzhugh (circa 1678-1713) of Eagle's Nest, Saint Paul's Parish, who married Ann Lee (1683-1732), daughter of the Honorable Richard Lee; she married secondly Captain Daniel McCarty (1679-1724) of Cople Parish, Westmoreland County, who was the widower of Elizabeth Pope (1667-circa 1716). Colonel William and Ann (Lee) Fitzhugh had an only son, viz:

    (i) Colonel Henry Fitzhugh (circa 1706-1742) who succeeded his father at Eagle's Nest. He married on July 28, 1730 Lucy Carter (171?-1773), daughter of Colonel Robert Carter; she married secondly Colonel Nathaniel Harrison (1713-1791) of Brandon, Prince George County, widower of Mary Digges (1717-1744). Colonel Henry Fitzhugh represented Stafford County in the House of Burgesses 1736-1742. Colonel Henry and Lucy (Carter) Fitzhugh had an only son, viz:

        (a) William Fitzhugh, Esq. (1741-1809) who built Chatham in 1769. By the laws of primogeniture, he was the heir of his great-grandfather, Colonel William Fitzhugh the immigrant, who by his last will and Testament entailed his estate male. As his great uncle Thomas Fitzhugh (circa 1689-1719) died without male issue, his extensive land holdings eventually devolved upon William Fitzhugh of Chatham, so that he inherited two full shares of the estate of his great-grandfather Fitzhugh. He held thousands of acres of land in Stafford, Westmoreland, King George, Richmond, Spotsylvania, Fauquier, Prince William and Fairfax counties and spent his declining years at Ravensworth in Fairfax County, maintaining a town house in Alexandria. He was an intimate friend of General George Washington. The last time the General was away from Mount Vernon before his death was on Sunday, November 17, 1799; he records in his diary: "Went to Church in Alexandria and dined with Mr. Fitzhugh." William Fitzhugh married on April 2, 1763, Ann Randolph (1747-1805), daughter of Colonel Peter and Lucy (Bolling) Randolph of Chatsworth, Henrico County. Their only child to leave issue was Mary Lee Fitzhugh (1788-1853) who married in 1804 Mr. George Washington Parke Custis (1781-1857) of Arlington, grandson of Mrs. George Washington, and their only child to survive infancy was Mary Anne Randolph Custis (1808-1873) who married in 1831 Lieutenant [later General] Robert Edward Lee (1807-1870).

(2) Colonel Henry Fitzhugh (January 15, 1687-December 12, 1758) of Bedford, Saint Paul's Parish, married on February 24, 1718 Susanna Cooke (December 7, 1693-November 21, 1749), daughter of Mordecai Cooke, Gentleman, of Gloucester County; their tombstones are in the family cemetery at Bedford. Henry Fitzhugh was a meticulous record keeper and these coupled with the many records concerning him on the court records give us an excellent account of his family. Colonel Henry and Susanna (Cooke) Fitzhugh had nine children; four sons survived infancy, viz:

    (i) Colonel Henry Fitzhugh (1723-1783) succeeded his father at Bedford. He married Sarah Battaile of Caroline County on October 23, 1746 and had fourteen children. Their handsome portraits painted by John Hesselius in 1751 now hang at the Virginia Historical Society.

    (ii) Captain Thomas Fitzhugh (1725-1768) of Boscobell, Overwharton Parish; see pages 221-222.

    (iii) John Fitzhugh, Gentleman, (1727-1809) of Bellaire, Overwharton Parish;

see page 224 et seq.

(iv) Colonel William Fitzhugh (1729-1785) of Loudoun County; he never
    married and vested the greater part of his estate by deeds of gift
    in his nephew, William Fitzhugh (1757-1803) [son of John and Alice
    (Thornton) Fitzhugh] of Prince William County, Virginia.

(3) Thomas Fitzhugh, Gentleman, (circa 1689-1719), received by the will of
his father nearly 5,000 acres of land. A tract of 1,100 acres lay near
the falls of Rappahannock River immediately opposite the present city of
Fredericksburg. At the time of Thomas Fitzhugh this property was in
Richmond County and his last will and Testament is recorded there. He
served as clerk of Stafford County a few years, dying in office. Thomas
Fitzhugh married Anne Fowke (Mason) Darrell, daughter of Colonel George
and Mary (Fowke) Mason, and widow of William Darrell (16 -1715) by whom
she had a son Sampson Darrell (1712-1777) who died testate in Fairfax
County. Thomas and Anne Fowke (Mason) Fitzhugh had an only child, Mary
Fitzhugh, who died in infancy. Anne Fowke (Mason) Darrell Fitzhugh married thirdly Thomas Smith (1   -1764) who died testate in Fairfax County;
his will mentions three children, viz: (1) Susanna Smith; (2) Mary Smith
[married Mr. Hancock]; and (3) William Smith (172?-1802) who died testate
in Mason County, Kentucky.
As Thomas Fitzhugh, Gentleman, died without male issue and his father had
entailed his estate, his property came into possession of William Fitzhugh,
Esq. (1741-1809) and in 1769 he built the handsome brick mansion called
Chatham upon the land overlooking Fredericksburg.

(4) George Fitzhugh, Gentleman, (169?-1722) married Mary Mason, daughter of
Colonel George and Mary (Fowke) Mason. He represented Stafford County
in the House of Burgesses in 1718. His widow married circa 1726 Major
Benjamin Strother and had three daughters who have been mentioned on pages
220-221. The only child to survive infancy of George and Mary (Mason)
Fitzhugh was their son William, viz:

(i) Colonel William Fitzhugh (1721-1798) who was an intimate friend of
    General George Washington. He married first Martha (Lee) Turberville,
    widow of Major George Turberville of Hickory Hill, Westmoreland Coun-
    ty, and secondly in 1752 Ann (Frisby) Rousby (1727-1793), daughter of
    Peregrine Frisby and widow of John Rousby (1721-1751) both of Maryland,
    - "a Gentlewoman of excellent accomplishments and a handsome Fortune,"
    says the Maryland Gazette of April 16, 1752 in announcing their mar-
    riage. After his second marriage Colonel Fitzhugh removed to Maryland;
    he left issue by both wives.

(5) Major John Fitzhugh (169?-1733) of Marmion, Saint Paul's Parish, which
handsome mansion now standing was built by him about 1725 upon lands bequeathed to him by his father. He married Anna Barbara McCarty, daughter
of Captain Daniel and Elizabeth (Pope) McCarty of Westmoreland County, in
1715 and had four daughters and three sons. His last will and Testament
remains of record at Stafford County court. His sons were:

(i) William Fitzhugh (1725-1791) who succeeded his father at Marmion. He
    married first Ursula Beverley, daughter of Colonel William Beverley
    of Blandfield, Essex County; and secondly Hannah [surname unknown]
    (17 -1799). He left issue by each wife. In 1797 Marmion was pur-
    chased by Major George Lewis (1757-1821), nephew of General George
    Washington, and is now in possession of his descendant Mrs. Robert

Carter Nicholas Grymes (nee Lucy Lewis). Doctor Robert Wellford
(1753-1823), physician of Fredericksburg, was several days at Marmion attending Catherine (Daingerfield) Lewis (1764-1820), wife of
Major George Lewis, in her last illness. As Doctor Wellford sat by
the fire in the little parlour at Marmion on a cold day in February
1820 he wrote in his diary, reflecting upon former days:

> "At the particular desire of Mrs.Lewis I remain-
> ed the whole day in the house and slept on the sub-
> sequent night once more and for the last time in the
> little parlour in which room in time past I have wit-
> nessed much sociality and more merriment than in any
> other room in the whole course of my life. ... Mr.
> William Fitzhugh, the hospitable owner of the mansion
> [Marmion] and the estate surrounding same, his sons,
> his brother Daniel, and his son William; the Rev. Thomas
> Thornton; that truly respectable Gentleman, the late
> William Fitzhugh (of Chatham); Mr. Grymes of the Wild-
> erness and his namesake of Eagle's Nest; Mr. Robert
> Allison; Mr. John McCoy (with the musicians, Victor,
> Olliver, &c. in the subordinate range of assembly)
> formed a group not often collected together in the
> Northern Neck of Virginia. But they are all gone and
> 'the place that hath known them shall know them no
> more.' The worthy proprietors of this most hospitable
> mansion are also removed from the cares of this world
> and are (I sincerely hope) at rest in Heaven although
> the place of their interment in the Graveyard of the
> Old Orchard cannot (from the changes that have occur-
> red) be easily found by their former friends and acq-
> uaintances."

(ii) John Fitzhugh (1730-1772) married in Saint Paul's Parish on January
31, 1760 Elizabeth Harrison, daughter of Colonel Nathaniel Harrison
then of Eagle's Nest. They settled in Prince George County upon
the Church Pasture Quarter of her father and by will he bequeathed
her a life estate in this property with reversion to his only son
Benjamin Harrison, Esq. (1743-1807) of Brandon, Prince George County. John and Elizabeth (Harrison) Fitzhugh were survived by seven
children.

(iii) Daniel Fitzhugh (1733-1786) married three times and left issue a
child by each wife, viz: (1) Catherine, probably nee Hore, who is
mentioned as a granddaughter of John Triplett of King George County in a deed there in 1766 - she was the mother of his only son,
William Fitzhugh, mentioned by Doctor Wellford; (2) in 1771 to Alice
Riden [Riding] and (3) in 1772 to Susanna Potter. By his last will
and Testament of record in Westmoreland County, William Fitzhugh requested that he be buried "in my brother William's burial ground."
Daniel Fitzhugh's will was dated September 17, 1777 and recorded
March 28, 1786; it indicates his three wives predeceased him. Jane,
his daughter by his second wife, married on June 17, 1790 Henry Dade
Hooe, and Susanna, his daughter by his third wife, married on May 13,
1790 Rice Wingfield Hooe.

Like his father, John Fitzhugh (1727-1809) of Bellaire was afflicted with poor vision and was blind from the age of about 45. The Reverend Jonathan Boucher of Caroline County was intimate with the Fitzhugh family having once paid his addresses to Sarah Fitzhugh, daughter of Colonel Henry and Sarah (Battaile) Fitzhugh of Bedford. In 1765 Boucher recorded a discourse in his journal on Virginians as he had come to know them; he concluded his observations thus:

.... "The family character both of body and mind may be traced thro' many generations as for instance, every Fitzhugh has bad eyes; every Thornton hears badly; Winstons and Lees talk well; Carters are proud and imperious; Taliaferros mean and avaricious and Fowkeses cruel."

Handsome portraits of Mr. and Mrs. John Fitzhugh of Bellaire are in the possession of their descendants. Their obituaries, which appeared in Fredericksburg newspapers, are interesting and quoted verbatim:

"On Friday last died, of a short illness, Mrs. Eliza Fitzhugh, wife of Mr. John Fitzhugh, of Stafford County, in the 61st year of her age. She was the mother of thirteen children, all of them bred up and settled out in that regular decent manner as to be patterns of sobriety, industry, and good behaviour to all around them; these, with their children, amount to the number of 54. And what is very remarkable, that amidst all the cares, troubles and difficulties, of so laborious a task, and the additional misfortune of her husband being blind for near twenty years, she lived with him in so constant a tenor of conjugal affection, that not a harsh word or untoward expression ever passed between them; such are the comforts of the matrimonial state when rightly conducted. Her loss is much deplored by her acquaintances and affectionate children, but it is and must be peculiarly distressing to her surviving husband, who has now no one left to live with him to cheer the meloncholy residue of his days of darkness." [1]

"DIED: On Thursday morning, at his seat in Stafford County, John Fitzhugh, Esquire. Though near the commencement of his 83rd year when he died, he had never been confined a single day by sickness and though a gentleman of affluence and family, he never sued nor was sued in his life." [2]

The unusual family register of the Bellaire family has been preserved and from this and other sources I am able to present an account of the thirteen children of John Fitzhugh, Gentleman, (1727-1809) and Alice Thornton (1729-1790), his wife, viz:

1 - Fredericksburg Virginia Herald of March 11, 1790; Eliza is a typographical error for Alice.

2 - Fredericksburg Virginia Herald of May 13, 1809

(1) Henry Fitzhugh was born February 9, 1748 and "was baptized by the Rev.[d]
Mr. Sympson[1] and had for surities Major John Fitzhugh of Brandon and Mr.
Sympson, also Miss Jean Moore and Mrs. Elizabeth Thornton, his aunt."
He was married on October 23, 1777 to Elizabeth (Stith) Fitzhugh, dau-
ghter of Colonel Drury Stith of Brunswick County and widow of Henry
Fitzhugh (May 7, 1750-June 9, 1777) of Fitzhughsburg, King George County,
who was the son of Colonel Henry and Sarah (Battaile) Fitzhugh of Bed-
ford. Elizabeth Stith (June 23, 1754-May 13, 1786) married first on
October 28, 1770 Henry Fitzhugh and had an only child, viz:
Henry Fitzhugh (July 11, 1773-August 10, 1830) who "was baptized by the
Rev. Mr. William Stuart the 10th of September following and had for surities his grandfather Col. Henry Fitzhugh, Col. Francis Thornton and his
Lady, Col. Robert Stith and his Lady, Warner Throckmorton, his cousin
Henry Fitzhugh of Bellaire, Mrs. Ann Stith and his aunt Susanna Fitzhugh."
Henry Fitzhugh (1773-1830) married in 1792 Elizabeth C. Conway [their marriage bond in Orange County is dated April 17, 1792] and succeeded to the
family estate, Bedford, in the family cemetery of which his tombstone may
be seen. He died testate in King George County, leaving issue several
children. Henry Fitzhugh (February 9, 1748-January 15, 1815) of Bellaire
and his wife nee Elizabeth Stith, had five children, viz:
  (i) John Bolling Stith Fitzhugh who was born at Fitzhughsburg on October 1,
      1778 and "had for surities (being baptized by the Rev.[d] William Stuart)
      his mother who stood proxy for his grandmother Fitzhugh, John B. Fitz-
      hugh and his father. He married on December 29, 1807 at Twinford his
      cousin Frances Tabb Fitzhugh. She was born on February 1, 1794 at
      Nanzatico, the daughter of George Fitzhugh and Humphrey Frances Toye
      Tabb, his wife, of King George County, and died June 29, 1868; she is
      buried in the Fredericksburg Cemetery near her only son George Henry
      Bolling Fitzhugh (February 17, 1818-March 24, 1874), who was a bache-
      lor. John Bolling Stith Fitzhugh died at Bellaire on April 23, 1825.
      There is some account of his several daughters in Tyler's Quarterly
      Historical and Genealogical Magazine, Volume 15, page 263 et seq.
  (ii) A son born dead the 2nd October 1780.
  (iii) Lucinda Fitzhugh was born February 1, 1782 and was "baptized by the
      Rev.[d] Mr. William Stuart at the Eagle's Nest and had for surities, Mr.
      Benjamin Grymes and Lady, Dr. William Gibbons Stuart and Lady, Miss
      Mildred Grymes and Mr. John Alexander Stuart.
  (iv) Caroline Matilda Fitzhugh was born June 4, 1784 and was "baptized by
      the Rev.[d] Mr. Robert Buchan at Bellaire & had for surities Mr. John
      Pratt & Lady, her grandfather Fitzhugh, Col. William Fitzhugh of
      Loudoun, Miss Elizabeth Strother, Henry F. Thornton and Mr. Thornton
      Fitzhugh.
  (v) Alice Thornton Fitzhugh was born August 15, 1785 and was "baptized by
      the Rev.[d] Mr. Robert Buchan & had for surities Henry F. Thornton, his
      wife her aunt, grandfather and grandmother Fitzhugh, Miss Fanny Rich-
      ards, Peter Thornton and Daniel McCarty Fitzhugh."

---

1 - He was probably born at Crow's, the residence of his widowed maternal grand-
mother Elizabeth (Catlett) Thornton (1689-1751), in Hanover Parish, King George
County where the Reverend Mr. Joseph Simpson was then curate. He married in
1749 Mary Skinker, born April 19, 1732, illegitimate daughter of Colonel Samuel
Skinker (died 1752) of King George County, who made her a wedding gift of £ 500.
The Reverend Mr. Joseph Simpson died intestate in Richmond County in 1762.

(2) John Fitzhugh was born at his Grandmother's on September 29, 1749 and was "baptized by the Rev.^d Mr. Campbell [1] & had for surities Capt. Francis Thornton, his uncle, Col. Presley Thornton and Mrs. Elizabeth Thornton, his grandmother. While his name is entered simply as John in this record he was known as John Thornton Fitzhugh; he died testate in Prince William County on February 9, 1809. He married Margaret (Helm) Foote, widow of Richard Foote who died in 1778; she died February 13, 1814 aged 62 years and 22 days. They left issue.

(3) George Fitzhugh was born at his Grandmother's on April 24, 1751 and was "baptized by the Rev.^d Mr. Davis and had for surities his father & Uncle Thomas Fitzhugh, Mrs. Peggy Arnold and Mrs. Peggy Murdock." He died in November 1810 having been twice married; first to Humphrey Frances Toye Tabb (17 -1794) and secondly to Mary (Fitzhugh) Stuart, widow of William Gibbons Stuart, on July 18, 1797. George Fitzhugh left issue.

(4) Thomas Fitzhugh was born at his father's house in Stafford, Bellaire, the 15th June 1753. He was baptized by the Rev.^d Mr. Moncure and had for surities his Uncle Thomas Fitzhugh and Mr. Daniel Fitzhugh, Mrs. Mary Washington and Mrs. Thomas Fitzhugh, his aunt." Thomas Fitzhugh married Lucinda Helm and died testate in the fall of 1829 in Prince William County where his will remains of record; they had issue several children.

(5) Elizabeth Fitzhugh "was born in Stafford on Friday the 10th day of October 1754, was baptized by the Rev. Mr. McDonald, and had for surities her Father and Uncle Thomas Fitzhugh & her two aunts Susanna and Betty Fitzhugh. She died Friday, 21st February 1823, aged 68 years and 4 months." She married two distant cousins, viz: first on March 20, 1770 Francis Conway, Junior, (March 7, 1749-February 13, 1794) of Mount Sion, Caroline County, by whom she had ten children, and secondly Colonel James Taylor, son of James and Alice (Thornton) Taylor, of Orange County, Virginia. The portrait of Elizabeth (Fitzhugh) Conway Taylor is now hanging at the Virginia Historical Society.

(6) Susanna Fitzhugh "was born in Stafford on Thursday the 5th of February 1756, and was baptized by the Rev. Mr. Moncure & had for surities Mr. & Mrs. Moncure, Mr. Henry Tyler and Miss Betty his daughter. She died 15th day of March 1819 aged 63 years one month and 10 days." She married in 1775 Captain Catlett Conway of Hawfield, Orange County, who was born December 25, 1751 and died September 14, 1827. He was the son of Francis Conway (December 27, 1722-May 17, 1761) and Sarah Taliaferro (October 8, 1727-January 17, 1784), his wife, and brother of Francis Conway, Junior, (1749-1794). Captain Catlett and Susannah (Fitzhugh) Conway had a large family; their daughter Elizabeth C. Conway married in 1792 Henry Fitzhugh (1773-1830) of Bedford, King George County, Virginia, mentioned on page 229.

(7) William Fitzhugh "was born in Stafford on Thursday the 11th of August 1757, and was baptized by the Rev.^d Mr. Moncure & had for surities Charles Carter, Esq., of Stanstead & Lady, Mr. William Hedgman and Mrs. Hannah Hedgman. He died the 4th of October 1803, Aged 46 years." He married in Orange County on February 24, 1783 Ann Taliaferro, daughter of Colonel Lawrence Taliaferro (1734-1798) of Rose Hill, Orange County, and Mary Jackson (1742-1773), his wife. The will of William Fitzhugh (1757-1803) remains of record in Prince William County, Virginia. They left issue.

---

1 - The Reverend Mr. Archibald Campbell (17 -1775) of Washington Parish, Westmoreland County, is referred to. The child's maternal grandmother, Elizabeth (Catlett) Thornton (1689-1751), widow of Rowland Thornton, is referred to.

(8) Alice Fitzhugh "was born in Stafford on Saturday the 20th of January
1759, was baptized by the Rev? Mr. Moncure and had for surities Mr.
Samuel Selden, Mr. & Mrs. Tyler, and mother." She married first in 1779
Henry Dixon, Gentleman, (circa 1749-1783), only child to leave issue of
Captain Edward Dixon (circa 1702-1779) of Port Royal, Caroline County,
and his wife Sarah Turner, only child of Colonel Thomas Turner (1698-1758)
of Walsingham, King George County, and his first wife Sarah Taliaferro.
She married secondly in 1784 John Birkett Pratt (September 4, 1761-January
15, 1843), son of Thomas Pratt, Gentleman, (1721-1766) of Eden in Saint
Paul's Parish, and Margaret Vivion (circa 1724-1818), his wife. John
Birkett Pratt dropped his middle name; the handsome tombstones of himself and his wife are in the family cemetery at Camden, their plantation
on the Rappahannock River in Caroline County which is in the possession
of their lineal descendants. Alice (Fitzhugh) Dixon Pratt left issue by
both marriages.

(9) Francis Fitzhugh "was born in Stafford on Thursday the 4th of February
1761, was baptized by the Rev? Mr. Moncure and had for surities Messrs.
William & Francis Thornton Jun? and Miss Jane Massey afterwards the wife
of Mr. John Waugh." [1] "He died 30th of March 1821 at his seat in King
George and was buried at Bellaire." Francis Fitzhugh paid his addresses
to Frances Carter, daughter of Robert Carter, Esq., of Nomini Hall, Westmoreland County; this match must have been agreeable with his father, but
the young lady rejected him as the following letter will testify:

> "July the 24th 1781
>
> "Sir,
> I have received your favor of last Friday propos-
> ing therein an alliance between your son Mr. Francis
> Fitzhugh and my daughter Frances, which letter I com-
> municated to my wife and daughter F. Carter the latter
> of whom informed me that she intended to desire the
> young gentleman to desist in making any further adv-
> ances to her as a suitor.
>
> "I do highly approve of your Idea in making tem-
> porary provision for your children and it is my sin-
> cere wish and desire that Parents would make more
> equal distributions of their Estates among their sons
> and daughters.
>
> "Pray present my respectful compliments to Mrs.
> Fitzhugh and the relatives of your Family.
> "I am
>   Sir
>
>   Your Most Obedient Servant
>   Robert Carter"
>
>
> "To,
>   Mr. John Fitzhugh
>   Bell-Air
>   Stafford County"

---

1 - John Waugh and Jane Massey were married on April 22, 1761 by the Reverend Mr.
William Stuart. It is recorded in The Register of Saint Paul's Parish, page 150.

On December 27, 1781 Colonel Robert Carter wrote to Mr. Richard Bernard, Clerk of Westmoreland County court, giving his consent for the marriage of his daughter Miss Frances Carter to Colonel Thomas Jones, Junior, of Northumberland County and directs him to issue the license. About 1791 Francis Fitzhugh married his distant cousin Lucy (Alexander) Taliaferro (1757-18   ), daughter of John and Lucy (Thornton) Alexander and widow of John Taliaferro, Gentleman, (1745-1789) of Hayes, King George County; they had no issue. By will dated October 22, 1798 and recorded April 5, 1821 at King George County court, Francis Fitzhugh bequeathed to his wife Lucy his entire estate for life, and after devising a few chattels to others, made his nephew Edwin Conway (1785-1844) [son of Francis and Elizabeth (Fitzhugh) Conway of Caroline County] his residuary legatee.

(10) Daniel McCarty Fitzhugh "was born the 9th of May 1763 on Monday at ten o'clock at night, was baptized by the Rev.d Mr. Moncure & had for surities, Mr. Daniel McCarty, his cousin, and Mr. George Brent, also Miss Molly Mercer and Miss Betty Tyler; the Godmothers stood by proxy. He died 2nd May 1823 aged 59 years, 11 months and 23 days." His obituary appeared in the Fredericksburg Virginia Herald of May 7, 1823. Daniel McCarty Fitzhugh (1763-1823) resided at Cherry Point on the Rappahannock River. By his will dated April 13, 1823 and proved June 5, 1823 at King George County court, he bequeathed his estate to Caroline, Ann, Mary, John Thornton and Francis Cullom - the children I had by my housekeeper Elizabeth Cullom. These children assumed the name of Fitzhugh and John Thornton Fitzhugh (181?-1843) succeeded his father at Cherry Point and left issue. Caroline Fitzhugh (1812-1874) married Joseph Lee of King George County, Virginia, and left issue.

(11) Sarah Ann Fitzhugh "was born the 13th February 1765 on Wednesday, was baptized by the Rev.d Mr. Brooke and had for surities Mr. John Knox and Mr. Joseph Meninger [?], Miss Susanna Fitzhugh and Miss Ann Tyler. She died November 1820 in Kentucky." She married about 1781 Captain Charles Thornton (1754-1824) of North Garden, Caroline County, widower of Mary Jones, and son of Colonel Anthony Thornton (1727-1782) of Ormsby, Caroline County, and his first wife nee Sarah Taliaferro (1729-1762). They moved to Kentucky and the Fredericksburg Virginia Herald of May 26, 1824 announced the death of Captain Charles Thornton in the 70th year of his age at his seat near Louisville, Kentucky; this account states he was "an officer in the Revolutionary War." Captain Charles and Sarah Ann (Fitzhugh) Thornton left a large family some of whom lived in Oldham County, Kentucky.

(12) Thornton Fitzhugh "was born the 4th of June 1768, was baptized by the Rev.d Mr. Brooke and had for surities Mr. Robert Dade, Henry Fitzhugh, his uncle, Mrs. Sarah Douglass and Miss Eliza Strother. Died June 29th 1804, aged 36 years 25 days." His obituary notice appeared in the Fredericksburg Virginia Herald of July 3, 1804.

(13) Ann Rose Fitzhugh was "born the 25th of December 1769 early in the morning, baptized by the Rev.d Mr. Clement Brooke and had for surities Alexander Dick, Roy Mercer, Charles Rose and Henry Fitzhugh of Fitzhughsburg, also Molly Selden, Peggy Rose, Fanny Dade and Sarah Fitzhugh of Bedford." She married on September 22, 1785 her cousin Doctor Henry Fitzhugh Thornton (1765-1830) of Caroline County, son of Colonel Anthony Thornton (1727-1782) of Ormsby and his second wife Susanna Fitzhugh (1731-1795), daughter of Colonel Henry and Susanna (Cooke) Fitzhugh. Dr. and Mrs. Thornton left issue.

JOHN PEYTON, GENTLEMAN

John Peyton, Gentleman, of Stony Hill, Stafford County, was born in 1691, the son of Henry and Anne Peyton. He died testate in Stafford County on May 18, 1760. He represented Stafford County in the House of Burgesses 1736-1740 and again 1757-1758; he was a justice in 1745 and probably until his death. He married first Anne Waye by whom he had six children, and secondly, Elizabeth (Rowzee) Waller (circa 1715-1782), widow of Charles Waller (17 -1749) of Essex and Stafford counties, heretofore mentioned, by whom he had two children. She married thirdly on December 6, 1760, Major Benjamin Strother (circa 1700-1765) by whom she had no issue. [See pages 220-221] The Reverend Horace E. Hayden in his Virginia Genealogies, page 495 et seq., gives an account of John Peyton of Stony Hill and his family. His tombstone, originally at Stony Hill, was moved to Aquia Churchyard some years ago. It is inscribed: "Here lie the Remains of John Peyton, the son of Henry and Anne Peyton, who was born An. Dom. 1691, and departed this life May the 18th, 1760. He was a kind Husband and a tender Parent. To his Memory this Tomb was erected by His son Yelverton Peyton."

* * *
* *
*

THE WAUGH FAMILY

The Reverend Mr. John Waugh (1630-1706), minister of Overwharton Parish, and some members of his family, have appeared so frequently in The Register of Overwharton Parish perhaps a brief genealogical account will be of interest to some. It is stated in the William and Mary College Quarterly, First Series, Volume 15, page 190, that the loss of so many of the Stafford County records renders it impossible to accurately account for all members of the family, but it is a foregone conclusion those of the third generation are the grandchildren of the Reverend Mr. John Waugh. By consulting the records of adjoining counties and a few unindexed sources, I have ascertained some information which has not heretofore appeared.

The Virginia Magazine of History and Biography, Volume 19, page 186, gives an abstract of the will of David Waugh, planter, of Stafford County, Virginia, which was written on December 27, 1692 "A Board the Elizabeth of London, Captain George Hill, Master," and admitted to probate on February 20, 1693 at the Prerogative Court of Canterbury. He bequeathed his entire estate to his brother, Peter Waugh, sailor in New Castle upon Tyne. It is probable that the testator was a brother of the Reverend Mr. John Waugh.

Elizabeth Waugh appears in the records as the wife of the Reverend Mr. John Waugh from 1674 to 1691. She may not have been the mother of Joseph and John Waugh, the elder sons of the Parson, as they seem to have been particularly favored with an equal division of two of his most valuable tracts of land, and they were considerably older than his other children. Elizabeth Waugh probably died in the late 1690's as in 1700 the Reverend Mr. Waugh conveyed several tracts of land and there is no mention of his wife or her dower interest in the several deeds. The Parson's last wife was Christian [surname unknown]; I first find her as his wife on May 13, 1702 when she relinquished her dower right in certain land sold by him. She survived her husband and married prior to December 11, 1707, John Hawkins who died November 20, 1717 in Saint Paul's Parish. Christian Waugh Hawkins died testate in Saint Paul's Parish on November 12, 1721 and her last will and Testament was recorded in now missing Stafford County Will Book "K" [1721-1730], page 34. She had no issue by the Reverend Mr. John Waugh.

On May 9, 1700, probably shortly before his last marriage, the Reverend Mr. John Waugh conveyed to his two sons Joseph Waugh and John Waugh "for love and affection," 2,246 acres in Stafford County and directed that it be equally divided between them. Parson Waugh died intestate in the spring of 1706 and the detailed inventory of his estate remains of record; mentioned is "Mr. Waugh's apparel, wig and gloves &c." His sons Joseph, John and Alexander Waugh were his administrators and the accounts show a debit for the schooling of their brother, David Waugh, in 1706.

The large quantity of land acquired by the Reverend Mr. John Waugh, by purchase and patent, cannot be detailed here; those interested in such details are referred to the land patents and grants and the court records of Stafford County and the counties formed from it.

Included in the land holdings of the Reverend Mr. John Waugh was 6,350 acres on the headwaters of Potomac Creek which he patented on March 2, 1691, and dying intestate, this land together with all his other land not conveyed before his death, descended to his eldest son, Joseph Waugh (circa 1660-1727). The year following his father's death, Joseph Waugh divided this tract into five parcels of approximately 1,200 acres each and put his brothers John, Alexander and David Waugh in possession of an equal fifth part of it. As this division is of genealogical import, it will be mentioned later.

In spite of the many gaps in the Stafford County records, it is possible to accurately ascertain considerable information concerning Joseph Waugh (circa 1660-1727) and John Waugh (circa 1661-1716), the elder sons of Parson John Waugh, and their families. Of the Parson's other three sons, we are in dire need of some of the missing records for positive information. Richard Waugh was living in 1691 [see page 203] but as there is no further record of him it appears very likely he died before his father and without issue. Alexander Waugh (166?-1722), third son of the Parson, was one of the administrators of his father's estate. He is believed to have procreated a family and for want of a more satisfactory explanation, I am crediting him with issue. The reason I assign the children I do to Alexander Waugh is that the records lead me to the conclusion that David Waugh (168?-1753) left no issue and thus he is the only eligible person to be their father.

The names of five sons and two daughters of the Reverend Mr. John Waugh appear on the records, viz:

I.   Joseph Waugh (circa 1660-1727) is described in several records as the eldest son and heir-at-law of his father and as such he inherited all of his father's landed estate. Shortly after the Parson's death one land patent for 6,350 acres on the head of Potomac Creek was divided into five parcels of approximately 1,200 acres each and Joseph Waugh vested each of his young er brothers with a parcel. The mansion house tract of Parson Waugh, containing 1,000 acres and lying on Potomac Creek between Whipsewasin Creek and the lands of Captain Joseph Sumner, was equally divided between Joseph Waugh and John Waugh, Junior. There is a plot of the division of this valuable tract of land which overlooks broad Potomac Creek near its conflux with Potomac River and the peninsula on John Waugh's part, now owned by Mrs. Martha (Forbush) Beckham, is yet called Waugh Point. In 1717 Joseph Waugh patented 436 acres of land in Essex County and sold it in 1724 after it became a part of Spotsylvania County. His last will and Testament was dated April 1, 1726; it was recorded in now missing Stafford County Will Book "K" [1721-1730], page 214, in 1727. He married first Rachel Gowry, daughter of John Gowry (16 -1721), who had land patents adjoining his land on Whipsewasin Creek and by her had two children who appear on the surviving records. He married secondly, circa 1720, Mary (Crosby) Mountjoy Mauzey [see Tyler's Quarterly Historical and Genealogical Magazine, Volume 26, pages 99-104] and by her had an only daughter. Mrs. Mary Waugh, widow, appears on a Stafford County Rent Roll of 1742 with 3,381 acres of land; she died testate in 1756.

The three children of Joseph Waugh were:
(1) Joseph Waugh, Gentleman, inherited land from his father and mother. He married circa 1732 Million Travers, daughter of Giles Travers, Gentleman, (16 -1717) of Potomac Creek, by whom he became vested with 625 acres on Occoquan Run in Prince William County. Joseph Waugh appears on a Stafford County Rent Roll of 1742 with 2,404 acres of land. He died on September 4, 1747 in Overwharton Parish and his widow in 1748; both of their last wills and Testaments remain of record at Stafford County court.

Joseph and Million (Travers) Waugh had three sons and one daughter but only their sons survived them, viz:
  (i) Gowry Waugh, Gentleman, is styled captain in some contemporary records. He erected a handsome dwelling house at Belle Plain and seems to have attained the greatest wealth of any of the colonial Waughs. He appears on a Stafford County Rent Roll of 1776 with 1,570 acres of land and in 1783, the year in which he died, paid tax in Stafford County on 39 Negro slaves, 19 horses and 57 cattle as well as 429 acres of land and 1,100 acres in King George County. Captain Gowry Waugh (circa 1734-1783) married Letitia Turberville, daughter of Major George Turberville of Hickory Hill, Westmoreland County, and Martha Lee, his wife, who married secondly Colonel William Fitzhugh (1721-1798). Letitia (Turberville) Waugh predeceased her husband; their only two children were under age on February 3, 1781 when their father wrote his last will and Testament devising them a handsome estate and carefully providing for their education, viz:
    (a) George Lee Waugh died unmarried and intestate in 1796. He was a lieutenant of a Company of Horse in the Stafford County Militia in 1789.
    (b) Robert Turberville Waugh died unmarried and intestate in 1795. With the death of these two young men the Waugh

name terminated in the eldest male branch of the family.
Both were possessed of handsome real and personal estates
which reverted to their heirs-at-law, thus provoking lengthy suits in the chancery courts which pended for years
and which are quite informative genealogically. On their
paternal side, the only heirs-at-law were their two first
cousins, daughters of their uncle Joseph Waugh, Gentleman
mentioned below.

(ii) Joseph Waugh, Gentleman, (circa 1736-1763) is described
as "a man of Handsome property" at the time of his marriage in January 1758 with Mary Bronough (17 -1799), daughter of Captain David Bronough of King George County;
they had two daughters. Mary (Bronough) Waugh married
secondly Colonel Elijah Threlkeld and they had an only
child, Ann Threlkeld (1772-1828) [see page 206 and Tyler'
Quarterly Historical and Genealogical Magazine, Volume 21
pages 265-268].

Joseph and Mary (Bronough) Waugh had two daughters,
viz:

(a) Hannah Waugh (November 10, 1761-March , 1814) who
married on December 18, 1783 George Morton, son of
George and Lucy (Baylor) Morton; they moved to Mason
County, Kentucky, and left issue.

(b) Million ["Milly"] Waugh (circa 1763-April , 1799)
who married her cousin Rawleigh Travers Brown (July
13, 1753-November 24, 1803) of Windsor, Stafford
County, and left issue.

(iii) Elizabeth Waugh (March 31, 1740-ante 1747); she is not
mentioned in the last wills and Testaments of either of
her parents.

(iv) Travers Waugh (January 24, 1743-1765). The inventory of
his estate remains of record at Stafford County court;
he died intestate, unmarried and without issue.

(2) Elizabeth Waugh was the daughter of Joseph and Rachel (Gowry) Waugh.
She married on October 16, 1737 in Spotsylvania County, John Gregg.

(3) Mary Waugh was the daughter of Joseph and Mary (Crosby) Waugh. She
married on June 17, 1740 in Overwharton Parish, Captain Alexander Doniphan (171?-1768) [see Tyler's Quarterly Historical and Genealogical
Magazine, Volume 26, pages 99-104 and 275-285]. In a deed dated November 18, 1785 of record at Stafford County court, the sons of Mary
(Waugh) Doniphan conveyed to Thomas Fitzhugh, Esq., of Boscobel, 1,126
acres of land on the waters of upper Potomac Creek and this instrument
recites that Joseph Waugh, deceased, by his last will and Testament
dated April 1, 1726, devised to his two daughters Elizabeth and Mary
Waugh land on Potomac Creek and that it was afterwards divided between
them, and Elizabeth was allotted the upper half and Mary the lower half
which is the 1,126 acres now conveyed.

II.   John Waugh, Gentleman, (circa 1661-1716), second son of the Reverend Mr.
John Waugh, served in several official capacities of trust. On March 19,
1701 he received a commission from Governor Francis Nicholson to be sherif

of Stafford County and on November 3, 1704 the Honorable Robert Carter,
Virginia agent for the Proprietors of the Northern Neck of Virginia, appointed him his subagent in Stafford County. In 1714 John Waugh, Gentleman, served in the House of Burgesses. He owned lots in the Town of Marlbrough and had land patents issued to him in what are now the counties of
Prince William, Fairfax and Fauquier. From the court records of these last
mentioned counties we are able to learn some of the provisions in his last
will and Testament which was dated October 8, 1716 and admitted to probate
at Stafford County court on November 16, 1716 although that document is now
among the many missing records of Stafford County. John Waugh was the most
progressive of the sons of Parson Waugh and resided on Potomac Creek near
Waugh Point. John Waugh married Martha Vandegasteel, widow of Giles Vandegasteel (16 -1701) who died testate in Stafford County. Colonel George
Mason in a letter to the Governor of Virginia dated July 10, 1700 mentions
that Ensign Giles Vandecastill (sic) and six men are to range on the upper
Potomac River and Cornet Burr Harrison is to range from Occoquan Creek down
to Potomac Creek. John Waugh's wife probably predeceased him as the records state he appointed as his executors his brothers Joseph, Alexander
and David Waugh and Priscilla Vandegasteel [daughter of Giles Vandegasteel]
who later married a Mr. Hay.

    John Waugh, Gentleman, was survived by four sons, viz:

(1) John Waugh (circa 1703-November 17, 1742), planter, of Overwharton Par-
    ish. As early as 1732 he conveyed land in Prince William County as the
    eldest son and heir of John Waugh, Gentleman, deceased, and was joined
    in this deed by David Waugh, planter, and Priscilla Hay, widow, the
    surviving executor and executrix of his father, John Waugh, Gentleman.
    A Stafford County Rent Roll of 1742 indicates he was possessed of 2,858
    acres of land; this was probably entailed by his father's will as it is
    mentioned in the will of his brother, Captain James Waugh. John Waugh
    died testate in Stafford County and by will provided for his illegiti-
    mate children by Elizabeth Monk [see page 81].

(2) Captain James Waugh (circa 1705-May 9, 1750) married on August 22, 1740
    Betty (Brittingham) French, daughter of Nathaniel Brittingham of Pocko-
    moke, Accomac County, and widow of Hugh French, Junior, by whom she had
    two children, Mason French and Rachel French. A Stafford County Rent
    Roll of 1742 indicates he was possessed of 1,543 acres of land; it ap-
    pears he inherited the 2,858 acres of land which were charged to his
    brother John Waugh on the same Rent Roll. In 1745 with John Mercer,
    Mott Doniphan, John Wheeler, James Withers, William Harrison, Henry
    Tyler, James Scott and William Mountjoy, Captain James Waugh served as
    a vestryman in Overwharton Parish when the replacement of the wooden
    edifice at the Aquia Church site was first considered. The building
    of a brick church at Aquia met with opposition in the House of Burgesses
    from Major Lawrence Washington, acting in behalf of himself and other
    proprietors of the Accakeek Iron Works. He contended "that there is at
    present a very good Church at the same place which might be repaired at
    a moderate expense," and as the Accakeek Iron Works is in Overwharton
    Parish "and employ many Tithables in carrying on the same, they will
    labour under great hardships" if the proposed contract is let to William
    Walker to build a new brick church for 153,000 pounds of Tobacco. Captain
    James Waugh was a member of the House of Burgesses at this time and was

doubtless influential in having the petition of Major Washington rejected. Nothing more in regard to building the new brick church in
Overwharton Parish appears until 1751 when the project was finally
set in motion [see page 192].

Captain James Waugh succeeded Colonel Henry Fitzhugh (circa 1706-
1742) as a member of the House of Burgesses from Stafford County in
1744, however, his election was contested by John Peyton of Stony
Hill. Peyton's complaint failed to provoke action and on April 9,
1746 he withdrew it. Captain James Waugh served in the sessions of
1744-1746 and was replaced in the fall session of 1748 by William
Fitzhugh, Esq.

Captain James Waugh died testate in Overwharton Parish on May 9,
1750 and his widow married thirdly on May 7, 1751 Andrew Edwards (1725-
1788). Captain James and Betty (Brittingham) Waugh had five children;
two of them predeceased their parents and the guardian accounts of the
surviving three remain of record, viz:

(i) John Waugh (October 20, 1741-circa 1772) married on April 22,
1761 in Saint Paul's Parish Jane Massey (February 8, 1744—
17), daughter of Sigismund and Mary (Stuart) Massey. By
the terms of the last will and Testament of his father, John
Waugh was possessed of all his lands in Stafford County. By
the alteration of the Stafford County - King George County
boundries of 1777 it appears some of John Waugh's land fell
into each county. In 1776 John Waugh's Executors are charged
on a Stafford County Rent Roll with 1,700 acres and when the
land tax lists begin in 1782 John Waugh's Estate was charged
with 1,200 acres in King George County. John Waugh died
testate circa 1772 and his last will and Testament was recorded in now lost Stafford County Will Book "N" [1767-1783], page
166. The King George County records prove conclusively that
John Waugh had a least two sons, viz: John Waugh (176?-1801)
and Lewis Waugh (176?-1808), but it appears very likely that
he was also the father of Charles Stuart Waugh, Townshend
Waugh and Betty Waugh.

Mary (Stuart) Massey, above mentioned, as the widow of
Sigismund Massey, married secondly in Saint Paul's Parish
on January 14, 1753 Horatio Dade, Gentleman, and had issue
among others, Charles Stuart Dade and Townshend Dade - they
were the much younger half-brothers of Jane (Massey) Waugh.
It may be that after the death of John Waugh (1741-circa
1772) his widow married his younger brother James Waugh and
that he was the father of Charles Stuart Waugh and Townshend
Waugh, but such marriage I have not been able to prove. The
conclusion is, however, that in view of their names, it is a
foregone conclusion that Charles Stuart Waugh and Townshend
Waugh were the children of Jane (Massey) Waugh and they will
be mentioned under her only husband of whom we have positive
proof, John Waugh.

(a) Lewis Waugh (176?-1808) appears to have been the
eldest son of John and Jane (Massey) Waugh. He was
probably born in 1762 as he appears on the personal

tax lists of King George County in 1782 with 9
Negro slaves, 3 horses and 9 cattle. On December
10, 1804 Lewis Waugh conveyed to Peter Hansbrough
of Culpeper County, 500 acres of land whereon he
then lived lying on Potomac Creek and Potomac
River, reciting the grantor had title to the said
land from the will of his father, John Waugh, who
had the same from the will of his father, James
Waugh, late of Stafford County, deceased.

Lewis Waugh married Mary Peyton, daughter of
Colonel Francis and Frances (Dade) Peyton of Loudoun County. Lewis Waugh died testate in King
George County in 1808. By his last will and Testament he mentions his two daughters, the children
of his deceased brother John Waugh, and devises
his landed estate equally to be divided between
his nephew Lawrence Lewis Waugh and his daughter
Mary Peyton Waugh. Although the land of Lewis
Waugh was carried on the King George County land
tax books for years as 700 acres and later divided
between Lawrence Lewis Waugh and Mary Peyton Waugh
and carried on the said books as 350 acres each,
upon a survey in 1822 it was found to contain 582
acres. In 1821 Lawrence Lewis Waugh sold his part
to Peter Hansbrough, Sr., of Culpeper County and
in 1840 Mary Peyton Waugh of Loudoun County sold
her part to James G. Taliaferro of King George
County. These deeds recite the title of this
property.

The elder daughter of Lewis Waugh was Jane
Waugh; she married on August 17, 1802 in King
George County, John Murphy. Frances (Dade) Peyton
died testate in Loudoun County in 1814; her last
will and Testament mentions her granddaughter Mary
Peyton Waugh and her grandson-in-law John Murphy.

(b) John Waugh (176?-August 5, 1801) appears to have
been the second son of John and Jane (Massey) Waugh.
He was probably born circa 1766 as he first appears
on the personal tax lists of King George County in
1788. He married on November 4, 1790 in King George
County, Mary Watts Ashton daughter of John Ashton
(1735-1788) and Mary Watts, his wife. The Fredericksburg Virginia Herald of August 14, 1801 announced the death in King George County on August 5th of
Mr. John Waugh, leaving a wife and two small children to lament his death. Oddly his will was not
admitted to probate until October 6, 1803; it mentions his wife Mary Watts Waugh and children Mary
Stuart Waugh and Lawrence Lewis Waugh. John Waugh
bequeathed to his brother Lewis Waugh all the land
bequeathed to him by his father's will upon the

condition that the said Lewis Waugh would make
the testator good title to the land on which he
then resided. Mary Watts (Ashton) Waugh shortly
remarried and I suppose to deprive her of any
dower interest in a landed estate, Lewis Waugh
never made a conveyance to his brother John's
estate but to set things to rights bequeathed
Lawrence Lewis Waugh half of his landed estate;
this he sold in 1821 when a resident of Culpeper
County, Virginia. In 1830 Lawrence Lewis Waugh
was married to Lavinia Ward (Farish) Wiglesworth,
widow of Major Claiborne Wiglesworth of Fredericksburg, Virginia. [See Tyler's Quarterly Historical and Genealogical Magazine, Volume 21,
pages 258-259]

(c) Charles Stuart Waugh was a doctor of medicine
and lived in Culpeper County. In 1790, without
explanation, he is first taxed on 606 acres in
Stafford County and the land tax books of Stafford
County carry this property for many years after-
ward. In 1826 Charles Stuart Waugh mortgaged this
property and this instrument states that the said
606 acres lies on Potomac Creek and that the grant-
or has a right to it by the will of his father but
he is not named.

Charles Stuart Waugh married his cousin Mary
Waugh, daughter of Major Richard Waugh (1732-1805)
of Culpeper County, and left issue.

(d) Townshend Waugh appears infrequently on the King
George County records. On August 7, 1806 there
is an order stating that "Townshend Waugh having
obtained a license to practise as an attorney at
law in the Superior and Inferior courts of this
Commonwealth, and having taken the oath prescribed
by law, is thereupon admitted to practise as an
attorney at law in this court." By his last will
and Testament dated February 8, 1808, Lewis Waugh
of King George County appointed Townshend Waugh
one of his executors. I have no further information in regard to him.

(e) Betty Waugh was married in April 1797 in King
George County to Cuthbert Harrison Scott, son of
Captain James Scott (1742-1779) and Elizabeth
Harrison (1740-1823), his wife, of Fauquier Coun-
ty. For the ancestry of Cuthbert Harrison Scott
and the issue of C.H. and Betty (Waugh) Scott see
Hayden's Virginia Genealogies, pages 600-601.

(ii) Sarah Waugh, daughter of Captain James and Betty Waugh, was
born May 27, 1744. In 1758 John Mercer, Esq., was her guardian.

(iii) James Waugh (February 4, 1746-September 3, 1746).

(iv) Betty Waugh (September 4, 1747-September 14, 1747).

    (v) James Waugh, second son of the same name of Captain James and Betty Waugh, was born September 26, 1748 in Overwharton Parish. In 1758 Travers Cooke, Gentleman, was his guardian as well as for his elder brother John Waugh (1741-circa 1772). James Waugh, by the terms of his father's will, received all his land in Fairfax County, and his elder brother was bequeathed all the testator's land in Stafford County. Captain James Waugh's holdings in Stafford County were upward of four thousand acres and as his eldest son John Waugh does not appear to have been possessed with this amount of land at the time of his death, it appears likely that he may have deeded his younger brother James a thousand acres. On a Stafford County Rent Roll of 1776, James Waugh appears with 1,000 acres, but by 1782 when the land tax books begin he is absent from both the Stafford and King George County land tax books. The loss of all the deed, will and court order books for Stafford County for this period coupled with the testimony that Joseph Robinson, clerk of King George County court and his deputy John Bithiway Lampton Grigsby, were very lax during the Revolutionary period and failed to properly record many instruments presented to them, renders it impossible to accurately resolve many genealogical situations.

      On page 238 I suggested that James Waugh may have married Jane (Massey) Waugh, his brother's widow.

      Another possibility is that he moved to Fairfax County and settled upon the lands bequeathed to him there by his father. These records were checked without finding conclusive proof such was the case. On February 19, 1785, James Waugh and Henrietta, his wife, of Fairfax County sold to Peter Mauzey of Fairfax County, 72 acres of land. There are several deed books of Fairfax County missing and I was unable to find any instrument which would positively identify James Waugh of Fairfax County as the son of Captain James Waugh. Perhaps a more exhaustive search there might prove fruitful.

(3) Thomas Waugh (circa 1707-ante 1733) was the third son of John Waugh, Gentleman. A Prince William County deed dated March 19, 1733 states that John Waugh, Gentleman, by will dated October 8, 1716 devised 1,200 acres of land which had been granted to him by his brother Joseph Waugh [March 9, 1708, Stafford County Book "Z", page 456] to his four sons John, James, Thomas and William Waugh and that prior to this date Thomas Waugh died intestate and without issue. By this instrument his three surviving brothers, John, James and William Waugh, agree to a division of this land among them.

(4) William Waugh (circa 1710-1748) married in Overwharton Parish on September 10, 1738 Margaret Tyler, only child of John Tyler of King George County [see footnote on page 125]. Shortly before his death he moved to Prince William County where he died testate, but his last will and Testament is among the many missing records of that county. In 1749 his widow, Margaret Waugh, made a deposition in Prince William County in regard to

the efforts of her late husband, William Waugh, to purchase certain land
in Orange County from Dr. Thomas Houison. By February 5, 1752 Margaret
Waugh, widow, was the wife of Daniel Royalty of Overwharton Parish and
they were parties to a deed of record in Prince William County in regard
to her dower right in the lands of William Waugh, deceased. Some of
William Waugh's land fell into Fairfax County upon its formation in 1742,
and some of it fell into Fauquier County upon its formation in 1759 and
the court records of these two counties are enlightening as to this family.

John Tyler of King George County in his last will and Testament
proved in 1757, mentions the five children of his daughter Margaret and
her husband, William Waugh, viz:

    (i) Tyler Waugh was born on February 29, 1739 in Overwharton Parish.
He was an early dissenter from the Established Church and appears
as a subscriber to the Covenant of the Chapawasmic Baptist Church
in 1766. He married on August 25, 1773 in Fauquier County, Mary
Crump, daughter of John Crump. They were living in Fairfax County in 1776 when he sold a portion of the land inherited from his
father, William Waugh, and this deed further recites the land
was patented in 1710 by the grantor's grandfather, John Waugh,
Gentleman, deceased, of Stafford County. Tyler Waugh appears on
the personal tax list of Fairfax County in 1787 paying tax on 2
Negro slaves and 2 horses.

    (ii) Priscilla Waugh was born on October 22, 1741 in Overwharton Par-
ish. On July 12, 1755 her grandmother, Mary Tyler, gave bond
to Thomas Ludwell Lee, Esq., "first justice in the Commission of
Peace for Stafford County," as guardian to Tyler Waugh and Priscilla Waugh, orphans of William Waugh, deceased, and guaranteeing
to deliver to them all such estate as may be due when they came
of age. It appears she married Peter Mauzey of Stafford County
as on May 15, 1763 Tyler Waugh for five shillings deeded 250 acres
of land in Fairfax County to Peter Mauzey and Priscilla, his wife,
with reversion after their deaths, to their son John Mauzey. Peter
Mauzey was an early dissenter from the Established Church and appears as a subscriber to the Covenant of the Chapawasmic Baptist
Church in 1766.

    (iii) William Waugh was probably born in Prince William County as his
birth is not of record in The Register of Overwharton Parish. On
1 June 1767 William Waugh of King George County conveyed to Peter
Pearce of Fauquier County for £45, 150 acres of land in Fauquier
County. This instrument recites that this land is the same that
was conveyed to the grantor's father, William Waugh, by Joseph Dun-
com and Lydia, his wife, and by the said William Waugh devised to
his son William Waugh, the grantor herein, by his last will and
Testament by "the name of the plantation whereon he then lived"
same being of record in the county court of Prince William.

    (iv) Thomas Waugh

    (v) Million Waugh

III. Alexander Waugh (16 -1722) appears to have been the third son of the
Reverend Mr. John Waugh. On May 12, 1703 Diana Webb made a deed of gift

of various chattels to her daughter Catherine Waugh; she is presumed to be the wife of Alexander Waugh as the wives of his elder brothers are known and his brother David was then under age.

On June 11, 1707 Joseph Waugh, planter, of Overwharton Parish, made a deed of gift for 1,200 acres of land to his brother Alexander Waugh, describing it as part of 6,350 acres on the head of Potomac Creek which was patented by their late father, the Reverend Mr. John Waugh. He did not retain possession of this tract long as on October 9, 1707 Alexander Waugh, planter, of Overwharton Parish conveyed it to his brother-in-law George Mason, Gentleman, also of Overwharton Parish. Colonel Robert Carter of Lancaster County was apparently interested in purchasing this land as on May 23, 1728 he wrote John Mercer, Esq., attorney-at-law, in Stafford County, that he had sent him Alexander Waugh's deed to Colonel Mason, "but you have not sent me Joseph Waugh's deeds to his brothers John, Alexander and David Waugh."

The records indicate that Alexander Waugh died intestate in 1722 and that David Waugh acted as his administrator. There seems to be no surviving record which will give us the names of his children. My reasons for assigning him the children below mentioned have been given on page 234.

(1) Alexander Waugh seems to have been the overseer for Colonel John Taliaferro (1687-1744) of Spotsylvania County at his plantation in what is now the county of Orange. John Mercer, Esq., of Marlborough debited Major [later Colonel] John Taliaferro in 1730 with cash paid to John Asher for going with Doctor Mungo Roy to show him the way "to your Quarter to visit Alexander Waugh at the Mountains." On November 23, 1733 Theophilus Eddings conveyed to Alexander Waugh of Spotsylvania County, 230 acres in the fork of the Robinson River; this property fell into Orange County in 1734 when it was severed from Spotsylvania County. On April 27, 1738 John Taliaferro, Gentleman, of Spotsylvania County, made a lease for 150 acres of land in Orange County for the natural lives of Alexander Waugh, Sarah Waugh, his wife, and Richard Waugh, his son, and thereafter there are many records of Alexander Waugh and his family in the records of Orange and Culpeper counties.

Alexander Waugh died testate in Orange County in 1793 and this document mentions his wife Sarah and their seven children, viz:

(i) Richard Waugh (1732-July 3, 1805) married in Orange County on November 11, 1782 Margaret Brown, widow; she was probably his second wife. He died testate in Culpeper County and the Fredericksburg Virginia Herald of July 16, 1805 said: "Died: In Culpeper, 3ᵈ day of July, Major Richard Waugh, in the 72ᵈ year of his age." Major Richard Waugh in his last will and Testament mentioned his wife Margaret, his daughter Mary, then the wife of Doctor Charles Stuart Waugh [see page 240], and entailed certain landed estate upon their son Richard Waugh. The Fredericksburg Virginia Herald of October 15, 1823 carried the obituary of the last mentioned young man: "Died: In this town on Monday morning last, Mr. Richard Waugh, son of Dr. Charles Waugh of Culpeper County."

(ii) Alexander Waugh, Junior, was born in 1734 according to a deposition which he made in Orange County on November 24, 1756. His father deeded him 270 acres in Culpeper County in 1761 and there are records concerning him there.

(iii) John Waugh (circa 1736-July 10, 1802) resided in Culpeper
County and appears on those records as Captain John Waugh.
He was probably the John Waugh, Jr., who petitioned the
House of Burgesses on May 17, 1769 in regard to an incident
which happened in 1760 when he was marching a group of en-
listed me to join the Virginia Regiment under authority
vested in him by Lieut. Governor Francis Fauquier. The family
Bible record of Captain John Waugh is preserved in the Archives Division, Virginia State Library, #22612.

(iv) Abner Waugh (circa 1738-September 13, 1806) was a student at
The College of William and Mary 1765-1768. He subsequently
studied theology and was licensed for Saint Mary's Parish,
Caroline County, on March 11, 1771. He served as a chaplin
in the Second Virginia Regiment in 1775 and on the Committee
of Safety of Caroline County in 1776. [See The Virginia
Magazine of History and Biography, Volume 41, page 303, and
T.E. Campbell's Colonial Caroline (1954)]

The Reverend Mr. Abner Waugh married Philadelphia (Claiborne) Carter, daughter of Colonel Philip Whitehead Claiborne
(17 -1772) of King William County and widow of Colonel John
Carter (174?-1773) of Cleve, King George County, by whom she
had an only child, viz: Ann of Cleave Carter (1772-1828) who
married John Lyons, Esq., of Studley, Hanover County, Virginia. I have no record of the issue of the Reverend Mr. Abner
Waugh, if any.

The Richmond Virginia Argus of September 20, 1806 said:
"Died: At the seat of Col. John Taylor, in Caroline, on the
13th inst., the Rev. Abner Waugh, minister of the Protestant
Episcopal Church."

(v) George Waugh

(vi) Mary Waugh married first on May 31, 1756 in Orange County the
Reverend Mr. Musgrove Dawson (17 -1764), rector of Saint
Mary's Parish, Caroline County, by whom she had an only child,
the Honorable John Dawson (1762—1814), Member of Congress; he
died testate in Spotsylvania County without issue. Mary (Waugh)
Dawson married secondly the Honorable Judge Joseph Jones (1727-
1805) of Spring Hill, King George County, whose many positions
of trust are detailed in the Biographical Directory of American
Congress, page 1163. Judge Jones was the only maternal uncle
of President James Monroe, and at the time of his marriage to
Mrs. Dawson, was the childless widower of Mary Taliaferro (17 -
1777), daughter of Colonel John Taliaferro (1687-1744) of Snow
Creek, Spotsylvania County. Judge Joseph and Mary (Waugh) Jone
had an only child, Joseph Jones, Junior, (circa 1780-circa 180?
who died unmarried. John Dawson and Joseph Jones, grandsons o
Alexander Waugh of Orange County, are mentioned in his last wi
and Testament as the children of his deceased daughter Mary.

(vii) Elizabeth Waugh married Joseph Thomas of Orange County and lef
issue.

(2) Solomon Waugh is believed to have been a son of Alexander Waugh (16 -
1722 for reasons stated on page 234. Solomon Waugh appears to have

been a man of no real estate and the surviving Stafford County court
records fail to enlighten us in the least. His existence is known,
however, by the three entries on page 126 of The Register of Overwharton
Parish and in 1763 he signed a bond for his indebtness to William Allason, merchant at Falmouth. His signature on this bond appears to be
that of an old man.

Solomon Waugh was married on April 13, 1748 in Overwharton Parish
to Betty Chinn; she had an illegitimate daughter named Lizzie Chinn
born on October 18, 1745. She was the daughter of Rawleigh Chinn who
died testate in Stafford County in 1760, but he was not the son of Rawleigh and Esther (Ball) Chinn of Lancaster County as stated in Hayden's
Virginia Genealogies, pages 74-75. The Lancaster County records conclusively show that Rawleigh Chinn (17 -1756), son of Rawleigh and
Esther (Ball) Chinn, died intestate in that county leaving two daughters, viz: Catherine who married Francis Christian and Anne who married
Thaddeus McCarty. Furthermore a case in the Virginia Court of Appeals
in 1793 recites the facts as follows: that Rawleigh Chinn by will in or
about 1741 devised the residue of a certain tract of land for which he
had a patent from Thomas, Lord Fairfax, to his son Rawleigh Chinn and
"he died in or about 1756, intestate, leaving issue as co-heiresses,
two infant daughters, Anne and Catherine, the former of whom intermar-
ried with McCarty and the latter with Christian, before they attained
their ages of 21 years."

The births of two children of Solomon and Betty (Chinn) Waugh appear on The Register of Overwharton Parish, viz:

   (i) Micajah Waugh was born on January 9, 1749 in Overwharton Parish.
       I am unable to find him on the county court records of either
       Stafford or King George counties and the tax books fail to show
       that he owned any real estate or slaves. In 1783 he appears on
       the Stafford County personal tax lists, being charged with three
       horses and twelve cattle. In 1787 McChagby Waugh appears and he
       also paid tax on David Waugh, aged between 16-21 years, residing
       in his household. Micajah, McChagy, McCagby, Waugh appears with
       David Waugh for the next several years on the Stafford County
       personal tax lists and in 1800 they appear to have slipped across
       Potomac Creek as we find them on the King George County personal
       tax lists for that year. In 1801 Micajah Waugh sans any taxable
       personal property, David Waugh with two horses and James Waugh
       sans any taxable personal property, appear on the King George
       County personal property tax lists with Lewis Waugh (176?-1808)
       and John Waugh (176?-1801) [see pages 238-239], whose children
       are established. I submit that the pedigree has now reached a
       very unstaple stage as it is impossible, from the scanty records
       which these indigent people left, to identify them positively -
       yet we know they are descendants of the Reverend Mr. John Waugh!

  (ii) Grace Waugh was born on July 21, 1751 in Overwharton Parish. The
       Register of Saint Paul's Parish, page 150, records the marriage
       of Gracey Waugh and Elisha Perry on January 30, 1783.

David Waugh and Elizabeth Waugh appear separately on the King George
County personal tax lists for 1783 and shortly fade away; they may have

have left issue.

The first quarter of the Nineteenth Centuary witnessed the complete obliteration of the great name of WAUGH from the Stafford and King George county records. The following unidentified persons are the last to tantalize the genealogist:

James Waugh first appears on the King George County personal tax lists in 1801. He was again listed in 1802, was married in King George County on December 31, 1803 to Elizabeth Jones, and then appears on the Stafford County personal tax lists in 1805 for the last time. The so called Old General Index to the Stafford County court records indicates that in Will Book "Z" [1804-1809], page 173, the inventory of the estate of James Waugh was recorded; this record book is among the many now missing from the clerk's office of Stafford County. In 1806 James Waugh's widow, Elizabeth Waugh, was taxed on two horses; she shortly removed to her native county of King George and in 1810 paid tax on one horse in that county. She is listed each year thru 1815 on the personal tax lists of King George County being the sole person by the name of WAUGH mentioned on those personal tax lists for the period 1810-1815 and the last to so appear.

The inventory of the estate of Elizabeth Waugh was recorded on June 1, 1815; William G.A. Jones was her administrator. On December 2, 1819 Charles Jones gave bond as guardian of Tabitha Waugh, orphan of Elizabeth Waugh, deceased, and various accounts of the estate of Elizabeth Waugh, deceased, for the years 1815-1819 were admitted to record.

Catesby Waugh was married on August 6, 1801 to Sarah Simms in King George County, per the recording in King George County Marriage Register No.I, page 21. This may be a contortion of Micajah, McChagy and McCagby as is evident from the personal tax lists.

Travers Waugh was married on April 26, 1804 to Rebecca Jett in King George County per the recording in King George County Marriage Register No.I, page 22. He may have been a seafaring man. The will of Travis (sic) Waugh was dated 24 September 1817 and recorded in Fredericksburg, Virginia, 13 August 1818; therein he describes himself as of the town of Fredericksburg. To his wife Rebecca he bequeath his schooner, The Swallor, and all the rest of his estate for life; after her decease he decreed it was to be equally divided among the testator's brother and sister, John Waugh and Hannah Waugh, and Nancy Jett and her brother William Jett.

IV. David Waugh (169?-1753) was under age in 1706 when his father died; see page 234. During the years 1721-1724 David Waugh is frequently mentioned as a party in various suits which pended before the King George County court but the surviving brief notations in the Court Order Book are without genealogical import except that in 1723 he is mentioned as the administrator of Alexander Waugh, deceased. In an action of trespass which pended before the Fairfax County court, David Waugh of Stafford County made a deposition on October 2, 1746 in regard to the extensive Alexander properties on Hunting

Creek. He stated that about 35-36 years ago [circa 1710], he was on a
survey in Fairfax, then Stafford, County with his brother John Waugh and
Thomas Gregg, surveyor of Stafford County, and relates his knowledge of
early land marks in that area.

David Waugh received 1,200 acres of land by deed of gift from his eldest brother, Joseph Waugh, and must have purchased 300 acres later. David
Waugh appears on the Quit Rent Roll of 1723 [see page 154] with 1,500 acres
of land in Stafford County and was a tobacco tender there in 1724 [see page
163]. However, David Waugh is absent from the Stafford County Rent Roll of
1742 and it must be presumed that he had disposed of his landed estate by
this time, but there are no surviving deeds at Stafford County court to
show the disposition of the said land. As Prince William County had been
formed from Stafford County in 1731 and Fairfax County from Prince William
County in 1742 it is possible some of David Waugh's land was not within the
bounds of Stafford County by 1742 and thus not on that rent roll. There
are several deed books missing in each of these counties but from those
surviving I do not see any disposition made by David Waugh of his land
holdings.

David Waugh seems to have lived quietly and died on March 22, 1753 at
the home of the widow Priscilla (Vandegasteel) Hay as is recorded in The
Register of Overwharton Parish. The record books for this period for
Stafford County are preserved but they are silent as to any estate which
David Waugh may have left. I believe David Waugh was a bachelor.

V.   Ann Waugh was the daughter of the Reverend Mr. John and Elizabeth Waugh.
Mrs. Elizabeth Waugh and her daughter Ann are mentioned in a deposition
taken on November 11, 1680 shortly after the Reverend Mr. John Waugh returned to their home on Potomac Creek from Jamestown [see page 176]. With
her brothers Richard Waugh and Alexander Waugh, Ann Waugh was bequeathed
land in Stafford County by Henry Thompson, Gentleman, in 1691 [see page
203]. She was married to Giles Travers, Gentleman, (16 -1717) and on July
12, 1700 Parson Waugh made over by assignment on the reverse of a deed 400
acres of land on Potomac Creek which he had purchased on March 14, 1695
from Edward Smith. This valuable tract of land at The Landing Run on Potomac Creek was bequeathed by Giles Travers, Gentlemen, to his daughter
Elizabeth Travers [only child of Ann (Waugh) Travers] by his last will and
Testament dated June 1, 1717 and proved at Stafford County court on September 11, 1717. Ann (Waugh) Travers predeceased her father.

(1)   Elizabeth Travers, only child of Giles and Ann (Waugh) Travers, married
first John Cave (16 -1721). On August 5, 1707 Sampson Darrell, Gentleman, of Gloucester County deeded to John Cave, carpenter, of King and
Queen County, 300 acres of land on the south side of Potomac Creek and
this deed recites that the said land is one half of 600 acres formerly
sold by Captain William Heaberd to Captain John Norgrave by deed dated
March 6, 1667. John Cave must have moved from King and Queen County to
Stafford County about this time, settled upon his newly acquired land,
and married Elizabeth Travers. John Cave's will was dated August 6,
1714 and proved in 1721 at Stafford County court; it was recorded in
now lost Will Book "K", page 2. He devised 200 acres of land on Axton's
Run and adjoining the property of John Gowry and Giles Travers to his
son John Cave but he "died so that the above mentioned land fell and

reverted to" David Cave of Orange County who was joined by his wife
Sarah in conveying the said property to Keene Withers of Hamilton
Parish, Prince William County, on September 12, 1748.

Elizabeth (Travers) Cave married secondly Lewis Ellzey and on March
8, 1726 they conveyed to Hugh French of Washington Parish, Westmoreland
County, "400 acres of land which was devised and bequeathed unto the
said Elizabeth by the last will and Testament of Giles Travers, her
father," and adjoining the property now in the possession of William
Cave, Joseph Waugh and Townshend Dade. About 1730 Lewis Ellzey moved
to what is now Fairfax County and before that court on April 6, 1743
he stated his age to be 41 years and gave a lengthy deposition in regard to the land holdings of the Travers and Cave families on Potomac
Creek in Stafford County, Virginia.

After the death of Ann (Waugh) Travers, Giles Travers, Gentleman, (16 -
1717) married a second wife whose name is unknown to me; she predeceased
him leaving two daughters, viz:
   (1) Anne Travers who married as her first husband William Cave; he died
       testate in Stafford County in 1742 and she married secondly in 1747
       Thomas Dent. Her only child to survive infancy was Elizabeth Cave,
       successively the wife of Keene Withers (1728-1756), Andrew Edwards
       (1725-1788) and Thomas Walker [see pages 32 and 134]. Giles Travers,
       Gentleman, by will bequeathed to his daughter Anne Travers his dwell-
       ing plantation on The Landing Run which flows into Potomac Creek a
       short distance upstream from Belle Plain. Upon this property William
       Cave erected a tobacco warehouse and Cave's Warehouse became a very
       well known shipping point. By virtue of his marriage to Cave's only
       heir, Andrew Edwards held this property at the time of the Revolu-
       tionary War. On November 5, 1776 he petitioned the Virginia Legis-
       lature in regard to his warehouse on Potomac Creek, "called Cave's
       Warehouse being appointed a Naval Depot." There are other petitions
       concerning this property in the Stafford County Petitions to the Leg-
       islature in the Archives Division of the Virginia State Library. This
       property, after the death of Elizabeth (Cave) Withers Edwards Dent,
       descended to her eldest son and heir, James Withers; he was a vestry-
       man in Overwharton Parish and attended Potomac Church.
   (2) Million Travers, younger of the two daughters of Giles Travers, Gent-
       leman, by his second wife, married Joseph Waugh, Gentleman; for in-
       formation in regard to them see page 235.

VI. Elizabeth Waugh, younger daughter of the Reverend Mr. John and Elizabeth
    Waugh, married Colonel George Mason (16 -1716) widower of Mary Fowke. She
    is mentioned on the Stafford County records in 1707 as Madam Elizabeth Mason,
    wife of Colonel George Mason. She is believed to have died shortly after the
    birth of her only child, Catherine Mason (June 21, 1707-June 15, 1750), who
    married John Mercer, Esq., (1705-1768) of Marlborough. Their family has been
    detailed in The Virginia Genealogist, Volume 4, pages 99-109. Colonel George
    Mason married thirdly Sarah Taliaferro (16 -1716), daughter of Francis Tal-
    iaferro and Elizabeth Catlett, his wife, of Essex County, and left issue. The
    last wills and Testaments of Colonel George Mason and his widow Sarah (Talia-
    ferro) Mason were admitted to probate on November 14, 1716 at Stafford County
    court. Colonel Mason left issue by each of his three wives.

I N D E X

THE REGISTER OF OVERWHARTON PARISH [1-136]
IS ARRANGED ALPHABETICALLY BY SURNAMES IN
CHRONOLOGICAL ORDER AND THESE NAMES ARE NOT
CARRIED IN THE FOLLOWING GENERAL INDEX

INDEX